AMAZONS
THE FORGOTTEN TRIBE

MARTHA MATTSON

AMAZON PRESS

Copyright © 1997 Martha Mattson

All rights reserved. No part of this book may be used or reproduced in any manner whatsoever without the written permission of the Publisher. Amazon Press, P.O. Box 26383, San Diego, CA 92196-0383.

The stories in this book are true. Some names, places, and details have been changed to protect some people's identities. You may think you recognize the identity of some character as your next-door neighbor. You're probably wrong. And you're probably right.

Library of Congress Cataloging-in-Publication Data
Mattson, Martha
 Amazons : the forgotten tribe / Martha Mattson — 1st ed.
 ISBN 0-965-89474-6
 1. Homosexuality — United States   2. Lesbians — United States — Case Studies   3. Gay Men — United States — Case Studies   4. Homosexuality — Law and Legislation   5. Homosexuality in the Bible   6. Homosexuality — Religious Aspects   I. Title
HQ76.3.U5M38
305.9' 0664 — dc20   97-73679
                                                                                                    CIP

INK DRAWINGS   CHRIS BRISCOE
COVER ART AND DESIGN   ANDREW GILL

Printed in the United States of America
First Edition

*For Tom and John—
your love and encouragement make all things possible*

My friends are my treasures—thanks

*Chris
Nikki
Charlene*

*And to the women and men who told their stories
in the hope of a more loving world*

Wounded Amazon. Marble copy of bronze original, thought to be by Polyclitos or Cresilas, fifth century B.C. *(Courtesy The Metropolitan Museum of Art, Gift of John D. Rockefeller, Jr., 1932)*

Contents

PREFACE

Amazons   9
Myth or Reality? Yesterday and Today

INTRODUCTION

Definitely Not Mindy   23

THE FORGOTTEN TRIBE

1 Surprised by Passion   29

2 Young Warriors   35

3 CEO   53

4 Sally from Santa Fe   104

5 Mother Superior   129

6 Ted and Fred   154

7 Anniversary Waltz   176

8 Bishop's Tale 215

9 A Journey 263

APPENDICES

I Fox in the Hen House 331
How to tell if your best friend is a lesbian

II The Last to Know 334
How to tell if your husband is gay

III Glossary 337

IV Two Men and a Baby 347

V Time Line 352

EPILOGUE

Lesbian Myths 393
Delusion and Disillusion

Acknowledgments 414

To Order Book 414

Preface

Amazons
Myth or Reality?
Yesterday and Today

STORIES OF AMAZONS, women of exceptional strength and beauty, warriors who carry arms and fight fiercely, have pervaded our culture since before the time of written history. Were they real and do they exist today?

The first Amazon story is the ninth labor of Hercules, from prehistory. Hercules' task was to capture the sacred girdle of the Amazon queen Antiope. After a fierce battle which Hercules eventually won, he gave the queen her freedom in exchange for her armor and girdle. (One can imagine this battle as brutal but respectful. See the battle between Arnold Schwarzenegger and Brigitte Nielsen in the film *Red Sonja*. I've seen this film, because I have two sons, who, like heterosexual men throughout time, love a mighty warrior woman.) Some versions of the story say King Theseus of Athens was with Hercules, and he took the queen's Amazon sister Hippolyta back to Athens as his bride where she was a boon to the royal bloodline.[1]

The Greek sailors headed back to Athens by ship with some captured Amazons, but were overpowered and killed by their captives on the way. The Amazons didn't know how to sail the ships and soon ran aground in strange

---

[1] The historical Amazon stories in this Preface are told in Abby Wettan Kleinbaum's book *The War Against the Amazons,* New Press McGraw-Hill, 1993, in which she traces Amazon stories through history. All page citations in the Preface are for her book.

territory. They found wild horses and learned to ride them, and then came upon the Scythian people whose men fell in love with them. Greek myth says this was the beginning of the fierce Sauromatian race of people whose women rode horses into battle with their men. Modern Soviet archaeologists have confirmed the existence of warrior women by excavations of Sauromatian graves in the Caucasus (north of the Black Sea on Asia Minor) where women have been found buried with their weapons.

The next Amazon tale has the Amazons attacking Athens in the 13th century B.C. in retaliation for the theft of the sacred girdle and the Amazon women. The Greek men drive them back and win the battle. This battle is part of the classical Greek consciousness and is reflected in the art and funeral speeches of classical Greece. Whenever Greek men talked about bravery in war, it was always this war against the powerful Amazons. Yet there is no evidence that such a battle ever occurred.

The important battle that did happen was the Greeks drove the Persians out of Greece in the fifth century B.C. However, when they rebuilt the city of Athens after this victory, the stories in their art and architecture, the figures on the Parthenon, didn't show them battling the Persian armies, but Amazons, giants, and centaurs—all mythical creatures. Greek art from the fifth century B.C. shows Amazons wearing short tunics, on horseback, and with one breast bared. Stories of Amazons removing a breast came centuries later, in literature.

When the Romans conquered Greece in the first century B.C. they picked up and continued the Amazon legends. Now the Amazons are the enemy in their ancestral stories, fighting on the side of the Trojans in the Trojan War (thought to be about 1250 B.C.). Achilles kills the Amazon queen Penthesilea, daughter of Ares, but he falls in love with her when he sees her corpse.

Men (and women) make myths to confront, explain, and sometimes, conquer their fears. Greek and Roman men preferred to make up tales of conquering the creatures of their fears and fantasies to telling true stories of battles with men who are like themselves and thus not so formidable to conquer. Amazon women in the classical stories are fierce fighters and beautiful; and they are always eventually overcome by men, either in battle or in passionate love. Amazon myth scholar William Blake Tyrrell (*Amazons: A Study in Athenian Mythmaking,* The Johns Hopkins University Press, Baltimore, 1984) sees the genesis of the Amazon myths in men's fear of powerful women: a fear that women could survive without men, govern themselves without men; fear of women's powerful fertility and the chaos they could create in bloodlines if men did not control them. Men feared that women, not controlled and kept submissive, could destroy the patriarchy. Thus in the myths, the Amazon, the strong woman, is always conquered. The ancient Greeks, and later the Romans, sought transcendence by overcoming the powerful Amazon women. To best an Amazon in battle or in bed was the mark of a hero. (Kleinbaum 36)

Although there was never evidence of Amazons, throughout the centuries men continued to write the stories. In medieval literature religious writers saw Amazons as too sexual for Christianity (but they still saw them). The beautiful warrior woman always ends up brutally hacked to pieces at the end of the battle. Too many pieces for her ever to be resurrected.

On Columbus's first voyage (1492) he thought he'd found the Island of Female which Marco Polo said he'd visited in the thirteenth century, proving to Columbus he was in China. (Why was it only in the last year that scholars began to doubt Marco Polo traveled to China?) Columbus believed, from natives' stories, that The Island of Martinio (present-day Martinique) was an island of Amazon women archers, living apart from men, and mating once a year with cannibal men from another island. Unfortunately he was not able to approach the island because of fierce winds. Later explorers also got Amazon tales from natives. It's hard to say if the natives really had Amazon tales or were just responding to the explorers' excited questions with answers that made the explorers very happy. On his second voyage (1493) Columbus was attacked by female archers on the island of Guadaloupe. This time he was sure he'd found Marco Polo's island and was in the Orient. (108) In the 18th century when several American Indian tribes (e.g., the Iroquois and Huron) were found to be matriarchies, with matrilineal lines, where women governed and were archers, explorers and scholars felt they'd found proof for their ideas of Amazon heritage or influence. (149-156)

In the fifteenth and sixteenth centuries all of Europe thrilled to romantic tales of Amazons. My favorite Renaissance Amazon story is in Book V of the *Amadis de Gaule* series which ran twenty-one volumes by the end of the sixteenth century and had five different authors—Spanish, Italian and German. In this story the tall, black woman warrior Califia comes from her island California (on the edge of Paradise) in a fleet of ships filled with 500 man-eating griffons in golden harnesses and thousands of warrior women in golden armor. She'd been hired by a pagan sultan to take Constantinople from the Christians. She was winning the battle when she fell in love with a beautiful Christian knight. Not able to marry him because he was betrothed to a Spanish princess, she asked him to choose a

Christian husband for her. She married the knight's cousin, embraced his religion, gave him her island where gold and jewels lay on top of the ground, and taught all her warrior women to be good, submissive Christian wives. This was a big change for women used to carrying the heads of men about on the tips of their spears. (84)

In 1533 a rumor spread through Spain that seventy large ships bringing ten thousand Amazons had entered the ports of Santander and Laredo, that the Amazons had heard of the celebrated valor and virility of Spanish men and wished to mate with them. It was said the Amazons would pay fifty ducats to any man who got them pregnant. This forced prostitutes in the capital district to lower their prices. (Dream on, guys!) (86)

There were Amazon stories about every unknown piece of geography where Amazons could possibly exist in secret—Africa, the Americas. Every explorer "almost" found them. They were always just beyond reach, a mountain or two valleys away, when the explorers had to turn back. The Amazons often were on an island where they could isolate themselves from men. They were always warriors, strong and beautiful and a physical challenge for any man. They were adorned in gold and precious metals and were always associated with wealth and riches. Many stories talk of green stones as their unique jewel—called Amazon stones. Some stories said they removed their right breast to strengthen their bow arm. Amazons mated once a year with men they imported from another island annually or with captive males who fell into their hands and met their criteria. Some tales have Amazons raiding countries for males for procreation, after which they return them or kill them. Some stories have them kill their male offspring. In others the Amazons give the males to the fathers when they return to mate the next year, or when the males are fourteen. Seventeenth century scholar/physician Pierre Petit thought they crippled the males for servants and craftsmen and as procreators for children. His theory was that cripples not only cannot become warriors, they make passionate lovers. (145)

Is it any wonder that when Juan Rodríquez Cabrillo sailed up the western coast of North America in 1542 he named the land he saw California? (125-126) Amazons were finally seen in South America, also in 1542. Francisco de Orellana was carried (against his wishes) down the great river by its strong current, from Peru where he was with Pizarro, to the river's mouth. A Dominican friar on board wrote a first-hand account of a battle they fought with Indians where twelve tall, white, women archers with long, braided hair came to help the Indians. Each one fought with the power of ten men. They took the front line of battle and clubbed any Indian who tried to turn back. (121) The Indians told the Spaniards they served the women warriors who lived seven days journey inland from the river in a large, developed civilization of seventy villages of women. The Spaniards had planned to name the river Marañón; it became now the River of the Amazons.

Wonder Woman, the comic book Amazon, was created in 1941. She left Paradise Island and came to the United States to help fight against Nazis. Today we have *Xena, The Warrior Princess,* a television series, so popular that we can find it being played several days a week on various channels and twice on Saturday. Xena is strong and beautiful, never beaten in battle, and able to be romanced by the rare worthy male. Men love her for the classic reasons—she's a formidable fantasy, the ultimate trophy, either for the males on the show who are sure they can beat her in battle because she is a woman, or the males at home in their living rooms who revel in the sensuality of her strength.

Men are attracted to Amazons and strong women. They are a challenge for one thing. (Studies have shown that bitchy women always get married.) The mystery is, if men like strong women, why are women taught to look helpless to attract them? Women have trouble in the boardroom because they aren't aggressive in conversation. They're polite to the point of sounding submissive—and this in an atmosphere where men bulldoze into conversation and try to take the floor the way they try to gain yards on the playing field. Men eye Amazons with admiration and lust to conquer them, and women are tripping around in high-heeled, crippling shoes acting helpless to attract men. A woman may well ask herself, "What do men want?"

Women like Xena because for them she's a role model, a woman with power. Xena doesn't fear anything, nor does she need to ingratiate herself for the protection or approval of a man. She has the independence and confidence women dream of. She wears clothes she can fight in and soft leather boots she can run in.

Western cultures are not the only ones with Amazon women and warrior princesses in their myths and fantasy life. Like all classic myths, Amazon stories appear in cultures around the world as if they'd sprung from a universal unconscious. Maxine Hong Kingston's *The Woman Warrior* is about Chinese warrior women stories. The legend is that a woman can either be a wife and slave (the word is the same in Chinese), or she can be a warrior woman and save her village. On Sundays when she was a little girl in California Maxine went to the Confucius Church in Sacramento and watched Chinese movies about women warriors. They could jump over houses without a running start. (Xena also is a great jumper.) The role model was impossible to achieve.

The Chinese had Amazon warriors who rode horses—they had to—their feet had been bound as girls and they couldn't walk. These Amazons were women who had escaped from their oppressed lives and become a band of swordswomen, a mercenary army. The story is that they raised the girl babies that families didn't want and they killed men and boys. When a slave girl or daughter-in-law ran away, it was said she went to the "witch Amazons."

Is this a fantasy tale invented by powerless females, or is it a male tale—fear of the subject females taking vengeance on their oppressors? In the book Kingston reflects on why the women of China had their feet bound. She thinks: "perhaps women were once so dangerous they had to have their feet bound." In Japan (when I lived there in 1980) women were not allowed to study martial arts, not allowed to become fighters. The traditional Japanese woman in traditional dress walks in tiny shuffling steps on tippy platform shoes, eyes to the ground.

When the women's movement began in the early seventies in America, men in both civilian life and the military feared losing their jobs to women. They responded by calling women in the workplace "dykes." Calling a woman a lesbian in the military was especially effective, because it took only a suspicion of lesbianism for a woman to be dishonorably discharged. Actually there was a smaller proportion of lesbians in the military in the '70s and '80s than ever before because the women's movement had led heterosexual women into nontraditional jobs. Previously a high proportion of women in the military were lesbians. The military appealed to them and many didn't marry or have family ties that held them back. They were patriotic and wanted to serve their country. In Post-World War II in General Eisenhower's occupation army in Europe he had a WAC battalion of 900 women serving at his headquarters. These women estimated that 95% of them were lesbians. It was one of the most decorated battalions in the Army.[2]

Myths grow out of fears. Men's fear of losing the status quo power of the patriarchy produced the Amazon myths. Strong women—Amazons, Xena—are great romantic figures for men. But maybe only because they're mythic, not real. In real life women who are perceived as strong are vilified by most men. Gloria Steinem is thought to be a lesbian (she's not) by many men because she talks about equal rights for women. They hurl the insult "dyke." Hillary Clinton, even more than Rosalyn Carter, is considered a threat because she's educated and articulate and is viewed as strong. The insult men (and their wives who follow suit) hurl at her is the jokes about her "wanting to be president"—a patriarchy position not open to a woman, in their minds.

Men have an extreme attraction/fear response to lesbians. They fear the lesbian's lack of female submissive (read that sexual) behavior around them and the idea she'll sexually reject them. They are mesmerized by the idea that the ultimate proof of their sexual power would be to give a lesbian such "amazing" sex that she becomes "converted." The ultimate stud. A bar tale bar none. (Except, it never happens. One is born with his or her sexuality.) Men's need for sexual conquest is probably their dominant trait. A woman priest friend of mine in Santa Fe said, with a sigh, that she'd discovered in her counseling that men find it hard to keep their pants on, a sign she thought that their social development was still close to primitive urges (see the Discovery

---

[2] Data is from Randy Shilts' book *Conduct Unbecoming*, see "Time Line" chapter.

channel.) An intellectual debate in the thirties was whether men's primary drive was for power (money) or sex. The answer then was sex. And reading the newspaper this July, 1997, with about six prominent men involved in sex scandals, that does seem true. Careers in jeopardy over what seems thoughtless sexual involvement. So men relate sexually to women, looking for dominance. That relationship is void with lesbians, leaving men confused.

For centuries the "proof" given by scholars (men) that Amazons cannot exist is that women could not build a civilization and govern it. Women are too weak and too inferior to build a society without men's help they say. So, do women who can live without men exist or not? I became interested in the Amazon myths in the summer of 1993 when I met a community of women who live in an insular community without men. Many have been warriors (in the military), some wear men's clothes and do "men's" work. I found them two valleys to the north in (where else?) California.

One woman, the CEO of her own multi-million dollar company, says she has to wear men's clothes. "Otherwise they wouldn't take me seriously at the Pentagon," she laughs. Others say they wear men's clothing for comfort. "I never wear pantyhose." The tiniest and most fragile one drives a city bus. Others are lipsticked and high-heeled. The most feminine one, always in silks and jewels, was the Mother Superior of a monastic order.

They are lesbian women—born not made—and they're not to be feared. Men, they don't want to replace you, they want to join you. Those who are masculine-oriented are the best friends you'll ever have, in the boardroom, on a Harley, for sports, tall stories, and action movies. And they're not sexual competition for you—you may *look* at the same women, but you won't *get* the same women. (You'll get the heterosexual women, they'll get the lesbian women.) The feminine-oriented ones, soft and perfumed, may prefer to live with a woman, but they enjoy the company of men.

These lesbian women shared their inner lives with me and I found them amazing. Relationships between the sexes are complex—especially when you take into account that there are more than two sexes. Come with me on my journey into modern myths—about lesbian women, gay men, homosexuality and heterosexuality—myths and reality about sexuality.

Introduction

Definitely Not Mindy

I FIRST MET ANN BISHOP in the spring of 1993. I was teaching at a small community college in Southern California. The first day of class I asked the thirty-five students to put their chairs (desks) in a circle. I'd take roll and we'd introduce ourselves—to begin to build the familiarity necessary to make the students comfortable enough to express freely their thoughts and ideas in class.

When we were in a circle, I called the first name. Mindy Bishop. There was no response, and I went on calling names, listening to people talk. In a few minutes a pleasant looking young woman came in. She was slightly plump, wearing no makeup and hoop earrings. She was maybe slightly over thirty. She pulled a desk over from the side and put it next to mine. When I finished the roll and introductions, I called again for the missing people.

"Mindy. Mindy Bishop."

The plain, slightly overweight young woman raised her hand.

"Here. *Ann* Bishop. Call me Ann."

After class she stayed to explain. "My mother named me Mindy, but I don't feel like a Mindy. Somehow I think of Mindy's as being cheerleaders. So I call myself Ann."

Ann was a wonderful student—the rare student who revels in learning and drinks up whatever wisdom or knowledge the teacher can give. And she had enormous patience with the slower students. It didn't take them long to gravitate to her for help. She always stopped what she was doing and listened intently to their problem. In the first week of class we did a "free writing" to show the students how much creative thought was in them if they started writing and kept going in a free manner. Ann's writing talked about her partner Elizabeth and the legal problems of making wills and being considered family in times of health crises.

I realized Ann was a lesbian and did not hide the fact. I admired her openness.

Soon Ann was waiting for me after class every day, walking to the parking lot with me for the chance to discuss the work, or some personal topic. We talked about her friends and she told me about one who was a CEO of a corporation. She told me her partner, Elizabeth, had been a nun in contemplative order monastery for over twenty-five years. She had in fact been the Mother Superior.

I know I gulped. Ann laughed. "She'd surprise you. She's not like what you'd expect. She's sixty-one—I think—but you'd never know it."

"Have you ever thought about the mystical aspect of your names? I mean she's a Mother Superior and you're Bishop?" I asked.

Ann smiled. "Yeah. I noticed that."

One day on the walk to the car we were talking about the new President Bill Clinton's wanting to allow gays to serve openly in the military. There was a lot of angry rhetoric in the press and Congress against gay men.

Ann said to me, "Did you notice that it's all about men? Men in the military don't want to shower with gay men.

They're so afraid. They don't know they already are. Do you notice the women in the military aren't screaming about lesbians? They aren't afraid. Women aren't threatened by lesbians. Homophobia is all about men who doubt their masculinity. You always hear about gay men, but never about lesbians. We're the invisible people. No one knows we're here. No one cares if we're here. Lesbians melt into society. We're not a threat to the heterosexual male."

"Ann," I said, "why don't you write a book—about lesbians. You can do it. You're a wonderful writer, and you have these amazing women for friends. Write about who they are, where they are. Introduce these lesbians to the world."

She looked at me very seriously and went home.

Several days later she walked with me to the parking lot after class again.

"I can't do it," she said. "I've thought about it and thought about it and I can't do it. Not now."

She had small beads of sweat on her brow. I could see she was very emotional about this—very intense. I looked at her and waited. Her next words stunned me.

"You write it," she said.

At first, of course, I said, "I can't." But Ann was patient. In a few days I said, "I'll try. I'll start and see what happens."

I felt it was important. Maybe my naive heterosexual view was a perspective that might be useful. Maybe straight people would be more likely to read the book if a straight person wrote it. I was going to enter a world I had no knowledge of—as most heterosexual people have no knowledge of it. I was going to meet these invisible people and tell their stories. Ann would bring the people to me, Ann would encourage me.

Although I was frightened that maybe I couldn't do them justice, I felt the chance to write their story was a gift—a gift from God I couldn't turn away from, and a gift of trust from Ann and the women who would talk to me. I prayed to God to guide the writing of this book.

The Forgotten Tribe

1

SURPRISED BY PASSION

SANDY CAME to my house for lunch on a hot July day in San Diego. Ann brought her on their lunch hour from work. Ann wanted me to meet her friend before Sandy moved away to Georgia.

Sandy sat at the table looking like the round, merry-faced grandmother she is. Her body was soft and round. Her face was soft and round. Her hair was snow white and her eyes were twinkly and bright blue behind round, blue-rimmed glasses. She could have been Mrs. Santa Claus. She could have been anyone's ideal grandmother. She was warm, and soft, and huggable. At the engineering firm where she is a technical writer the young engineers come to her for advice and brownies. She is their grandmother. She also is a mother who raised seven children and discovered in her forties that she is a lesbian. She was sitting at my kitchen table to tell me her story.

I grew up in a rural area, Watkins Glen, New York, Schuyler County. My father was a journalist and my mother wrote book reviews at home. So I guess you could say I came from an educated family. I had one brother one year younger and one brother ten years younger. My mother was a prescription-drug addict. She had so many pills that she kept them organized in a fishing tackle box. She was always having surgeries too. She was in and out of hospitals so we had a housekeeper or nurses at home. I really didn't understand this because I was young.

By the time I was in the eighth grade I had this pretty body. For that time it was the perfect body. I had a voluptuous figure. I had the same measurements as Esther Williams. Boys started bothering me, grabbing me. Asking me out but only to try to get my body. From the eighth grade on I was always being attacked for my voluptuous body.

Actually I never felt self-confident about my looks. I felt unattractive. My hair was straight and fine, light brown, called dishwater. I wore wire-rimmed glasses, round glasses, not fashionable at that time. My face was chubby, I thought, and round. I always had my nose in a book.

Yet some boy was always trying to get me into a hayloft. I was curious about sex. I didn't know much about it but it seemed natural. The boys wanted sex and finally I thought, "I'm a virgin and this is a nuisance—let's get it over with."

I think I unconsciously wanted to get pregnant. I wanted to hurry up and start living. And I was desperate to get away from home, from my mother. I wanted to get away from the craziness. My parents didn't get along and there was fighting. I thought my mother hated me. I didn't understand that she was addicted.

I got pregnant my senior year of high school and married in May. My first baby was born in December. I had seven babies in ten years.

My husband wanted sex all the time. He didn't care if I was well or sick. He only hit me once. It was during an argument in the eighth year of our marriage. The argument was probably over sex. That was what we argued about. The only birth control we had was jelly. After my fourth baby I tried to get a tubal ligation. It was the 1950s and you had to get three doctors to approve the operation. I couldn't get three. No matter how I begged one would always say, "But you might want more children—something could happen to yours." I didn't want more children, but I couldn't convince them. After three times applying, after each next child, I finally was able to get the tubal ligation after my seventh child.

I was twenty-eight when I had my last baby. I enjoyed my kids. I seldom saw my husband. He didn't bond with the kids. He planned on spending time with them when they were older and actually he did. When they were little he was working several jobs.

I had five girls and two boys. I felt like a good mother to the girls, but not the boys. They both had problems. One had a learning disability. The other was hyperactive and also had a learning disability—he couldn't comprehend material.

I realized within a year of my marriage that my husband and I were hopelessly ill-matched. He was a kind man but we were intellectually ill-matched. We shared no interests. We couldn't communicate and sexually I was not excited. I had close women friends but I'd never felt attracted to them. In the eighth grade I had a crush on a girl friend, but it wasn't sexual. It was more Ayn Rand, whom I was reading—I wanted to be her. I had heard of gay men but not gay women. I thought I had a low libido or was undersexed. I wasn't interested in sex. My husband said to me, "There's something wrong with you. Get some shots or something."

After seventeen years of working for the school transportation department my husband was laid off. He moved to Florida and I was to follow. I was working at Cornell University and I'd met this wonderful, vibrant girl, Greta. Greta confessed to me that she was bisexual. She told me about her sexual adventures. She would be with women and then she'd up and go to the Bahamas and stay on a yacht with her married male lover and his wife.

I had fun with Greta. I felt excited just hearing about her lifestyle. There was nothing sexual between us. Actually we're both fems—that doesn't mean anything usually, but in our case it did. Greta was only twenty, a graduate student, and I was forty-five but we ran around together and we laughed and talked and had fun. I didn't think I was a lesbian, but I thought the idea of lesbians was interesting.

When Greta would run off to the Bahamas with her lover, I'd stay in her apartment. It was convenient for me because it was close to school. Suddenly one day I looked at the woman I worked for and saw her with new eyes. She was fifteen years younger than I and she was dating my older son.

One time she came to Greta's apartment to see me and we looked at each other and flew into each other's arms. We didn't know what to do. We knew nothing about being lesbians. We just desperately clutched at each other, groping and gasping with passion neither of us had experienced before.

Jane, I'll call her, had known she was attracted to women but had never done anything. She didn't want to be a lesbian. She thought being a lesbian was a terrible thing. She wanted to be married. She wanted a husband and a child.

We continued to work together and sometimes when I was staying at Greta's Jane would arrive and rush desperately to put her arms around me. Then sometimes in her anger and frustration she would beat me.

I never went to Florida. Greta had moved to California and she phoned and asked me to come too. She wanted to help me get away from Jane. Jane never did marry and have a child. The last I heard she was living with a woman.

I've been happy in my new life. Now I know who I am.

All my children accept me and my friend Karen. Only one of my daughters, the lawyer, hasn't discussed it with me, hasn't said the word. But she comes to visit and is happy here and likes Karen. My husband, ex-husband now, knows too and he's fine with me. He's in Florida still and we talk about the children and sometimes get together as a family. I think he's happy for me that I'm happy. He's remarried.

I see my life as divided into two halves. In the first half I was a mother. I raised my babies and I liked being a mother. I knew nothing else and I had pleasure from my children. Now I have a different life. At forty-five I discovered I had a sexual identity and I entered a new life. I have good friends and I know who I am and I'm happy.

We'd overrun Sandy and Ann's lunch hour and they had to rush back to work. My fourteen-year-old son had come in while we were talking and met Sandy. That afternoon when my seventeen-year-old son came home he asked his younger brother, "Did you see the lesbian?"

JOHN: Yes.
TOM: What did she look like?

John thought a moment, remembering his favorite warm grandmother figure, the nun who ran the preschool he'd attended in Maryland.

He smiled as the connection came in his mind.

"She looks like Sister Julie," he said. "She looks just like Sister Julie."

"Cool," Tom said as he picked up his basketball and they headed out to do some serious shooting.

2

YOUNG WARRIORS

AFTER I'D MET SANDY, Ann wanted me to meet a young couple and see what their views were. She arranged for me to meet Linda, a young woman, at her house. Linda arrived and we both were a little nervous. She was attractive, blond, blue-eyed, in stonewashed jeans and a white shirt. Her hair was short and stylish, like a successful businesswoman's. It swept back from her forehead in an expensive cut, well-coifed look. We went out to Ann's backyard and sat at the patio table where we could talk privately.

Linda was twenty-nine. She grew up in a farm community in Colorado. This is her story.

I was a tomboy to the max. I never liked girl clothes. Even as a baby I screamed if they put me in a dress. I played with trucks and G.I. Joes. I didn't like Barbies.

My aunts thought I didn't walk like a girl, even though I was very young, only five or six. They'd try to pouf up my hair and put ribbons on me. I hated it when they'd do that. I had a pixie haircut. The other little girls wanted to hold hands and skip. I didn't. I said, "Don't hold my hand. That's gross."

I loved dirtbikes and playing with boys. I loved all sports—football, basketball, baseball. We built a high jump in a neighbor's yard. I loved to take things apart and put them back together—lawnmower motors, bikes, toys.

My dad was a mailman and a bricklayer. My mom was at home. I remember helping my dad lay bricks for our house. I liked to cook with my mom too. My parents let me be natural.

I have one sister, four years older than I am. We never got along. My father was physically abusive to my mother so the family kept separate, except I was close to my mother. My dad was moody and couldn't communicate so we were on pins and needles all the time. One day he got into a fist fight with my mother and cut her with a can opener he carried on his key chain. After that he left and went to California.

I was in the fifth or sixth grade when my parents divorced. At first we lived in a trailer but we couldn't afford it and lost it. My sister got pregnant at sixteen and moved out. When I was in the seventh grade my mother and I started living in motels—trucker motels—my mother had trucker boyfriends. I dropped out of school in seventh grade. No one seemed to notice. At one motel I spent my days helping the owners clean it. I hung around.

I had so much going on inside me that school seemed, well, trivial—the social life, the fads and fashion. The froufrou hairdos and makeup. I didn't fit in in seventh grade.

I worked at a flower shop too, where my aunts worked. We could never get ahead to rent an apartment. My mother had high blood pressure. I had to take care of her. I walked her to her doctor appointments to make sure she went. I was worried I'd lose her. I still take care of her. [now she's upset—pain crosses her face] CRIPES. I've got to stop it. I've got to say, "Mom, I'm not your mother—you're going to have to take care of this yourself."

My father went to court to get custody of me. The judge said my father had money, so he gave me to him. But my father didn't want me, he only didn't want to pay child support to my mother, so I didn't go with him.

I asked him for money, but he said, "If I give you money your mother will spend it on herself." So he didn't give me any. Now he's an alcoholic.

We were so poor. I collected bottles. I remember my aunts going to a store opening to "buy one item and get a free loaf of bread." Eventually we got on welfare and got into a trailer. We never had enough, but we had more than before. I was put back into school but dropped out again in the eighth grade.

When I was sixteen we had an apartment. I became interested in martial arts and hung around the martial arts club. I worked for the family who owned it—they didn't pay me but they let me take free lessons. They treated me like family and let me eat there. I met wonderful people who fed me. I spent all my time there. My mom's boyfriends lived with us in our one bedroom apartment. We had two beds in one room. I don't specifically remember anything but I know things went on that didn't feel right. I know something there affected me. [She holds her head in both hands in an involuntary gesture of pain.] I had to be aware. It had to affect me.

I know this probably makes my mom sound like a lousy person, but she's not. I feel close to her.

The life was crappy—but she wasn't.

My experiences in martial arts were educational—in self-esteem and different ways of life. I spent seven years in martial arts. I started at Carlos and Carmine's club. They were young and Italian. We taught Kung Fu. They always told me "you can do it," and at sixteen I studied on my own and got a GED diploma for high school and started junior college. I went for one and three-quarters years. I remember Carmine had a lesbian sister and they talked really bad about her being a lesbian. They were very homophobic and I listened. I didn't know anything. I agreed with them. After a while I began to feel used by Carlos—teaching and working hard and not getting paid. And I was meeting people and going to college. So I quit. I went to X-ray tech school and worked in a hospital for a while but I missed martial arts and went back to it, at a different school. But soon I felt used again. I taught all day long, did all the teaching and had low pay. After a year I left.

During the years I was in martial arts I dated guys. In fact I was homophobic about any women who came to martial arts. I'd say, "I'm not going to teach them—ugh—I'm not going to hug them." [as in a martial arts hold] And probably all the time people were looking at me and saying, "She's a dyke." I say that now because of pictures of me at that time. I look at them now and I can see that. [Actually I don't see it looking at her now. To me she just looks like an attractive woman.]

But I thought lesbians were gross. I was dating guys—great guys, kind guys. They loved me . . . but I always felt I could do without them. Lovemaking was hollow. I felt like I knew what love should be but I wasn't feeling it. I was looking for a certain feeling in my *heart*—a feeling of being engulfed by love. I had a sense that love should be all-encompassing. I knew in my heart that the feelings I was experiencing with these men weren't special. I had sex with them but thought, "Is it over?" "Are you done?" I remember one man, one night, gave me a good time.

I went back to school—this time at Colorado State. I studied premed. I wanted to pull myself out of the hole I was in. I was reaching.

After leaving martial arts I was really depressed. I was suicidal. Martial arts had been my life. I used to cut myself, with a knife. Physical pain was easier than emotional pain.

I lived in a rooming house and then in my grandmother's basement. At a neighbor's hot tub party I met Anna. She was an older woman student and she gave Swedish massages and taught piano to support herself. We became friends and she gave me massages. She listened to me and talked to me. Her compassion opened me up. She helped me learn to feel. She made me feel safe enough to allow myself to feel. We weren't lovers and she wasn't a lesbian. But through her compassion and the physical touch of massage I learned to allow myself to feel. I found I craved to be touched.

I asked Linda if she'd received affection as a child. She said, "Yes . . . I remember . . . from my mom. I remember things . . . sitting on her lap learning to do a button. I remember feeling close to her. I still feel close." She continued her story.

Anna belonged to the Non-traditional Students Club, a club for older women and men on campus. I used to go with her. The club room was right next to the Alliance Club room, a lesbian club. We used to walk by and I looked in and thought, "Those women are weird." I had no feeling of identity with them.

Anna left school and that summer I worked in Nevada. I hung around bars and picked up men. I kept thinking, "This doesn't work." When I went back to school I started getting massages from Angel. She was a lesbian and a member of the Alliance Club. I'd first seen her on a panel discussion about lesbians. Eventually I asked her about lesbians and she explained it to me. I listened and it felt right. The feelings she expressed struck a chord—like, hey, this feels right.

I went to my mom and told her I felt I wanted to try

dating women. My mom said she just wanted me to be happy.

The first woman I went out with was a bellhop named Gilda. She had blue eyes and blond hair. I got so giddy I ended up staying all night. She kissed me. I didn't know what I was doing—it was so easy. It was like a light went on in me. Then I was lovesick. I couldn't eat. The relationship was so *intense.* Women have this compassion and this intensity.

I dropped out of school. I had too many loans and my grades were not good enough. I moved around. Estes Park. Boulder. Ft. Collins. I went to a rooming house to rent a room and saw Carol there. I didn't rent the room but I remembered Carol. Later I saw her come into a gay bar where I was bartending. She had been in a relationship for six or seven years. One night she sat at the bar and I was mixing her drink. I told her, "I want to meet the person who will make my heart go WHOOOSH." Then I looked up at her and my heart did go POP! . . . that was it.

I took her out and I was all nervous . . . I tried to impress her. We parked and held hands . . . I thought, "This touch is what I want—this is what I've been looking for." We were soulmates.

I've been with Carol for four and a half years now. Her family treats me well. We live a normal life. We're married. It seems strange to me now how society, Carmine, had taught me to hate lesbians.

February 11 is our date. I met her on February 11. A few weeks later I asked her to "marry me." I'd never even thought those words before, and they just came out. Then she asked me. We both verbally said what we'd felt on February 11.

We sat in the bathtub one night and talked about what

"marriage" meant. We made a commitment: to be monogamous; to be mutual—we are both to help one another; to let the other person know if you are unhappy; to never devastate the other by being disloyal.

We had our wedding March 31. We had a reception at Carol's house, champagne and fish on the grill. At first we had JCPenney rings. Later we saved for better rings.

My mother said, "This isn't what I wanted for you—I wanted you to marry, have a home, have kids—"

I told her, "That's what I want too."

I asked Linda what her life is like now.

It's normal. We worry about bills. We're making a major move. Carol is going back to school to get her master's degree. Sometimes we worry about our relationship. We want kids. Someday we want to be called grandma.

We have no real problems. I'm not good at saving money. I guess it goes back to those motel days—if I got a dollar I spent it—not on anything good for me, but on a Pepsi and a candy bar . . . something that made me feel good.

Sometimes we get emotional. First—women do that. And then we find out we're saying the same thing. "Well, that's what I was saying!"

Sex? I used to think "ugh." Now I say, "I've never had it so good." I've never faked it.

I love Carol more than half the men in America love their wives—and they call me crazy.

Last Sunday evening we were walking down at the cove. It was so beautiful and I wanted to take Carol's hand. But I can't. Society says I can't. I can't hold her hand, or kiss her, or dance with her in public—I'm afraid someone will bash her head in.

People stare at us. "Look at those dykes."

Some people say, "You have a right to show affection in public." Yeah. They don't know—someone around the corner could just decide to bash your loved one's head in. They don't know.

Society says I'm wrong. Religion says, "God says it's wrong." I don't believe it. I love her. I love being with her—she's my best friend. We wrestle, we play, we make love—not sex, love. We're married. We made a commitment.

I don't believe God says it's wrong.

It can't be wrong. It feels too right to be wrong.

I ask her, "Are you angry?"

Yes, I'm angry.

When we finished talking, she said she felt terrific. Telling her story had been cathartic. We met once more because I wanted to ask her about her cutting herself.

I started doing it after I stopped martial arts. I didn't have that physical release for my pain anymore. I needed to inflict pain on myself. I cut myself with knives, with pieces of glass. I think I changed my inner hurt into anger, and then took it out on myself. The feeling of pain was at least feeling.

I think I cut myself because of my childhood pain—my mother giving love to men and to their children, but not to me. As a teenager I really wanted her love. Now my mother apologizes. I love her, but I don't want to be that close anymore. She wants me to be a caretaker.

When I met Carol I found out she had done it too . . . cut herself. We pledged to not cut ourselves anymore.

I asked her how she sees herself now.

As a warrior.

The following weekend I was to meet Carol. Linda had felt freed by telling her story and she wanted Carol to tell hers too. I was to meet them at Ann's house. My son John was with me. He was going to do some work for Ann.

Linda and Carol arrived together. I was waiting in the front yard with Ann. As they got out of their car and walked toward me I was struck by one fact—they looked like twins. Both slender, both blondes, both wearing white shirts and stonewashed jeans. I kept watching as they walked closer. Twins.

Linda had said they were soulmates, but they actually looked like each other. This was something I was later to see often in other gay couples.

Carol was excited to see Ann and tell her she'd been in an accident that afternoon. It wasn't her fault. She's a bus driver and a woman ran into her bus. "I was so angry. I really was. I told her off. That's not like me, but I did." Her face is fiery.

ANN: What did you say?
CAROL: I leaned out the window and shook my arm at her and said, "You're a terrible driver."

Ann laughed and said, "Right. You really told her off."
Linda laughed too. I noticed that Linda and Ann laughed at Carol's rather cute, sweet and harmless anger, the way men laugh at women sometimes.

I'm taking it all in. Carol is blushing at Ann's and Linda's reaction. She's looking at me with a certain hostility. I'm looking at her. She doesn't look as much like Linda close up as I'd thought. Linda has a polished and glossy look even though she doesn't wear makeup. She's a beauty. Carol is a little smaller. Her hair is reddish. It does not have the styled, coifed look that Linda's does. Its shape is undefined, it's fine and frizzy. It looks like it had a perm that didn't take well. Linda's complexion is smooth and translucent. Carol's is too pale and freckly—a redhead's complexion. Linda's figure is athletic and perfect. She moves with long-legged grace. Carol is a tad shorter, and has pear shaped, fuller hips, is wearing a different style jeans to accomodate her more female form. Linda fits in the slim legged jeans of men and super models. So up close they aren't quite twins after all. Carol seems smaller and more fragile.

I cannot believe she drives a bus—now for a hospital, but in Colorado she drove a city transport bus. She seems tiny with thin arms. No one would ever guess she is a bus driver. Once again these women surprise me. They have no preconceptions of what they can do or what their roles are. I see types and roles melt and change before my eyes again and again.

Carol and I settle on the patio to talk. She looks at me with suspicion and pulls back when I speak. Linda gives her a squeeze and a hug and sits down. I look toward the house. I felt uncomfortable about the squeeze and the hug and I was hoping my fourteen-year-old son had not seen it. I felt guilty about feeling uncomfortable.

I told Linda she had to leave. She told Carol, "It's going to be all right." To me she says, "I told her it would make her feel wonderful."

The moment Linda left Carol asked me, suspiciously, "Why do you want to know about me?" and I knew she'd been forced into it. I explained Ann's and my idea to let

people who didn't know any lesbians well learn who they are so they wouldn't fear them, and not thus hate them. Carol allowed that that understanding was important for lesbians to live someday without fear of that hatred. So she cautiously and reluctantly began her story.

I'm a Mormon. At least I was born and raised a Mormon. I have three older sisters and a younger brother. My mother was eighteen when her first child was born. She had two nervous breakdowns. They were only for a few days. My next older sister, Cathy, was hyperactive. She was athletic. I wasn't. I was overweight. We played ball together and walked downtown together. When she was nineteen and I was seventeen she tried to commit suicide, several times. She had these mood swings.

When I was in junior high school I was painfully shy. I was overweight and had braces and acne and stringy, straight hair and I thought I was ugly as hell. I was befriended by this girl Brenda. We did everything together. We talked on the phone all the time and played racquetball. She helped me lose weight. I lost weight but I still dressed like a fat girl. I wore big jackets, even when it was hot.

I spent a lot of overnights at Brenda's house. She smoked pot and drank. She had glamorous clothes and a nice house. Her father was a lawyer. I was impressed. I didn't take her to my house. I was ashamed of it. It was always messy and my mother was moody or yelling. I thought, "Why does Brenda want to be friends with me?" Our favorite thing was to play the piano together.

When I was thirteen or fourteen I kissed Brenda. Neither of us had kissed a girl before. Brenda had kissed boys. We instinctively thought what we'd done was bad and we should hide it.

We asked each other, "Do you think we're lesbians?"

"No," we decided. "No. It's just us—we have a special relationship."

We kept together through high school. In her junior year of high school Brenda was raped by a Mexican cousin and got pregnant. She never was the same after that. She never felt the same about herself. She went to another woman. I said, "But I thought you weren't a lesbian?"

I'd left the church in high school and now I went back to it. I started dating Mormon boys.

I ask Carol, "Did you ever have sex with a man?"

She bristles, angry. "Why do you want to know that?"

"I'm sorry," I say. "I just wondered how you felt about it if you did—I mean was it good for you, or was it different than what you have now, with a woman? I think people need to know that."

She accepts this and answers the question.

With a couple of the men I dated I had sex. I almost got married to one. We were good friends. We had fun together. He taught me how to surf. Once after we'd had sex he cried, "Why don't you love me?"

I told him, "I don't want to get married."

I had another boyfriend. We had sex. It was about the same. I liked it but it just felt like we were kids experimenting. Sex was—almost—a letdown.

He was romantic. He bought me flowers. He cooked dinner. He'd seduce me. But penetration was a letdown. I wasn't using any birth control. I thought I wasn't active enough to need it. Our plan was he'd pull out.

I was unhappy and dropped out of junior college. I started working at places around town and tutoring at the high school. Then I met Matty. She was Brenda's ex-lover. She called me. I was immediately—instantly and innately—attracted to her. On the surface everything was wrong. Number one, she was a woman. Number two, she had a terrible personality. But I couldn't stop thinking about her, listening for the phone. The excitement—it was thrilling. I didn't feel in control. This rang a bell. Then I remembered. This was how I'd felt about Brenda.

We moved to Colorado. She was going to be a graduate student in English. I was with her for seven years. Our relationship was bad. I was insecure in how to be a lover to her. She was demanding, and insecure too. Physically things were not good between us. She'd talk to me about literature and I'd feel stupid. We became friends but not lovers. We should have stopped living together after the first two months. For three years after that we lived together with the tension of her having another lover, Donna. Matty was intense and dramatic and loved playing Donna and me off against each other, of making us compete for her attention.

I wanted to leave but Matty kept saying, "You can't throw this away. You'll never find this again."

My mother finally asked, "Is Matty a lesbian?" (pause) "Are you a lesbian?"

CAROL: Yes.
MOTHER: That's what I thought.

She didn't talk about her feelings and she didn't like Matty. She only said, "I'll love you because you're my child—I'll never like what you're doing." Later Linda changed all that.

Dad said, "We'll always be here if you need us."

For a long time I had to stop talking to Mom. She always

had an undertone in her voice. Recently she told me, "I respect your courage for doing what you have to do—what you believe in."

Now I can use the words lesbian, gay, and homosexual in front of her.

My life changed when I met Linda. I called my mom and told her. I was so proud.

Carol's gestures have by now become expressive. She's talking with animation and openness. The hostility is gone.

Linda came to the house where I lived to rent a room. She didn't rent the room but I saw her. She was so attractive. She always dressed sharp—she looked like money, like Boulder money. I felt very nervous around her. I'd never felt like that before.

I'd been pushing myself to go out. I just sat around and read and didn't see anyone. Finally I made myself go out. I went to a bar and Linda came in. She was dressed so well. She was a real flirt. She had a lot of self-confidence. We danced together and I felt guilty about Matty. Linda said, "It's all right. We're just dancing."

I was a city busdriver at that time. I started stopping after work at the bar where Linda bartended. I'd find myself standing outside getting nervous about going in. I was scared. I knew I was getting feelings. I'd sit at the bar and read the newspaper, then go home early.

Once Linda said, "Let's go to the movies, like two Saturdays from now when I don't work."

I waited but she didn't call. I was upset. Linda says she said, "Maybe." "Maybe we can go to the movies."

Linda was a cool bartender. All the women liked her. Later I went back to the bar. I talked with Linda about

Matty. I looked at her and suddenly she just reached into my heart.

We'd been talking about the empty feeling about breaking up with someone. We talked about the feeling you *want* to have, when your heart goes WHOOSH.

And it happened.

The feeling was so spontaneous. Innate. We weren't trying. It just happened.

She asked me out for Saturday. The next day, Friday, I went in with a friend. Linda asked me for a hug. It felt so wonderful—not sexual—just . . . *right* . . . like we sank three inches into each other.

I said, "Why does this feel so comfortable?"

She said, "Why not?"

The intensity with Linda never stopped.

Everything with Matty was wiped out. The slate was clean. My feeling was so deep for Linda, so complete—there was no hurt or anger in me for Matty.

I told my mother I was going to marry Linda. I said, "Of course it isn't legal, Mom, but it's the same to me." I just kept calling my mom and talking to her like a friend. I had all this energy and I had to share it. My mom said, "I love you, but I don't approve of what you're doing."

At springbreak I took Linda home. I "returned" to my family. They liked Linda for bringing me home, for making me happy. Now we've been together four and a half years. Linda is more outgoing than I am. She speaks out. I've always wanted to do that myself. She's real genuine. She talks—she gives my family hugs—even if they don't want them.

She opened my family up—they weren't ever affectionate and didn't talk. Linda says, "I'm Linda, and here's what I think." My family respects Linda, and they respect my relationship with her like I respect their marriages.

Yeah . . . we still cry sometimes when we make love. Sometimes we get caught up in work—then we come back—one of us looks at the other and OOOSH! it all gushes up again, all the same old feelings.

Ninety percent of our relationship is not sexual. It's touching. But in public you can't touch. Linda says to me in a grocery store, "You can't do that," when I put my hand on her back. We have to open our space in public, move further apart—lose the look of intimacy. Then it starts seeping into our home, and that's when I get angry—when our relationship turns into a struggle. [She pauses.] That outside pressure keeps us working on our relationship.

You have to stop and take time for each other. Last night we went to the cove for a walk. It was dark. We held hands and kissed a little—there was no one to see.

I tell her, "It sometimes bothers me to see the open affection—I feel uncomfortable."

I understand—it used to me too. I thought, "Two women together!" Now I'm used to gay bars—and if I ever go to a straight bar, which is rare, and see a man and a woman together, it looks so strange to me—I think, "What is she doing with him? Why doesn't she find a good woman."

Now my family accepts Linda's and my relationship as natural—are comfortable. My mom doesn't say anymore, "I love you, but . . ." Just, "Carol, I really love you." And I can say, "Mom, I love you too. Mom, you're my best friend."

I worry about Linda. I worry that she's not as self-confident as she was when I first met her. I wonder if I took that away from her.

I say, "No—maybe she's just letting you see the real Linda."

The interview is over when Linda rushes out and sits in a chair. She pulls Carol onto her lap and kisses her cheek. "Was it great to talk? Do you feel great?"

Carol puts her arms around her, "Yes. I feel great."

I glance at the house. Is John seeing this? Would it seem freaky to him? I hate the mix of guilt and discomfort I feel. But Carol had said, "I understand."

I look at the two of them. So happy together. Both think they are the lucky one. Both worry about losing the other. For them they've found the "other" that makes them complete.

As I write this now and remember them with affection I think of something I heard on the radio, on National Public Radio, the other day. I don't know who was talking, I'd tuned in in the middle, but it was a gay man. Explaining. He said, "Homosexuality is not about sex. It's about love. It's whom you love."

People are surprised by love. People wait for a love that they've only imagined in their hearts. They are stunned when it suddenly arrives. People like Linda and Carol, like Sandy, are surprised when they find they feel this love for someone of the same sex.

[Linda and Carol asked that their real names be used. "Why not?" they asked.]

3
CEO

I KNEW IF I was going to write this book that I wanted Gillian Bergman in it. I had heard about her from Ann to the point she had taken on mythical proportions in my imagination. Strong, tough, owns her own company, drives a red Ferrari. She never showed up at the parties at Ann's. Ann had lived with her when Ann was going through the struggle of "coming out." Ann had said, "She let me drive the Ferrari and I went wild, driving around looking for girls. And I could bring anyone home. There was nothing romantic between Gillian and me. She just let me live in her house." I had seen a picture of her that summer in a national newsmagazine. She looked strong, she looked like Martina Navratilova. She was wearing a fedora-style hat. She was with a soft, slightly plump, young-Shelley Winters looking woman with blond hair blowing in the wind. They were climbing into the cockpit of a plane. It looked like Gillian was going to fly it. I had stared at the picture in absolute wonder. It was a full page. It was about this amazing, woman-owned corporation. They were the CEO and president. They brought hope to women that they could succeed. I wondered how many thousands of people would see that photograph and be charmed by it. I wondered how many, if any, would ever think they are lesbians.

I phoned Ann and said, "I want to interview Gillian for the book. Will you ask her for me?"

Two nights later the phone rang and I answered it in the kitchen. A voice I first thought to be a man's voice—strong, forceful, moderately deep and loud—said, "This is Dr. Gillian Bergman. What is this book about and can we do it over the phone?" I momentarily felt totally intimidated.

I said, "It's hard for me to say exactly what the book is about—it's about lesbians as people, so people will see them as individuals of worth. It's not about sex. I want to find out who you are as a person—I'd like to meet with you. I can't really know you over the phone."

"Okay," she said. "When does this book have to be done? I'm leaving Sunday night and I'm going to be at the Pentagon and in D.C. for ten days. I could see you—let's see, I get back on the 27th. I could see you on Wednesday."

"That would be great. I can wait. The book's going to take some time—I have no deadline."

Somehow I knew these concepts were foreign to Gillian—to Dr. Gillian Bergman, CEO. I felt almost sure that if I said I had to have the book finished in ten days she would have accepted that as matter-of-course and taken me on the plane with her to the Pentagon. As it was, it was a heady trip just talking to her on the phone. She was definitely "take charge," like the male CEOs I'd known in the corporate world.

"Meet me at 12:00 at the plant. Invite Ann. Find out when she's free. Have her call my secretary and set up the appointment. First you'll get a tour of the plant, then we'll go out to eat. I'll spring for lunch. Then we'll come back to the plant and we'll have some private time to talk. Will an hour be enough?"

I knew, although it was Saturday night and she was probably at home, she was writing in an appointment book.

"Call my PR person, Carol. Tell her I want her to send you a full PR package—company history, newspaper and magazine articles.

"I got Ann out of the closet you know.

"I've known I was gay since I was four.

"I'll give you some information to get you started. I employ over 200 people, straight, gay, and lesbian. Their livelihoods depend on me. And my security clearance. If it came out that I'm a lesbian I could lose my security clearance, would lose my security clearance and my company depends on that."

I asked, "Are you sure you would lose your security clearance?"

"Absolutely. In graduate school I would have been kicked out. I had a big scholarship. But things are better today. Have Sandy tell you about the gay bashing in the '60s, really violent.

"I sometimes wonder about my mother, if her life would have been different if the times had been different . . .

"I started my company with my lover Marilyn twenty years ago. We were together for fifteen years. Then she left me for a man. She went a little crazy—wanted to have a baby. So I bought out her half of the company and gave her cash. I kept the stock. In the end it turned out she couldn't have a baby.

"I'm forty-five years old. An old woman. (laughs)

"I want to get out of this business and start a camp for disadvantaged children. A few more years and I can do that. I can't do it now. I have too many employees to take care of. All those engineers. In this economy where could they get another job that pays what I pay them? Some of them have been with me twenty years.

"I chose to be gay. I had three men lovers. The woman I live with now, have lived with for ten years, is a wonderful woman. I'd lay down my life for her."

A few evenings later Ann and Elizabeth came by. Ann was going to repair my old computer. I told them I was overwhelmed by Gillian.

M: She totally made the plans. Unlike a woman—who would say "What would you like?"
ANN: That's her CEO mode.
M: She makes decisions like a man.
ANN: I hate it. When you want to talk to her, you have to run along—"Come on," she says, moving away, "walk with me."

(This reminded me of my ex-husband, the executive. I had to run along to talk to him at home. Follow him from room to room. He didn't even say "Come on" which would show interest. To me this is male behavior as I see my sons do the same thing. They view it as "efficient" while the runee-along feels denigrated, like a child or slave girl.)

M: What should I wear?
ANN: Well, she wears either jeans, or . . .
ELIZ.: Oh, not JEANS . . .
ANN: Or a man's suit. She has them specially tailored.
M: Does she have a Hong Kong tailor?
ANN: A woman. She comes to the office. *She* follows Jill around. Jill is always holding out little swatches of cloth to me as we walk (trot)—"Do you like this one? Do you

like this one?"
M: She told me she'd lay down her life for Joanna.
ELIZ.: She's always melodramatic.

Ten days later I was in the lobby of Jill's building waiting for Ann. I walked up to a mezzanine where I could look down on the lobby and out the two-story glass windows. I saw Ann's silver pickup truck drive in. Minutes later I watched a nice looking young man, slightly overweight, with neat, thick, brown hair, wearing a T-shirt and black pants with suspenders—a typical engineering type guy—walk through the door.

In a moment, shocked, I realized it was Ann. It was as if I'd looked at her in a mirror that gave me a different perspective. I didn't see the Ann that I tried to talk into buying some soft, flowered dresses. Now I knew that vision was ludicrous. This was Ann.

Upstairs we got our security badges, Ann gave me a tour, and I waited to meet Jill. Suddenly she burst into the room, smiling, and gave me a hug as naturally as if we were old friends. I was totally charmed and disarmed. She wasn't physically intimidating as I'd expected. She didn't have the strong, muscular body of a Martina. She was slender, almost delicate, not tall, and vibrant, with a blushy, girlish, smiling manner. I felt immediately comfortable. Her hair was straight, wispy, and blond, and in a little girl plain bob. She wore no makeup—her skin was pretty and fresh and her cheeks naturally rosy. She was wearing navy blue pinstriped trousers with suspenders and a white with red pinstripes tailored shirt with a mandarin collar and monograms on the sleeves. Standing there with her hands jammed in her trouser pockets, she looked much younger than her forty-five years—she looked like a little girl doing a funky dress-up.

"Thought you were coming yesterday. Did the three-piece suit thing for you. Damn secretary f---ed up. Got to fire her. She does that all the time, and worse. I'm too soft. Keep thinking she'll get better. I'll let her go next week. Come with me. I've got to make a couple phone calls before we eat. Busy schedule." The roller coaster ride of being with Jill had begun.

We walked into her office. On the wall was a giant poster of Paul Newman and Robert Redford as Butch Cassidy and the Sundance Kid. She smiled at it as she walked behind her desk, "My heroes." Yes, I could see it. She herself reminded me of Paul Newman as Butch Cassidy—quick, sharp, fast, wiry, tough. In her pinstriped suit it could have been her in the picture—a girl Butch Cassidy with his legendary high spirits, playacting, verve, and nerve.

I sat back in my chair and listened to four or five rapid phone calls. I was stunned at the rapid-fire style, the vocabulary that was cleaned up for women and tough and cussing with men. The roller coaster was picking up speed. I cursed myself for not having a tape recorder.

A phone call to a woman went like this.

"Hi, it's Jill. Returning your call. How are you? Um-hmm, um-hmm—um-hmm. Well, that's great." More um-hmm's. And she's shaking her head from side to side and making a yakety-yakety gesture to me with thumb and fingers, like a shadow-duck quacking. "Okay. I love you, hon." Hangs up. Lets out a huge sigh, raises her eyebrows at me, and dials the next number on her list of calls to return.

A phone call to a man.

"Hey, Jim. Jill. How's the family? Great. How's the job? Oh, that's shit. Uh-huh. No shit. A V.P.? That's great—you're the youngest? No shit. Congratulations—like me—I'm the youngest woman president of her own company.

Yeah? Well, there's always shit. You just have to get around it. Why I'm calling is I have this problem at DEX, Inc. I talked with this woman Sylvia—but I need to go higher up, so—who can I talk to? I don't want to step on any toes. Uh-huh. No shit. Oh, hell. (Writing) Okay. I'll call him. Can I use your name? Yeah, you'll probably end up out here and I'll be out there. Yeah. Shit. Uh-huh. Okay."

She hangs up. No good-bye. Men don't bother with the extra words, at least not men with power, unless they're talking to a woman.

Three more calls in about that many minutes. Then she said, "Lunch. We're going to eat here. I've got these Pentagon guys in town and I don't have time to go out. I made some pasta salad for us this morning before I came in."

Now we were three women. Setting up lunch in the large, posh conference room with charcoal-tinted windows, Jill's conference room. Everyone helping. Setting out the two salads, the pasta and feta cheese that Jill and Ann discussed how much to heat it in the microwave, and the cold green salad with oriental vegetables. It was a good lunch. (Later when I remarked that Jill is a good cook, Ann huffed—"That's her entire repertoire—salad and pasta.")

Ann had sold me for three dollars a little "Kidcorder" (child's tape recorder) that she had picked up in her garage sale business. It was bright yellow and red and Ann thought it would be nonthreatening. It didn't threaten Jill so I turned it on while we talked and ate. Later I discovered it made a whacking noise as it recorded and that Ann's aside comments were spoken too low to register.

JILL: Do you want to move that closer? I can't believe Ann charged you for this. She should have paid you three dollars to take the thing—the way it looks.

M: You were twenty-four when you came to California?

JILL: Yeah. I was twenty-four and Marilyn was twenty-seven. We came out driving two sports cars. I still have one of them. I just said I'm going to California, and she said I think I'll quit my job and go with you. It's not like we planned it. When you're twenty, man, you don't plan anything. You know, someone says to me, "How the hell did you do this? You started this company with no capital and no resources and this portable typewriter your parents had given you in graduate school that wasn't even *electric*." We had no name, we had no reputation, and the answer is, we were young—we didn't know any better. Had someone said to me, "Had it dawned on you you could fail doing this?" The answer is, "Absolutely not." Failure? We were trying to survive. We were trying to buy groceries. We came cross-country with two backpacks, two sports cars, and two puppy dogs.

We thought we had teaching jobs. They told me, "Be here by the first of the month." We thought they meant September. They meant August. Shit, we didn't know school in California started in August. We thought it started in September like it did back east. When we got here they said, "Where've you been?" They'd given the jobs to somebody else.

We decided we wanted to live where there were pine trees so we drove up to the mountains. This is after Marilyn told me we only had sixty-four dollars and change left. She panicked. "What are we going to do?"

"Shit," I said. "I don't know. I guess we're in the consulting business."

Little did it dawn on me that I had just told my father I would never be stupid enough to go into business because I saw my parents' design business—well, I knew, the only freedom you have owning your own business is what twenty-four hours a day you work. So I must have come to this, I sort of came to this, hereditarily I'm afraid to say.

You'll have to edit this. I'll tell you the true story. We arrived in this mountain town. It was a hundred and goddamn somethin' degrees, and it was right after Labor Day because we started the business September 7. I'm in business twenty years this month. We drove up to this real estate office we saw a sign for, and I'm in my bra, because it was so goddamn hot. I maintained I could pull into a gas station in my bra and with this bod no one would even notice, and I was usually right. But Marilyn went in alone because she thought I shouldn't go in in my bra. She was in there about an hour, so finally I went in and said, "What gives? I'm starving. It's getting a little hot sitting out in the car with the top down." This woman, Rita, wearing cowboy boots is sitting there with her feet up on the desk, insisting there is no place to rent. So we took her out to lunch and she told us to go to her friend Diane's house the next morning. The next day we show up at eleven o'clock in the morning. I had my shirt on this time—trying to make an impression of course. Now Diane has this stone house and a chicken coop and outbuildings, and she walks out and hands me a Coors and I thought, this is where I want to live. Now this is before Coors had a bad reputation. In those days Coors didn't exist on the east coast so if you could get a Coors, man that was the ultimate. I thought, beer in the morning, this California life is for me. Where I came from you couldn't even buy beer on a Sunday, never mind drinking it.

So we moved into a single room in the chicken coop.

Then Diane and Rita found out we had nothing but two backpacks so they hauled in some furniture and a victrola and records. And Diane was always inviting us over for dinner, having a few other people over so it looked like a party not like charity. And when she had to come over and get a hornets' nest out of the shower she discovered we didn't have hot water and used that as an excuse not to charge rent for three months. They did everything they could to help us, despite ourselves.

M: What is your educational background?

JILL: My undergraduate is in radio/television broadcast electronics. I started as a disc jockey, I thought that was what I wanted to do, but I spent one semester as a disc jockey and thought I'd go absolutely f---ing out of my mind if I had to talk to a microphone for the rest of my life.

M: With no people around?

JILL: Yeah. It was driving me crazy. Then I went to grad school and got an Instructional Systems degree and concurrently a teaching degree in Massachusetts. I was commuting about a ten and a half hour trip to upstate New York where my lover lived. Marilyn's best friend was my first female lover. Then I was teaching at a community college and got a post-grad degree in computer science and then my Ph.D. is in Systems Management. I got to design a multimedia center for the college which was really neat because high tech video equipment was just coming in and I got to draw on my architectural design experience from my background with my parents.

M: Were your parents well-to-do?

JILL: Not at that time. I worked in a pizza place in undergrad school—lived there, because I needed people around me. Ann's been there. My boss, Mr. Guiseppi, always said my real degree was from Guiseppi's Pizza. I did my undergrad degree in three years because my sister Katy was coming to school and I didn't want my parents to have to pay for two of us at the same time. I knew they couldn't afford it. They were in their early forties and their business hadn't taken off yet. I went off to grad school on a full scholarship the year my sister started school. She's a psychotherapist.

ANN: Tell her you're different.

JILL: Well, yes. (she laughs) We're night and day. Night and day. I'm a technologist. She's a psychologist. They're very, very different skill bases. I mean, I say, "Katy, I'm having trouble with the schematics," and she says (Jill uses a very deep voice), "How do you feel about that?" She's not a business person. She inherited my father's artistic capabilities.

We recently went back to the camp where we went as children. That camp experience was so important. It made us much stronger women. In those days there weren't women's sports in the schools. My parents didn't know what to do with us in the summer, they were working in New York, so they sent us to my aunt's in the mountains and this camp every summer.

My friend Stan Reicher was my longtime friend and high school boyfriend. He lives here in town. He moved out here and moved in when he got divorced. Maybe we should talk about that as well. I had three long term and very nice male relationships prior to deciding it just wasn't for me.

M: That would be interesting. Everyone I've talked to has a totally different take on that element. Look at Ann—she's saying "I told you so."

JILL: Stan was my first boyfriend. We were together from the age of fourteen and all through high school. We didn't lose our virginity until college and didn't tell my mother until about five years ago. Then I was with Bob for a while and I was engaged to be married.

M: This was in college?

JILL: Yeah.

M: Did you find them very attractive, physically, sexually? I don't mean were they attractive people, but I mean did you feel an enormous attraction to them? Or were they good companions?

JILL: Well, Randall was very attractive to me—very, very handsome man. He still is. He's Jonnie and my best friend. In fact my lover of ten years and Randall were born on the same day, which is kind of ironic. (Here her voice clouds with emotion when she mentions Joanna, Jonnie, as her lover.)

M: Did your heart go flutter-flutter? That sort of thing?

JILL: I don't remember flutter-flutter. I don't know if I knew what flutter-flutter was. (laughs)

M: Well, it can still flutter. (I'm laughing too)

Jill: (suddenly serious) What happened was Randall said to me, "Have you noticed that we're looking at the same women? And they're looking back at you, not at me. Maybe we should just be friends."

M: There was Stan and Bob . . . What age were you?

JILL: Stan and I were 15 and 16. Bob and I were 17, 18. Randall and I were 19, 20, and then I gave it all up. It was very simple. Jenny kissed me in the bathroom and I thought, "**This is wonderful.**"

M: Oh, it was a lot better than . . . all the other stuff?

JILL: No. It was different. It wasn't better. It was just different.

M: It was different.

JILL: Uh-hmm. It was just different. I thought, "This is

real . . ." and I knew . . . (the thoughts break off)
M: What's your earliest . . . kind of . . . memory?
JILL: Kindergarten. (pause, her voice has a choke of emotion) Probably.

I grew up in a neighborhood of sixteen boys and me. My mother is the tough, controlling strength of the family, and my father is the one who cries all the time, and is very, very sensitive, artistic.
ANN: I would characterize her as the grand patriarch. Oh, I don't mean that.
M: She said "grand patriarch"—she had to correct herself—
JILL: (laughing too) Same difference. Everybody finds her tough. I don't find her tough because I'm her kid. She's backed off on me. Particularly now that she's totally accepted me and my life. It took her fifteen years. We look a lot alike and that's a problem for her. I think if my sister had been gay . . . because my sister's much bigger and my sister looks like a dyke. (She lowered her voice on the last four words.)
M: See, I expected you to be . . . well, you had rich mythical proportions in my mind. And when you walked in and gave me a hug—you're not really tall, you're slender. I expected you to be imposing.
JILL: My mother's imposing. My mother's about six foot, before she broke her back. I'm about five-nine. My sister is a half inch shorter than I am and looks two inches taller. Her hands are half again larger than mine. She wears a size 10 1/2 shoe. I wear an eight. Katy's skinny weight is probably 155-160 and I weigh 118. I'm the runt of the litter. My sister's very dark, she has a dark, thick head of curly, brown hair, and a little nose. The only similarity between us is we're both left-handed. So is my mother. I told my father when we were eating dinner

the other day that I never knew the whole world wasn't left-handed until I went off to college. My father was the odd-man-out. Besides being right-handed, he was the only man in the house. Even our dogs were females. My father loves women. He's very, very . . . adorable. He's got a big handlebar moustache. He's really a cartoon caricature. He's got a great sense of humor, and his girls were going to succeed. My parents, if they ever gave us a message, it was to get educated . . . that was the only way.

My mother never graduated from high school. My father is self-made, only had one drafting course. How the hell these people ended up with the fifth largest interior design firm in the United States, I have no idea. They did very well in later years for themselves, employed 50-80 people which in interior design is a big outfit.

My mother ran the business and was chairman of the board, (she laughs) needless to say. My father and the staff did the designs. My father specialized in humanizing Wall Street facilities, which in the '20s, '30s, '40s were ticker tape offices. My parents are in their 70s. My father modernized and humanized the buildings. That was where they made their niche.

Anyway, my father was convinced he had to teach me . . . Katy grew up with girls. Everyone Katy's age, because there're four years between us, close to it, was girls.

M: She's older?

JILL: Younger. She's younger going on about **sixty**. A very serious, also controlling, old soul. I've got Dad's humor and kind of lightness about life. You'd have to see the dynamic to believe it. But I would guess that my father probably perceived—I mean here was this skinny, little girl, who's gotta survive with a bunch of boys, her age and older—my mother said, "Teach her how to throw a ball." Before we knew it I was "up" fourth and I was playing first base and I was the captain of the team. And it never stopped after that.

My mother was a semi-pro basketball player, after high school, then the war came. That was good though—you know, like you read about *League of Their Own,* that was a time there were probably more women's sports than ever before. She really gave up the career, in my opinion, though they don't talk about it, to marry my dad. And it was a good marriage for both of them. They've been married fifty-one years. But, I mean, very good—**these people are bizarre**. They not only drove two hours into Manhattan to work every day of their lives together for forty-seven years, but, when they got there, they **sat in the same office**. They didn't even have separate offices. Mom's desk was here, and Dad's desk was the other way, was there, and that was **corporate**. They didn't travel. I don't ever remember them taking a vacation until I was in college.

M: Let's go back to when you were four. You said when you were four you knew you were gay.

JILL: Four or five.

M: What kind of experiences . . . what kind of feelings let you know that?

JILL: I just felt like I was a boy.

M: Oh, you felt like a boy.

JILL: But I don't know if that was because I was surrounded by only boys. It's really hard to determine when you're that age. I had to survive. I mean, I could tell you funny stories. I remember we all went into the woods and we all lined up and we all showed everybody our pee-pees, and I don't have one. You know, so the guys liked me enough and I was a good enough athlete, that they made like I was special. "Jill is special," instead of picking on me because I didn't have one. From then on I was captain of everything. And I was. I was good.

M: And you were comfortable with the boy culture?

JILL: Oh yeah. I don't know. I never knew anything else. I mean I had a stuffed rabbit that wound up and sang something when I was a kid, but I didn't have dolls. I had one doll my parents gave me that we named Todd when Katy was born because they didn't want me to be without a baby, and it sat on the shelf for about thirty years I think, until the rubber rotted . . . you know.

Then Katy and I went to camp when she was five and I was eight and it happened to be a very small camp which really helped because all the sports were co-ed. Even this weekend we all played coed sports which was great. Two doubles. Two singles. Two RBI's. And I scored twice. I was rebel-god again. Yeah, I was very proud of myself for an old lady. I thought, "Hey, this Sunshine Creek Camp[3] shit's for me." I came in glowing. Jonnie said, "There's no living with her." Plus my volleyball team won three out of three—in a *dramatic* comeback.

M: So you had quite a weekend.

(We're all laughing.)

JILL: I didn't break any bones either. They were taking bets Gillian'd come back in pieces. I was remarkably pleased with myself—that was kind of neat. Anyway . . .

ANN: You were saying you felt different.

JILL: I think I always knew.

M: You didn't have anything to call it then, but you felt

---

3 Sunshine Creek is the summer camp Jill has started.

like a boy.

JILL: I got kissed when I was fourteen years old at camp. A woman threw me in a haystack and kissed me. Unfortunately one of the counselors saw it and called my mother.

M: This was a grown woman?

JILL: No. She was a year older. I was thirteen, so she was fourteen. And I thought, hmmm, this is pretty neat, but you know, we all had boyfriends we walked around holding hands with. You have to understand this is a pretty prudish generation. This is the '50s. This is Ozzie and Harriet. I'm an old lady. We went to that camp until I was in college. Many of those people are still friends of mine.

I'm not a person who gets rid of people. There are very few people I would X out of my life. I mean, you've got to really push me. I mean like that Francine person—she ran off with all my credit cards and I had to get the FBI after her.

(Ann is laughing. She must remember the event vividly. Jill is not laughing. She sounds sadly serious now.)

All my ex-lovers are friends of mine, women and men. I haven't had very many women. I stood up at Bob's wedding. What do they call you in a Quaker wedding? Best woman? No, monsignor, something. It sounded very religious to me.

M: Who did you lose your virginity to?

JILL: Stan. I slept with all three of them. Yeah. Randall always bopped in and out of my life—still does. We were always like best best buddies.

M: Was sleeping with men . . . good . . . for you.

JILL: Yeah, it was fine.

(off-hand attitude, what we used to call "eh")
(thinks a moment, then laughs)

It's not something I'd go out of my way for these days.

Now we are all three laughing, the way women laugh together when they feel very close because they've shared private or seldom expressed feelings. We laugh, and then we're quiet together. We both look at each other and look at no one. We feel the other's feeling. Whether it's our own or not does not matter. We feel it and that feeling is shared in the air we breathe in the room. And that's why we're silent. It's a sacred silence. I don't know if men do this, but women do. I've seen men in a room look around with "why are they laughing?" on their faces when this happens so I don't think men do it. I'm generalizing here, but my experience has been that men laugh at different things than women. Men worry "Are they laughing at me?" Women laugh at ourselves, with joy, the joy of the human condition—when it's shared.

That was the strange and comfortable joy of being with Ann and Jill that afternoon. Even though I had just met Jill I was totally comfortable with her as often women can be with women because of their openness. Yet there were the strange drifts between their masculine and feminine sides: one moment Jill is a competitive boy (as all men are) talking proudly about her prowess on the playing field (sports and business); the next moment she's your girlfriend—concerned, listening, feeding you, hugging, as only girlfriends do. I knew I wanted to be her friend. I think both women and men do, just because she is Jill—she is so . . . alive.

JILL: It was OK. These guys loved me. They wanted to

marry me.

M: They thought you were terrific in the sack?

JILL: I don't know. We didn't really talk about that. I don't know how to answer that.

M: Yeah, I think men would like you too. My son Tom wanted to get a T-shirt that said "I love lesbians."

JILL: Keep your voice down. I have a top secret clearance. Do me a favor.

(It was the word lesbian. She was genuinely upset—afraid that someone heard that word.)

M: (now I'm whispering) We called the Alternative T-shirt store. I'm so naive. The first time I called there, for a political shirt Tom wanted, I asked, "Alternative? What does that mean? Alternative to what?" But they didn't make one.

JILL: That's odd.

M: I wondered if it's because it can be taken two ways.

JILL: Yeah. I see. Some men view lesbians as a challenge.

M: I asked Tom, "Why do you like lesbians?"

JILL: That's easy. "I love my mom."

M: I'm not a lesbian.

JILL: Oh, you're not. Oh, that's interesting. I thought you were. So what was his answer?

M: He said he didn't know why. He said he thought there were both reasons involved—attractive ("hot") and a challenge. You said these guys really liked the idea of being married to you—I think it's like the reason I liked Ted, my gay friend—he was such a good girlfriend. A lesbian makes a great woman for a man. I mean you understand his talk, you do his things, you don't bother him with all the kinds of talk that . . .

JILL: Yes. Yes. I would say that particularly of Stan and Randall. Bob I don't have much access to. He married a very overbearing woman. We're good friends, we get along great, I mean I'm no threat or anything, but the reason I didn't marry him was he's a Polish Catholic from Minnesota and I'm a Jewish Italian kid from New York and we moved at very different paces, and he wanted six kids and a white picket fence and I figured *he* was going to have to have them if this was what he wanted. It wasn't going to work. At that point I was absolutely convinced that I was gay. There was no doubt in my mind. And he took it terribly. We were ready to get married and I said, "I have something to tell you."

M: Did you tell him?

JILL: Yes. I said, "I'm sleeping with your ex-girlfriend." He was in New Jersey. He was a biochemist. And after we broke up I put him through law school. I'm a good bud.

M: You put him through law school? What were you doing?

JILL: Let's see. I was earning ten dollars an hour. That was 1971. Plus they gave me thirty-two grand a year to go to school. I was on full graduate scholarship at Cornell. I was the token woman in a program with 166 guys.

At this point we're interrupted by a woman. Jill's next appointment has arrived. She asks the woman to take care of him—to find out if he's had lunch yet, to tell him she's running late. The woman says she can't do it, she's busy. So Jill goes out. I hear her talking saying he can wait in her office and make phone calls. She takes him there and comes back. (All this surprises me—not typical CEO behavior— more like a mother, picking up the slack.)

JILL: I'm running late.

M: That's all right. We can finish another time.

JILL: I forgot, what did you just ask me?

M: Do you think people know?

JILL: I think people function—they rise to the level of their knowledge base. People who don't want to deal with this or don't want to know aren't going to. You ask my guys what they know, they'll say, "My boss is athletic." Do they know about the lab people—all lesbian—ninety percent of them don't have a f---ing clue. To them it's such a foreign thing—I don't even think they know about Ann and Ann's as obvious as I am. I can tell you sure as hell they don't know about . . . (she whispers Joanna's name). Now Maggie will tell you otherwise, but I'm telling you until Brenda (a lesbian who works at the company) opened her big mouth, Maggie didn't have a clue. She used to sit here and carry on about Randall to me. She's our "honorary" now, and we all know what we all know. But the fact remains (she whispers now), I don't think they give a shit.

M: That's the thing.

JILL: That's the real issue . . .

M: If you don't talk about it . . .

JILL: It has nothing to do with their lives . . .

M: And they can deny it. So it doesn't matter.

JILL: And I take good care of them, and I run the most humanistic company you'll ever see in your life. They care about their jobs and their families, and I'm accessible to them. I have an open-door policy, whether or not they give a shit. My mother said to me years ago (she uses a mincing, whiny voice), "Do the people who work for you and Marilyn know anything about, you know . . . ?"

And I said to her (exasperated voice), "Mom. Do the

people who work for you and Dad know how many times a week you screw?" And she stopped dead in her tracks and never asked me that question again. And the fact remains . . . IT HAS NOTHING TO DO WITH ANYTHING.

M: That's what the book is about. You asked me at the beginning what the book is about. It has nothing to do with anything. That's what the book is about.

JILL: Your sexual preference and how many times a week you do it, has nothing to do with . . . well, (she laughs) it might have to do with your state of mind personally, but it has nothing to do with how people think.

M: . . . with what you are. That's what the book is about.

JILL: As far as Sunshine Creek camp goes, I made a deal with my partner—who's not really into camp stuff, the only thing she likes to do is watch me play ball—the staff think she's a very classy lady—you'll have to meet her—anyway she's impeccable, and I'm in a headband and sweaty, my arms are bloody—I'm worried about getting to second base, she's more worried about what they're serving for lunch. I promised her that when we run the camp we'll be out of the closet. We're in the closet here. We can't travel together. We go through this crap where we have to get separate hotel rooms. The P.O. box.

(Her voice sounds tired with the memory of the struggle.)

We had separate addresses for a while.

M: That has to be a strain. Do people here know that you live with her?

JILL: Maggie. But Jim, Gwen, Harold? No. Just trust me. I've felt it out. And it doesn't matter.

(now she lowers her voice)

We run into some very, very difficult problems with this merger because she's been hit on a couple of times—in front of me, (there's pain in her voice) by AMI people—what am I going to say? Get your hands off my woman?
M: Yeah. (whew) It's emotionally charged.
JILL: It's a real problem. We've just decided we've got to deal with this. Sunshine Creek needs the money.

(now her voice brightens)

But as far as Sunshine Creek is concerned we march around in our little matching sweaters, Jonnie with her clipboard and me with my whistle, and we do what we need to do to help these families. Frankly, culturally—they probably don't have a clue—because we've got Mexican families, Korean families, and black families and white families and my rich, Jewish Italian friends show up from New York. And my Mexican families don't even have enough money to buy a T-shirt—we have to give it to them—but when they get to that camp, (now her voice is triumphant) it's transparent, because nobody's got a wallet. When they get to Sunshine Creek we're all the same. No one knows who's who. And that's the key to this whole thing. My theory on Sunshine Creek is this—I don't go around with "gay" stamped on my forehead—but will I deny it as far as Sunshine Creek goes? Absolutely not. As far as I'm concerned, anyone who doesn't want to take advantage of the Sunshine Creek experience because the founder is queer, I don't need 'em. I turned away a hundred and twelve families this year. It's not like I need . . . so that's how we're handling it.

Here we have no problems. These guys know I can read a schematic, they know I'm good technically, they know I can do the job faster than anyone in the company. They know I'm not a bad boss, they know I hate detailed operation shit, and I don't like to fire people. I mean, none of this is particularly unique. (She looks at Ann.) Am I right here? Who would like to fire people? Nobody leaves here. So I must be doing something right. I can't get rid of some of the people I want to get rid of. (now her voice is rising in exasperation and Ann and I are laughing) I've got some of these people here nineteen, twenty years. I mean companies are all scaling down on labor, but layoffs? Where the fuck is someone going to go and make 40, 50, 60, 80 grand in this city? All our competition is going under. And I'm keeping these people and their families employed. And, I took a twenty percent cut in pay not to have an engineering layoff. I don't go around bragging or telling them about it, but you know the accounting people know about it.

M: You're great at doing this.

JILL: (a quick sigh) That's nice of you to say. But it also gets very old. I wanted to sell this company when I was forty, and Marilyn and I fought about it, and then she got sick. I could have gotten millions of dollars for it five years ago. Now I've bought her out—she got lots of cash, I've got lots of stock in this new company. The good news is I negotiated to keep all my people at all seven site offices. I'm still president. I still sign all the checks. I still make all the decisions. I get overridden once in a while, but the guy who bought the company is usually right. I respect him. He's bought and sold several companies. He's sixty years old and he's given me some very good guidance. But if he isn't a closet case, I don't know who is. The guy's the biggest swish I ever met in my life. He's been married. I respect him businesswise, but again, when a guy spends half a dinner telling gay jokes . . .

M: Umm. Anti-gay jokes?

JILL: Yeah.

M: Then you think they protest too much?

JILL: Yes.

M: Definitely.

JILL: And he and his brother do this all the time. And they can never get my goat about it. It's not like they're testing me. There can be twenty people in the room and it always comes up. It's bizarre.

M: How do you feel about that? (laughing) Listen to me. I sound like your sister. "How do you feel about that?"

JILL: (sadly serious) You know, ten years ago it would have bothered me. I'm much more bothered now by things closer to me, by things that hurt Jonnie.

M: Yeah. We change. Our lives go in different phases.

JILL: The thing that's different about Jonnie and me is we have very few gay friends. Maybe ten to twelve—people we've met through Ann. Ninety-five percent of what I do throws me into terrible . . . not just heterosexual environment, but male environment. We went to an engineering conference a week ago and I'm the only professional woman at this conference. The only other woman who ever showed up was a bisexual woman who worked for us for many years. I mean, my whole life has been with men, OK?

Jonnie's attitude is that she doesn't want to spend time with people just because they're the same sexual preference. She wants to have something in common with them.

Jonnie is the only woman I've ever been with that wasn't a trainee. She's the only woman that I didn't "bring out." I've only had two other women, so it's no big deal. But she's had a varied background with men and women and because of it she's much more liberal.

M: You've always gone to conferences and been with men, and you're the only woman, and when I heard about you and wanted to get to know you, I thought . . . darn, she has all this . . . achievement, and . . .

JILL: All these men . . . and can't take advantage of them.

M: No. No. All this achievement, and you can't be who you are. You can't just say this is who I am and this is what I've achieved—isn't it great?, and be relaxed and be able to enjoy people more because you don't have to be on guard. You should get respect for what you've done, without having to worry about who you are. It makes me feel angry. It's so unfair.

At this time the tape stopped running and we all realized how long we'd been talking. I don't think we would have stopped if we hadn't noticed the tape was up.

So we broke up and made plans to meet again, next time at Jill's house in the country. I did want to see her in a different environment, in her natural habitat. Jill spoke about a project of mine I was having trouble with. "Call Senator _____, call _____. Use my name."

We cleared the dishes and covered the food and went into the foyer outside the conference room. I was struck again by Jill's petiteness, her little girl straight blond hair and the two bright pink spots of natural color in her cheeks that made her look like a German music box doll. She and Ann and I hugged each other with polite, ladies-after-lunch hugs and kissed each other on both cheeks like European ladies. In fact, we were American ladies—one straight, two lesbians. Ann so boyish. Jill in her baggyish, stylish trousers. So comfortable, all of us together—just three ladies after tea. I was struck by the ordinariness, and the sweetness of it all. I wanted the whole world to feel like that, for them and for me, and for my children, and for everybody.

The next Saturday I had my directions and was driving to Jill's house. Ann said, "It's some modern thing, by some famous architect—all redwood and glass. I hate it because when you go in the bathroom the outside walls are glass and people are walking around on the deck. No privacy." Jill had called to tell me she only had an hour or so because she'd forgotten she had an obligation to take "two gay boys out for a celebration dinner." "You see, we're celebrating the one getting sober and back on his feet. I want them to feel good about themselves, so I'm taking them out—new clothes and everything. What a time we had shopping for George's new clothes. He's my gardener now, and the other boy is sort of a valet. You can talk to me while I'm getting my sports massage and getting ready. Is that OK?"

Sure it was OK. I already knew better than to think Jill sat still.

The turn off the highway was onto a private, unmarked road. I saw the driveway and the redwood house sitting up among trees far back on the property. I was early so I pulled up to the security gate and waited. After a few moments the electric gate opened and I drove through. I was excited as I saw the woodsy property set up as an attractive camp with colorful signs and playhouses and sports areas. I thought of Michael Jackson's property. It was like that in that someone had put a lot of thought into it to make it a happy, magical place—a place to delight a child and take him away from the worries of the world. At the house I was greeted by Jordan.

"I saw you down at the gate, so I let you in. Jill's having a massage. Do you want to wait out by the pool?"

So Jordan and I sat by the pool on the deck behind the house and talked. He told me he'd had some bad luck and Jill had taken him in. He started looking after the house for her and stayed on.

"What all do you do?"

"Well, I feed the dogs. And take her clothes to the cleaners. And make appointments for work on the house."

He wanted to know what the book was about and I tried to explain it.

"It's about gay people, what they're really like, as human beings, so people will understand them and not fear them."

He was very excited about it. He was a handsome young man with light brown hair and a short neat beard. He was wearing Bermuda shorts and a T-shirt and a headband. Soon he left to check on Jill. He came back and said, "She'll see you now."

Jill was in the living room—a large room surrounded by glass and greenery, and with a spectacular view of the valley below. She was wearing slim, faded jeans and a well-worn pale blue sweatshirt. She sat on a black leather sofa and tucked her legs under her. "Do you want a sports massage? You can keep your clothes on." I turned that down because of the time constraints.

"Then I'll give you my man's name. He's terrific, and he comes to your house."

Her two large Irish setters roamed the room seeking attention.

M: The grounds are beautiful—all the flowers and landscaping.
JILL: George did that. It was a mess before. But I brought George here and gave him a job and helped him get sober and he brought this place to life. Tonight we're going to

celebrate. You passed him leaving when you came in. That's his new truck. He's so proud of it.

I wished I had my camera to take a picture of her. She looked very beautiful in the late afternoon light in her home. But I knew this book wouldn't have pictures. Most of the women needed to protect their identities.

M: I was thinking since we talked on Thursday about all the roles you take on. You have a lot of masculine roles in your life. You're the hunter, the protector—you protect all these people at your company, and you do it in a way that every heterosexual woman wishes she had a man who behaved that way, you really care about all the people around you. A lot of men really don't.

JILL: Right. Women run businesses very differently, very definitely differently than men do.

M: And you're the hunter. You go out and get the business that provides for all these people. Yet, on the other hand, you made lunch for us. You got up early and cooked for us.

JILL: All women have dual roles. You have dual roles as a mother raising two boys single-handedly.

M: I see you with all these women roles and then the CEO stuff. I see this blending . . .

JILL: I can't divide the two. One of the most frightening things that ever happened to me, frightening is probably not the right word, but enlightening, was when Randall and I went to Australia. It was for his fortieth birthday and it was the first vacation I'd had in eighteen years. I took off four months, which is pretty unusual because I don't even take off a weekend. It was like being catapulted back into the late forties or early fifties. All of a sudden I had no identity. I was Randall's friend or Randall's woman. I couldn't get into a bar to have a beer (a really disgusted tone of voice about this) without walking in the side entrance, with an escort. If anyone asked me what I did for a living and I said I owned an engineering firm that booked out twelve million dollars last year, well they immediately turned away from me and talked with Randall and made like I wasn't there. At first I got angry with him and then he said, "Look, this is just another culture." And I had to go an entire month without identifying myself as being a CEO with one of the largest businesses, woman-owned businesses, in California.

M: No man wants to hear that in Australia because that threatens them, that means maybe their women could do that.

JILL: One day.

M: One day.

JILL: The point I'm bringing up is the shock was that I could not separate my life from my career. I don't know if that's healthy or not. I'm much better at it now that I have Sunshine Creek. I know now that I'm doing engineering so I can run this camp for disadvantaged families. It's an entirely different mode I'm in, but that also comes from being forty-five, not twenty-five.

M: What comes with it? . . . the learning to separate?

JILL: Yeah. The letting go, the moving on. My parents did the same thing their entire lives. Your parents did the same thing their entire lives. Making a job change in the forties was not something that was OK. It meant you were unstable.

M: Or the fifties. It meant you hadn't done your job well.

JILL: Twenty years of this shit's enough.

M: Even if you hated your job, you knew you were going to do it your entire life. Because that's the way our society was, but not anymore.

JILL: Right. And I've made a very good living at this, emotionally, financially, culturally. My parents always said the key was education, especially for a woman. They were probably thinking of job interviews, but I haven't worked for anyone since college. The other thing they said was the most successful thing they could see was for the children to go one step further than the parents. So if mom and dad had an architectural firm on Fifth Avenue in New York that employed eighty people, then Jill employs two hundred people. They did three or four million in bookings, we do ten or twelve million in bookings. Both my sister and I patterned our homes and our styles after theirs, very modern. Well, that's what we grew up with. That's what we're comfortable with. People make fun of me because the house is so organized. It's a standing gag if you talk with Ann. She used to say I alphabetized my pantry. Well, that's not really true. I don't. She lived here for six months. I never heard the end of it. But the fact remains that when you have the pressure I have at work . . . I color code the clothes in my closet so I don't have to think in the morning. I put on this blouse with the black pair of slacks or this three-piece suit. My pantry, I know where the Italian food, the Chinese food, the vegetarian this and that thing is. So everything is simple and organized at home.

M: It's efficient.

JILL: That's all it is. And it takes a lot more time to be inefficient.

M: You said you never worked for anyone since college. How did you get your first job when you arrived here? You said you arrived and had no money and the job you came for was gone.

JILL: My first job... well, the guy who had hired us to teach said he didn't know what he was going to do with us. So he sent us to this woman who worked in the engineering college. She had a $5000 grant to develop a science media capability at an extension campus. She said do you think you can handle the job and I said sure. Now she never told us it was in f---ing Calexico. It was in goddamn Mexico—I don't mean that "goddamn" negatively, but I'd thought "extension campus," but this, do you know where Calexico is? It's like you go east and if you get to Yuma, you're too far. It's hot, it's like hell and gone from the city—it's a three-hour drive to work every day. We had our first quesadilla and drank our first Tecate beer.

So I ended up staying out there and Marilyn stayed home and kind of built up our little chicken coop. I ran out there and wrote a report that was two inches thick and presented it, and two of the people in the meeting when I was presenting the report were from the military and said maybe we could use your services, and one thing led to another. It was a $5000 job. Marilyn ran the hours and figured we probably made 23 cents an hour.

M: You told me that back in New York you said to Marilyn, "I'm going to go to California," and she said, "Oh, well, I'll go too."

JILL: Right. She quit her job.

M: Were you lovers then?

JILL: Yes.

M: Yet you just said to her "I'm going to California."

JILL: I needed to get the hell out of there.

M: You didn't like, sit down and talk and say "Shall we go to California"?

JILL: I said, "I'm going to Australia . . . to shoot film." I always wanted to go to Australia. And Marilyn said,

"Why don't you go to California and I'll go with you. So I said OK. That was our compromise. She gave three months notice. I had to graduate. Yeah. We planned it.

M: Were you, close? I mean it sounds like you were just going to leave her.

JILL: No. I wasn't planning on going out and staying out there. I might have misrepresented that.

M: It was just a trip?

JILL: Yes. But when she decided to come that changed. I'd known her for about seven or eight years before we became lovers. Her best friend was my first female lover. Who subsequently doesn't speak to Marilyn or me which is kind of ridiculous since Marilyn and I've been broken up fifteen years. I've tried to renew the relationship, [this means friendship, for anyone who might misinterpret that word] but she doesn't want anything to do with anything that has to do with her past of being gay.

M: Oh, she's not gay anymore?

JILL: No. She's married with two kids. Lives across the street from her mother.

M: Really.

JILL: Whadda, whadda, whadda, whadda. (whew)

M: I was talking to Jordan about the research on gay people published last summer. Gayness is passed on the X chromosome. I was so excited because I'd seen that in three families I know well, and now that it was proven I thought it was going to revolutionize society.

JILL: I did too.

M: But when I mentioned it to Jordan, he said, "Oh yeah. Jill told me something about that."

JILL: I think the gay population low-keyed it because they were concerned it would be used to cut off homosexuality.

M: Are there other gay people in your family?

JILL: Not that I'm aware of. My sister probably could be AC/DC. Ann thinks so, she's talked about that. I'm the only one that's out there anyway. (now her voice perks up) It's kind of a trip too . . . because I'm probably the most successful person in the family. Not only have I met the challenges of going to top universities on full scholarships and coming out with awards, not only have I won national awards for entrepreneur, being the top woman in technology, but I'm in a business that's totally male dominated, and I'm successful at it. How much of that is my folks' business background and what I learned from them, and my Jewish New York type-A personality, and how much has to do with gayness—I can't tell you. I haven't a clue. I can tell you being gay made it more difficult. My family is all educated people, but I was the first one to go to graduate school. I was the first one to get a Ph.D. My sister was the second. My family has been incredibly supportive. They welcomed both Marilyn and Jonnie with open arms. My mother's biggest fear on earth was that the family would find out, and the family knew before my mother.

M: When you told your mother, how did she respond?

JILL: Terrible. She started crying and said she knew it. Well, the first time she found out about it, which she won't admit, was when this counselor at camp told her I'd been seen kissing a woman in a haystack. She said, "You'd better watch out for Jill. She might have homosexual tendencies." Well, my mother didn't watch out . . . she had me in therapy. Thirteen years old, fourteen. To change me. At one point I think I said to my mother, "You're the hardest woman I ever tried to make." She was relentless. And not because she wanted to be. She wouldn't go to therapy with me. This was like some kind of stigma she perceived. It's their generation. Gay was queer.

M: Yeah. Take this child and fix it.

JILL: Give them shock treatments.

My parents are in their seventies. They are depression mentality people to whom security and marriage and all this stuff are paramount. And it's great. It works for them. But like my sister says, "Mom, Dad, Jill and Jonnie have been together for over ten years. They're more stable than my husband and I. They probably have just as healthy, if not healthier, a relationship.

M: When did your mother start to accept it, that it was all right?

JILL: It took her about fifteen years altogether. I guess when I moved to California. She finally came out to visit Marilyn and me, and that's when the transition took place. By then we had the business started. We were far from successful. The house was so cold she slept in a trenchcoat. She finally carted us to the Sheraton Grand for the rest of the week, with Marilyn screaming, "But this is our house." But we did start doing things after that. The three or four of us would go to Palm Springs, or they'd come out and my dad would go on to China on business.

M: But until she accepted you, when she was with you, was she cold, or did she talk negatively about it?

JILL: Never.

M: Just would pretend it didn't . . .

JILL: Correct. If it ever came up, it was like someone stabbed her in the heart.

Finally I called my father and I said, "Dad, get . . . your . . . wife . . . off . . . my . . . back."

He said, "Well, I don't know what to do. I've tried talking to her. I've said if you're happy what's the big deal?"

But my mother to this day is terribly, terribly fearful

that someone's going to try to blackmail me because it's happened several times — that someone is going to ruin my career. And that's her concern.

M: Now this is the fear thing that I think is so unfair. It's hard for me to even perceive, from my mindset, how someone could blackmail you.

JILL: I'm illegal. You cannot be a government contractor and be homosexual. I'm not bisexual like Jonnie. I'm not bisexual like Marilyn. I'm . . . homosexual. (her voice is heavy with resignation) Just like Ann is.

M: Right. Do you think Jonnie and Marilyn are really bisexual? I mean, they can be with men, but what do they really enjoy? I mean, you could be with men too.

JILL: I don't know the answer to that. I believe, and I always believed, and I told my parents, and particularly my mother this, "You didn't bring me up to discriminate in terms of whom I love, and whether Marilyn is Marilyn or Martin, or Jonnie is Joanna or Jonnie, the bottom line is this is whom I choose as my partner and this is what works for me and this is what makes me happy. Jonnie will tell you that the minute she met me, (her voice melts, chokes slightly) it was love at first sight.

(As I write this listening to a tape of her voice, tears come to my eyes and my throat tightens to hear how moved she is by Jonnie's loving her. I know it's because I wish there were a man who would be that moved by my love.)

M: Had she ever been in love before?

JILL: Yes. I believe she had. Whatever she was capable of loving as a teenager, which is highly questionable because of our skills as teenagers. She probably had a concern and a love and an admiration for her English teacher, Karen, and I really believe there was another love in her life of all the men she dated, and God knows she's been with a hundred of 'em. I would say that this man, Leo, she was really in love with and it's lucky for her he didn't leave his wife because now she'd be with a seventy-eight year old guy she'd have to take care of. And looking back now, she's thankful. But she still talks to him all the time, and I encourage them to see each other. I really believe that's healthy.

At this time Jill had to get up and start getting ready for the evening out, so I followed her to the bathroom and we continued talking while she showered. The tape is really funny because I'm shouting the questions and Jill's in the shower shouting back and the water is running. When I got home and told my son John, he said, "She was hitting on you." I told him no, it was like a guys in the locker room thing, like a sports figure being interviewed while he changes clothes. She was totally unselfconscious so I tried to be too. She undressed and peed and showered and shampooed and never lost a beat in the conversation. It was no different than when people chat with me when I cook. I admit I was getting a kick out of trying to act natural at something that was unusual for me.

M: (shouting) I wanted to ask you about your and Jonnie's roles at home. What traditional male and female roles do you have?
JILL: I cook. She does the laundry. We both clean the house. We both have businesses of our own. We both have our own offices.
M: Who takes care of the cars?
JILL: Jordan and George. (laughs) I used to though. You

mean, who's the mechanic? Me.

M: What kind of car do you drive?

JILL: Well, I own a Ferrari. It's a classic sports car I've had for twenty-five years. Jonnie drives a Honda, and we own a Dodge pickup that belongs to the camp. If you ask Jonnie she'll tell you the pickup's hers. (laughs) She likes to feel macho in the pickup. It's the standing gag around here, because she's so small that when she's driving and you're driving behind her it looks like the truck is going down the road with no driver.

M: (I'm laughing too) By the way I'm glad I met her the other day. To me she's absolutely beautiful.

JILL: Yeah, she is. Very unique looking.

M: She has that mobile face with so much expression in it.

JILL: She's a very gentle lady. We're very different. She's very quiet as well. I have my mother's temperament.

M: About your mother. You mentioned once you thought she might be a closet case? And that might cause her fears and her anger with you and that sort of thing?

JILL: Right. The anger wasn't with me. The anger's with herself. In my opinion.

M: She took it out on you though.

JILL: Uhmm. Not intentionally. I think she was harder on herself than she was on me.

M: What did she do to herself?

JILL: She kept blaming herself.

M: Blaming herself that you're gay?

JILL: Yes. "It's my fault. How did I create this?"

M: Oh. That's terrible. But that makes you feel like she created something wrong.

JILL: Exactly. But do you know what? The catch-22 in this? What she forget to factor into the equation was that as strong parents, they raised two very strong girls. And those girls could overcome their own fears. It's easy to look back and say it was easy, but it wasn't as bad as a lot of people have. At least we didn't have to... it was better that I was out there in the open and not living a lie.

M: Right.

JILL: That would have bothered me. That I couldn't do.

M: Did your mother show any other signs that she might have been a lesbian?

JILL: No. But she told a story about being attacked in Grand Central Station once. Some woman made a pass at her and scared the shit out of her. Now she denies it, but she's in her seventies so she can claim she doesn't remember. Very convenient.

M: Sometime you'll have to ask her, maybe she'll talk about it now. Ask her if there were any gay people in her family. Tell her they know now it's genetic.

JILL: I wouldn't tell her. No. Let her find out for herself. It's just one more thing that she'll take on. Who needs it? She's seventy. Let her go.

M: I thought it might help her. She's blaming herself all the time.

JILL: I don't think she does that anymore. What's she going to blame herself for? The fact that her kid's the most successful one in the family? I mean it's not like I'm a bum. And I've helped a lot of people, and I don't just mean my employees.

M: I know that. I see it all around you.

JILL: That's what it's all about.

M: That's what it's all about. You're right. I agree. Do you have any other fears besides losing your security clearance that are connected with being a lesbian?

JILL: Not that I'm aware of. We're in a pretty low AIDS group statistically. So security is my major concern.

Associated with that is the fact that I'm concerned they could welch on the merger deal, claim I hadn't disclosed it and I was jeopardizing government contract business, and therefore the deal's off. But that's unlikely—I'm too valuable right now. Locally. And I told you I get real sick of people hitting on Jonnie.

M: Is she too . . . soft in her manner to push these guys away?

JILL: No. She pushes them away. She plays it cool. It's just irritating that . . .

M: . . . that they try?

JILL: Well, they should try. She's good looking.

(Jill is out of the shower now and toweling down)

M: Do people hit on you?

JILL: Yes. All the time. And sometimes it happens when Jonnie's there and it's pretty hysterical because . . .

M: When men come after you?

JILL: Yes . . . because she can't believe that men would be attracted to me.

(now I'm really laughing hard)

I try to explain to her it's very rude and kind of not nice for her to say that really.

M: I can see why they would be.

JILL: Well, you know, I say, hey, I'm kinda cute, and I've got a great bod.

M: You do have a great bod and you're very good looking. I'd like to photograph you sometime. Your pictures don't do you justice.

JILL: Most of them are just snapshots.

M: So you've not had any really bad experiences from being

a lesbian?

JILL: I've avoided them. With great duress and great work. People following me back to my room and calling me and putting the make on me. I just had a guy, since the merger, drunk as a skunk, wouldn't get out of my room. I had to say, "You know, Bill, you forgot one thing. I own the company. If you don't get out of here, you're fired." See I have a leverage Jonnie doesn't have.

(She's right. I'm thinking how wonderful it would be if women had "power" to protect themselves.)

Now we walk down the hall, through the living room and kitchen to the other end of the house where the master bedroom and bath are. We are in a large open bathroom facing a long, shallow closet where Jill's clothes are hanging. I feel an immediate shock in that it looks like a man's closet. Business suits and slacks and shirts are hung in order. I see no feminine clothes of any kind. Now she's brushing her teeth and using the hairblower so I have to shout again.

M: What feels good about your life besides your success?
JILL: My relationship with Jonnie. She's my lover and my best friend. That doesn't mean it came easy, we've worked on it for a long time. My business entertaining is the hardest thing. We have to run around and take down pictures of us, of Jonnie holding my sister's children. It's a bone of contention for both of us.
M: I want to ask you about your lifestyle. Do you ever relax?
JILL: Ya.
M: When?
JILL: Usually when we go away. I try to take a day or an evening that's not business. We spend the holidays with

our families. I try to relax when Randall's around.

M: You have all this energy and you really schedule your time. How much do you sleep?

JILL: I need ten to twelve hours a day. I'm an epileptic.

M: You're an epileptic? Do you take medication?

JILL: Not anymore. I haven't for years. I control it with a vegetarian diet and lots of sleep. I do biofeedback.

M: Can you tell if a seizure is coming on?

JILL: Yes. I've trained myself to know. My seizures are nocturnal, they come in the early morning, wake me up.

She's partially blown dry her short blond hair and now rolls it on large, bright red rollers. It's incongruously feminine. I tell her, "I like the red rollers" and she laughs. She goes to the closet, she's wearing only underpants and no bra. She studies the suits, her hand on her chin. She reaches into a drawer in the center of the closet and takes out a pair of men's calf-high socks and puts them on. Then she stands and studies the closet again. The closet is open and shallow and about eight feet long. The clothes are meticulously arranged, like a prince's closet—suits in a row, color-coded, followed by white shirts, white patterned shirts, and colored shirts. That's all there is—only men's suits and shirts—no dresses, no blouses.

M: Do you ever wear a dress?

JILL: Sure. Sister's wedding. Blue silk and three-inch heels.

She walks into the bedroom and brings back a photo to prove it. She looks gorgeous in the blue silk.

She goes back to the closet and stares again, then pulls out a suit of nondescript brown. She puts on the trousers and carries the jacket and vest into the bathroom and hangs them on the hanger of a wooden valet stand. Now she returns to the closet and stares at the shirts. The trousers are open but zipped just enough to keep them from falling down. As I watch this process I am struck by the masculine process of the dressing. It surprises me it is exactly the way my former husband used to dress. She pulls out a white shirt, holds it up to her, and turns to me.

"Is this OK?"

M: It's a little . . . plain, with the brown.
JILL: Yeah. I thought so. How about this?

She holds up a windowpane design shirt—still a white business shirt, but with pale brown stripes making large checks.

M: Still not it. You need something more festive. This is a party.
JILL: Ah ha! I know.

With great relief she holds out an orangy-red cotton business shirt.

M: Yes. That's good.

There was no other choice. This shirt was from the far right of the color-coded closet. This was as festive as it could get.

She takes out the big red rollers and her hair falls straight, just below her ears. She puts on the shirt, the vest (buttons every button), the suit jacket, then surveys herself with satisfaction in the full length mirror. (She considers a *three*-piece suit is "dressing up.") Then she went to put on shoes. The shoes were lined up on a shoe rack in the closet—all were perfectly polished. As I looked at them I felt a twinge of shock, of weirdness—they were all men's loafer shoes. I had accepted relatively easily the comfortable men's clothes as funky, or practical, or "George Sand," but I had really expected the shoes to be women's flats or loafers, feminine, but these were thick-soled men's shoes. They looked clunky on her delicate little feet.

(Days later at home I tried on a pair of my son's black dress trousers he'd outgrown and put out to be given away. I thought I could look very stylish in them with a silky, flowing sleeved blouse and jewelry. I tried them on and the fit was perfect, but when I looked in the mirror I saw I was wearing men's pants and they looked like men's pants and I felt suddenly freaky like I was cross-dressing. I thought I looked like a dyke and I took them off and put them in a bag to give to some ninth grade boy.)

M: Don't you ever want to wear something more feminine, like a silk blouse?
JILL: No. I have to dress like this, for business, to be taken seriously.

(She says this matter-of-factly, like a man. Everything Jill says is like a man—"this is it—fact—no other ideas entertained"—that authoritarian manner that allows no chit-chat, no feminine discussion of "what do you think? am I right? oh, maybe you're right, oh, I know this is all wrong.")

JILL: Feminine clothes do not work in my business. Dressing like this gives me an advantage, from a power standpoint.
M: They treat you differently when you dress like a man?

JILL: Absolutely. I wouldn't be taken seriously if I didn't. I'm the only woman . . . first of all they say things around me they probably wouldn't say around other women.

M: I think you talk back in their language too.

JILL: Yeah. I don't say "Gee, I'm sorry I said f--k in front of you." Well, I get that from my mother. I didn't get it from being in this business. My mother brought me up on it. You know these people are from New York. They have to survive.

M: Are both your parents Jewish?

JILL: Yes, they are. But we were brought up in an Italian town. Ninety-five percent of the people I grew up with were pure Italian.

M: If I were around I'd probably be after you to soften up your dress a little. You could wear a vest unbuttoned over the shirt I gave you, with no jacket, and still look dressy. I do that.

(She'd liked my shirt with Clint Eastwood dressed as a cowboy holding two smoking guns, so I'd given it to her. I knew cowboys were her heroes.)

JILL: Good advice.

(But I don't think she'll do it.)

M: Do you have all your clothes made? I noticed all your shirts are monogrammed on the sleeves.

JILL: Yeah. I designed this shirt. It has this little notch. (on the collar) See you can close it. So . . . when I go to the Pentagon I like to wear a scarf.

M: The reason I've spent so much time on the clothes is because, well, George Sand liked to wear men's clothes and . . . I wondered . . .

JILL: It gives me a serious advantage.

M: But also, you choose to do it outside of business . . .

JILL: Uhmm.

M: You're doing it tonight.

JILL: Yeah . . . I don't do it as much if I go out with Jonnie as I do with these gay guys. I spent three hundred dollars on this guy to get him dressed up to make sure it would be important to him.

M: I knew you bought him a tie.

JILL: I bought him a whole suit. Jordan went out and bought it and dressed him up. I said, "We've got to get George feeling good about himself."

M: Are Jordan and George just friends.

JILL: Yeah. They're not lovers or anything.

M: Is there anything you'd change about your life if you could?

JILL: I'd be running Sunshine Creek.

M: That's the only thing? . . . and you will be doing that.

JILL: Yes. If you're referring to my gayness . . . No. Absolutely not.

M: How will the camp change your life?

JILL: Number one, I'll be outside instead of behind a desk. Number two, I won't be in the closet. I told you that yesterday. If people don't want to send their kids to camp because the owner is gay, f--k 'em.

M: What do you like about being a lesbian?

JILL: Not much.

M: Not much?

JILL: Uhmm . . . I don't know anything else, so it's hard to . . . It hasn't given me any advantage, and it's given me a lot of challenges. Honestly. I like my life. I've made it a good, productive life. It's not as affluent as it could be, but that's not my focus. I have a great relationship as far as that's concerned. I'm certainly glad I didn't sell out, and decide to go the easy route. (marry a man) I'd have had to live with second best.

M: You'd have been unhappy?

JILL: Ahh . . . I wouldn't have been as happy, let's put it that way. And I would have done a terrible disservice . . . to me and to anyone I was with . . . if I was with Randall.

M: If you could choose what you wanted to do with your next life . . . this is a Baabaa Walters' question. Do you know Barbara Walters on *Sesame Street* is played by a sheep and they call her Baabaa Walters?

JILL: Yes. I would work less. And do Sunshine Creek sooner.

M: You wouldn't ask to change your gender?

JILL: (shakes her head) Uh-uh. I have this standing gag. I said it to Sandy and Jonnie one day. If somebody asked me what's the worst thing that could ever happen to you? I'll finally come back as a guy, and women will have taken over the universe. (she laughs) And I'll have to do the whole f---ing thing all over again. That would be it. That would be the worst thing.

M: I heard that, but it's tricky to absorb.

JILL: I'll tell you again. I'll finally come back as a man, and women will have become the superior race . . .

M: And you'll have to fight your way back up again.

JILL: Yeah. Let me get my wedding band.

M: Would you've liked to be a man in this life?

JILL: No. It just would've been easier. For business.

M: But you're happier being a woman . . . with all your power . . .

JILL: Yeah. I wouldn't want to have to deal with the lack of the ability to be sensitive. No, I wouldn't be happy changing my gender.

M: So, you're happy being a woman and you're happy . . .

JILL: . . . being in a same-sex relationship. I've achieved what any man could achieve and then some. I think I've had to work harder at it . . . because of being a woman, not because of being a lesbian. It's a male/female issue, not a gay/straight issue.

M: But most women don't have the strength and perseverance to make that fight you've made.

JILL: I doubt that. I don't know. I never thought about it. It's a family thing. It's a Bergman thing. It's in my family blood.

(now she's running the hairblower again)

You don't have to shout. I read lips too. And no, that isn't my nightgown.

I look where she's looking. There is a lacy, rufflely, see-through black nightgown hanging on a hook to my left. I laugh.

M: No. I knew that. I guessed that.

The tape recorder had run out and she was still blow drying her already dry, fine hair which now was alive with static. We discussed the sale of her business and financial aspects of the merger more. Then she went to the closet and started putting on hats. She likes to wear hats that look like men's fedoras from the forties. I don't like the hat on her. It hides her girlish blond hair. I suggest she not wear the hat.

She races through the house to her library/den and makes a call to her parents. She speaks briefly with both of them.

She asks about Aunt Lottie, and Aunt Sophie and a neighbor. She tells them about a couple business items and asks for advice. "Bye. Love you both."

M: How often do you phone your parents?
JILL: Every day.

Then we're out to the kitchen where she's getting some crackers out and putting in a call to Jonnie who's out of town at a convention.
"How's it going? Uhmm. Martha's here. We're waiting for Jordan and George. They're late. We have reservations. What time will you be here tomorrow? Okay. We'll play tennis, all right? Good." Then she blushes, and asks, "Do you love me?" Blushes deeper. "I love you too—see you tomorrow."
Now Jordan and George have arrived. Jordan is a big, handsome young man. He's especially good looking in his cream-colored suit and short, well-trimmed beard—he's the kind of man I fall for. He's rushing around. It's emergency rush.

JORDAN: Sorry we're late. Everything went wrong. George doesn't have any socks.

Jordan is adjusting and retying George's tie. George is red-faced from the apparent rushing, sweaty and embarrassed. He's a handsome, stocky man, with dark curly hair and a bushy moustache. He's wearing a good-looking dark blue suit, but Jordan lifts the pants leg to reveal George doesn't have socks.
Jill runs to get socks from her drawer for George.

JILL: Did you feed the dogs?

JORDAN: No. I didn't have time.

Now Jill is feeding the dogs. "We need drinks." She makes a vodka daiquiri on the rocks for Jordan, and pours Kahlua for herself. "We need photos."

M: I'll take the pictures when everyone is ready.
JILL: We need another drink.

Jill pours more drinks which she and Jordan gulp down. George can't drink. That's what this party is about.

JILL: George is driving.

Outside on the terrace I take pictures of the three of them by George's new, big truck which they're driving out to the most expensive restaurant in the city—Jill's treat. George gets behind the wheel and Jill climbs in the middle. I'm far down the drive at the lower level where my car is parked when I hear Jordan calling to me. I turn around and wave. Jordan is at the edge of the terrace waving and calling to me, "Hurry. Hurry with the book. We need you."

4

SALLY FROM SANTA FE

I MET SALLY at the swim club. We were thrown together by mutual misery. Sally was going through a terrible divorce. I was going through a terrible divorce. Her husband was a mean cad. My husband was a mean cad. She lived with her three girls in a nearly empty house in the country. Her husband, a brain surgeon, had taken the furniture. I lived in a nearly empty house in an elegant suburb with my two boys. Our children went to the same school. We consoled each other and exchanged our continuing horror stories. Sally had the worst one. The police arrived at her home, arrested her and put her in jail on Christmas Eve. Her husband had accused her of pushing open a door and injuring his nine-month-pregnant mistress. She didn't know the woman was behind the door. She was trying to push the children's school books through. The police dropped the charges and released her.

We became friends because no one else could fully comprehend the horrors of our lives at that time. We were both new in Santa Fe. We lost most of the friends we had during our divorce trials. Many of them were social friends interested in us because of our husbands' titles. The others, with successful husbands, were afraid to be near us. What was happening to us frightened them. We had a disease they didn't want to catch.

I saw Sally almost daily at the swim club in the summer.

It was where we entertained our children through the hot summer days of our misery. Her table and space were down the hill from mine. She sat in her chair all day wearing her boy-cut swimsuit (with shorts legs)—"to camouflage my lack of bosom and large thighs," she said—and always sunglasses. She never walked up to visit me. I always walked down to visit her. I would watch her when she got up to swim in the late afternoon. She is a tall, slim, awkward girl. She had short, dark brown, glossy hair—cut as short as a boy's. Her face was incredibly pretty, with beautiful hazel eyes and long dark lashes. In the loose skirts and shirts and the flat shoes she wore too big, she always looked awkward, like Huck Finn dressed in women's clothes, shifting from one foot to the other. But when she stood on the edge of the pool and dived she was athletic and graceful. I watched her swim with strong, long strokes, and I remember thinking one day—"She is so boyishly beautiful—I bet a lesbian would love her." But I didn't know any lesbians, or anything about them.

I sometimes dropped by her house when I was near and our children played and we talked and laughed. Her old mother who lived with her was cold and often rude to me. I try to excuse or overlook that kind of behavior but my children, as children always do, recognized it. They told me we weren't welcome there. Sometimes Sally came to my house when she was totally worn out and needed a moment of peace. I tried to get her to go out to dinner with me, finally she did once, but dashed off before the dessert. She was totally devoted to her three girls—as wild in their behavior as wild horses—her older sister and her mother. She spent all her time with them and on the blind dates her sister constantly set up for her. She sometimes phoned me the next day to tell me how awful they were. The worst was her date to the Sewer Contractors' Ball. After the dance he drove her to a construction site and tried to get her into a hot tub.

When my divorce was final I left Santa Fe and moved to California with my children. Sally began to call me frequently and we talked about our children and problems and laughed about them. She was bright and had a good sense of humor.

After I'd been gone from Santa Fe for a couple of years, one January, the calls became more frequent and longer. Sally was depressed. She began to phone everyday—the calls would go on for an hour, I couldn't get away. She was so blue I was frightened for her. I'd tell her, "You must go to a psychiatrist and get help. You can't go on this way." She said, "I can't. I went once and I said something I was sorry for. I didn't trust him. Once I started talking these things came out of my mouth that I didn't want to say."

The phone calls went on. I was exhausted and felt helpless. One night I said, "Sally, I can't help you because I don't know what's wrong." She was suicidal. I was scared. "Do you know what's wrong with you?" She answered, "Yes."

The phone calls went on. "Sally, you have to tell me if you want me to help you."

"I can't tell you. It's too terrible."

One night when she phoned in her depression I told her I couldn't go on with these useless phone calls. The daily phone calls had gone on for over six weeks.

M: You have to tell me what's wrong.
SALLY: I can't. It's terrible. It's terrible.

Finally I said, "Okay. Then I'll guess and you say yes or no." To my surprise she responded calmly with, "Okay."

I didn't know what I was going to guess. I thought. What

can it be that's so terrible she wants to commit suicide?
I bravely launched my first question.

M: Did you kill someone?
SALLY: (laughs, that's a new sound) Noooo.
M: Uhmm, well, I thought maybe a hit-and-run accident and you panicked and were afraid to tell anyone.

I wracked my brain. What is the next question? She seemed happier now. Finally—

M: Did you have an abortion?

(She's Catholic and we'd often discussed the abortion issue. She is very Catholic. I knew she'd have terrible guilt and think she was going straight to hell if she'd done that.)

SALLY: No!

(She laughed again, in shocked disbelief.)

Now what? I had no more ideas of what might be terrible enough in her mind to take her own life and leave the three wild children to whom she devoted herself. From somewhere I dredged up a question, a last-resort-I-give-up question.

Lightheartedly I asked, waiting for her laugh, "Are you a lesbian?"
This time she didn't laugh. She said, "Yes. (a long pause) Yes . . . that's it. (pause) I think so. (long pause) I don't know."

I was shocked. It had never entered my mind. Not my

conscious mind. I would have been less shocked and known better how to react had she told me she'd murdered someone.

When I recovered my voice I said, "Good. That's not so terrible—not worth dying about. See, now you've said it. Now you can stop being depressed."

She said, "Will you still be my friend?"

M: Yes. Of course. No one would stop being your friend for that.
SALLY: Janet would. (Janet was her friend in Santa Fe) She's a fundamentalist Christian. She'd never talk to me again if she knew. I don't want that.
M: I have to tell you I'm surprised and a little shocked. I have a couple of questions. Have you ever had crushes on women?
SALLY: Yes. A girl in high school.
M: What about now? Are you attracted to any of your friends now?
SALLY: Well. You, and Janet. (quickly) But only sometimes, not all the time.

Well. I thought I could help her. I certainly wasn't going to desert her. But there was so much I didn't know then. One of things I didn't know then was: there isn't anyone who doesn't know a lesbian—let's go further, there isn't anyone who doesn't know many lesbians. They're just firmly in the closet like poor Sally. And they are suffering. It's very scary and dark and suffocating in the closet.

That summer Sally went to her high school reunion at a Catholic girls' school in Kansas. One girl in her class was a lesbian. She said she was going to talk to her. ("I kinda had a little crush on her in school. She was real cute.") She took her girls and her mother with her on the trip. When she got home she phoned me. She was nearly hysterical. She had fallen in love with this old school friend. She wanted to turn around and go back to Kansas, without the kids.

SALLY: She told me she wasn't interested in me. That she's through with women. She told me not to think about her, that she didn't care for me. But I thought if I just went back there and started over, I could change her mind. What do you think?
M: You can't do that. Have someone tie you to the mast. You aren't thinking clearly. You'll get past this.

That should have been a clue to me of what was to come. The next spring I met Ann. She was open about being a lesbian so I talked with her about Sally. She is very kind and offered to write to her. Sally was always saying, "I don't know any lesbians." Sally decided to come to California to visit me. My boys and I were surprised because Sally would never before go anywhere without her mother and daughters. I encouraged her because I thought a break from their constant demands on her would help her calm down. I told Ann, "Sally is coming out this summer." Ann said, "Be careful how you use that phrase."

My boys and I picked up Sally at the airport. When she got off the plane I was shocked at how different she looked. Of course, we were both older. But mainly it was her ugly haircut—it was shaved from a line at the top of the ears down, the style favored by junior high boys that year, called a step (formerly a "bowl"). The top was short and stood up and had patches of gray. She was thinner, she had a scrawny, old-maid look in her oversized shoes and long skirt. We had talked incessantly about being overweight and diets over the last year as I was gaining middle-age weight and was struggling with it. She had said she was overweight too, but she wasn't today. I thought, she really looks like a lesbian. She was nervous but we were all happy to see her and looking forward to having fun.

The first night, Saturday, Ann and some friends picked her up and took her out, to a country western gay bar and dance place. I told her I didn't want to go, I wouldn't be comfortable. She said, "I'd better go. Do some research. See if it will cure me. Ha. Ha." Ted, my across-the-street neighbor, was invited to go along too. They all gathered in my living room, a merry crowd. Sally was laughing and excited. I waited up for her. When she was dropped off around midnight, she said it was "really neat. But no one wanted to dance with me."

The next day we drove to the mountains and ate lunch in a small town. I began to see what I was up against. She acted very foolish, making eyes at the plump and surly, fiftyish waitress. The service was slow, the food was thrown on the table, our bill overcharged us ten dollars, and Sally beamed blissfully and batted her eyes at the waitress. When we left, Sally threw a huge tip on the table. "Wasn't she cute? I loved her sense of humor."

"Sally," I said, "She didn't have a sense of humor. She was mean and rude. We had the sense of humor."

Sally had a thousand tics. For one thing when she was sitting she pumped her legs up and down constantly. At the mountain restaurant I asked her if she knew she was doing that. Our table was shaking up and down.

"Oh, yes," she laughed. "I do it all the time. Natalie (her daughter) does it too."

I told her she should try to stop that. That it was annoying to people. She did try but then she rocked, or bounced up and down. She had verbal tics too. It was like she had Tourette's syndrome. She made noises pretty much constantly.

"Upps, oops, that's good. Good idea."

If I said I had to get a chapstick, she said, "Good. Yup. Good idea. (now more firmly) Good . . . good idea . . . chapstick . . . ups . . . whoops . . . good idea . . . can't go wrong . . . chapstick . . . uh . . . huh . . . chapstick . . . yup . . . oops . . . wish I'd thought of that."

She had a terrible time getting dressed. She'd brought several heavy suitcases for her five-day visit. She'd bring her outfits into me. "Should I wear this? Should I wear this?" She always ended up choosing her jeans shorts. Then she began bringing in bundles of belts—most of them were ornate, jeweled, and ribboned belts. They didn't go with the jeans shorts. She'd try to put them on with her jeans shorts but the shorts hung low on her hips and the belts fit around her waist. I'd say, "Wear the leather belt." But she was never sure and would change several more times. By the time I'd viewed her outfit about twenty times I said, "Just choose one. How do you get dressed at home? You must make choices at home."

"No," she said, "I'm the same at home. My mother chooses for me."

Sunday night we were going to Ann and Liz's for a special barbecue party Ann had planned to introduce Sally to her lesbian and gay friends. I was going too. Ann had bought me a special T-shirt to wear. It said STRAIGHT BUT NOT NARROW across the front. Ann said, "So everyone will know you're not part of the family."

I had trouble getting Sally out of the bathroom. She was layering on makeup and perfumes. Then she would pat her face with a big powder puff of loose powder. I didn't know anyone who used that except for movies and TV, and old ladies and geishas. I wondered if her makeup ideas were from her mother's vintage. She smelled too strong of a too sweet perfume. I tried to get her out of the bathroom. She looked garish to me—I was reminded of the last scene in *Death in Venice* when the older man makes up heavily to attract the young boy. I was repelled. I felt dizzy. I felt ill.

"You're wearing too much makeup," I said. "It's better to look more natural."

"Oh, no," she said. She looked at me and laughed, "You have to look good if you want to attract someone," and continued with the pancake makeup and powder. In the end she looked falsely white with darkly made up eyes. Like a powdered old maid, or a Kabuki actor.

Ann was hoping her friend Patsy, an older woman, would take an interest in Sally at the party. When I got there I saw that would never happen. Both Sally and Patsy are "toolbelts"—the masculine oriented lesbians—they would never be interested in each other. I am constantly surprised that the lesbians I know don't see this. (Sandy had said she and Greta weren't attracted to each other: "I don't know why not—we should have been." No. They never would have been. They're both "lipsticks" or feminine lesbians. They're attracted to men, or toolbelt lesbians.) Sally and Patsy did not look at each other. Patsy was more interested in me.

Sally wouldn't eat at the party. She was too nervous, trying to attract someone. The food was good and plentiful and beautiful. I discovered there is nothing like a gay party for elaborate food. There were many gay men couples at the party and most of them had brought dishes to share: "Oh, I just had to." Ann had the lawn covered with rented, decorated, round tables with umbrellas. It was as pretty as a wedding.

Everyone treated me like I was special. I felt they

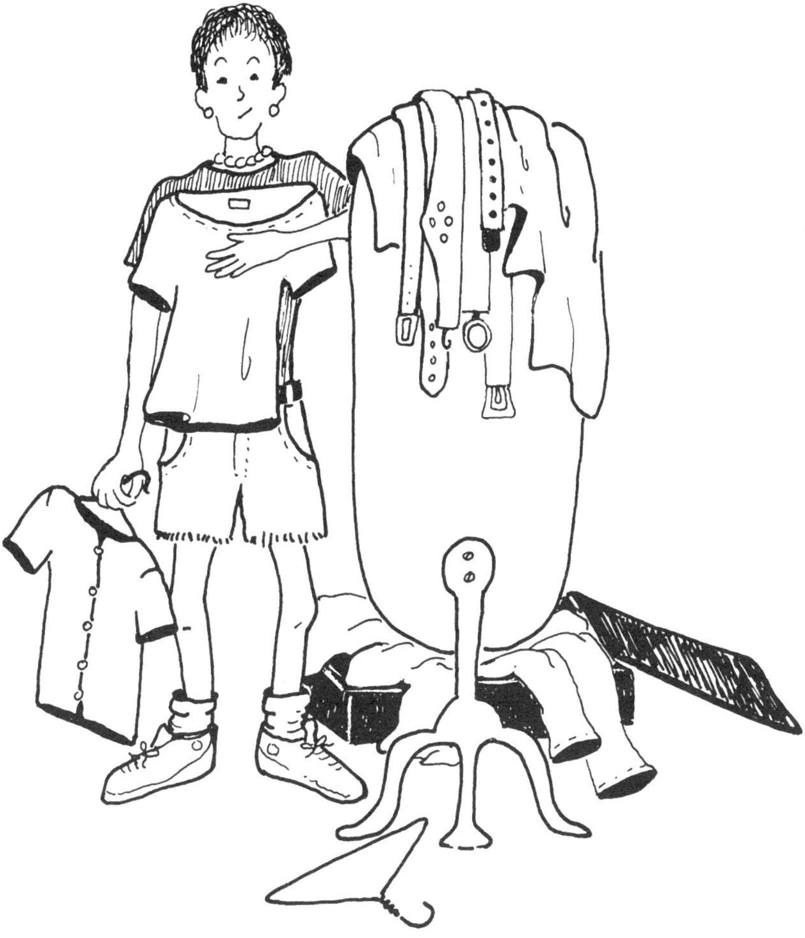

adjusted their behavior and talk to make me feel comfortable. I was reminded of the time in college when I was invited to a black wedding. I was the only white person at the reception. It was a new experience for me. People kept coming over to me and bringing me plates of food and chatting with me and making sure I was comfortable and happy and didn't feel left out or alone. I've never forgotten that. I wondered how many times whites had gone out of their way to make them feel comfortable when they were one in a sea of whites. Since then I've always been aware of the kindness of blacks and thought it must have grown out the many times they'd been mistreated or lonely.

The gay community is like that, so kind and loving and thoughtful of outsiders, wanting you to be comfortable with them and feel valued. I think it is for the same reason as with black people, they know what it is like to be left out, to be treated like an outsider. Their mistreatment has only served to make them compassionate. The thought in my mind is God must love them very much.

Sally flirted and bounced up and down. At the end of the evening she didn't want to leave. "I want to go home with Sarah. She is really cute."

I told her, "You can't. Sarah has a partner. It's like being married."

Sally pouted to Ann, "No one asked me to dance."

Ann, always kind, said, "Yes, but lots of people asked me about you."

SALLY: Really? Really? Then there's hope?

The rest of Sally's stay was bizarre. If we ate out she wanted nothing but cheeseburgers. She would study a Mexican menu at length and then duck her head down and lift her eyes like a child begging to the waitress and say plaintively, "*Can* I have a cheeseburger?" (Once I lost my patience and whispered to her, "Of course you can *have* a cheeseburger. It's on the menu, just order it.") It was all she ate except for plain tortillas. She tipped outrageously. In the Mexican part of town she insisted on tipping a Mexican woman with a tortilla cart one dollar for a fifty-cent tortilla. The Mexican woman kept trying to give it back. Sally said, "She's so cute."

For breakfast I would fix her an egg and tortillas. "What do you want to drink?"

"Uh . . . gingerale."

Other than that she ate Snickers bars, bananas, doughnuts, and jelly beans. She'd bound into my room in the morning, "Hey, want a jelly bean?" She swung on the kitchen counters. She heaped layers of butter on her bread then put it in the toaster, and then forgot it. She made coffee and filled the cup to the top. Then she'd dump handfuls of ice in it, causing it to overflow. She'd smile at me, "Can't drink it hot." When we were driving she would insist on stopping. "Gotta have a beer." She would take two quick sips and then get up and leave it on the table. "Ummm," she'd say, "that sure hit the spot." At the ocean she would jump up and down, then strike a hands-on-hips, legs-apart stance in front of me, asking me to play: "Wanna go look for sharks?" She was like a wild nine-year-old boy to entertain. She was a Peter Pan . . . but she was a forty-eight-year-old woman.

I didn't know where my old friend was. I could have no conversation with this wild child. She was nervous around me. If I walked down the hall she leaped aside and flattened herself against the wall, like a private leaping to the side when the general walks by. She actually looked like she was standing at attention. The boys and I were going crazy. One night I woke up screaming. It was a nightmare. I thought I woke up and saw her standing beside my bed in the night. My son John ran into the room, "It's okay Mom, it's okay—you're having a nightmare." My nightmare consoled by my child. It was a sweet first. I told him I thought I'd seen her standing over my bed. John said, "She was just up—she went to the bathroom." So I knew she'd heard me scream. John and I wondered if the nightmare could have been real. There was no way to know.

After that I felt strange around her. I shut my door at night. I told Ann I felt guilty about that. Ann laughed, "Well, her behavior is bizarre. I never told you how odd and obsequious her behavior was the night we took her out." Then she told me how she'd told her best friend and roommate in college that she thought she was a lesbian. "The next day when I came back from class she'd stacked all the bookcases down the center of the room between our beds. She was afraid of me. She was never my friend again."

Wednesday was her last day with me and I was at my wit's end about how to entertain her, but I thought I should speak to her frankly before she went home. I took her to the old Mexican area of town to a pretty little restaurant. I had Mexican food, she had a cheeseburger. I tried to talk to her. Most of the time with me on this visit she tried to talk cars, thinking that was a good topic. It was always, "See that Mercedes—that's like mine. Great car. Boy. I love that car." She'd asked Ted to take her for a drive in his car. "Oh boy, that Ted. What a car. A Datsun MZ. What kind of car do you want—if you could have any car—any car?" I tell her I don't really care.

"Of course you do. I want a Jeep Wrangler—really like that. And a Mercedes Sports Convertible—$90,000, SL500."

When we were driving she saw every sportscar on the road. She was especially excited when we saw a Testarosa. She told me she had car posters in her room. Just like Tom and John, when they were twelve and fourteen.

Another topic of conversation for her was *Baywatch*. "I know a great show you'd love. *Baywatch*."

"Sally, that's a show for boys to watch girls walking around in bathing suits."

"Love that show."

I tell Sally I want to talk seriously before she leaves.

M: Have you decided you're a lesbian and what you're going to do about it?
SALLY: (squirms) I'm not sure.
M: People know you're gay.
SALLY: No. How could they know?
M: For one thing, what you talk about. You talk about cars all the time.
SALLY: Yeah, cars. Everyone loves cars.
M: Only guys talk about cars all the time.
SALLY: Okay. Good. Glad to know that. I'll stop talking about cars.
M: And your hair. You have a boy cut.
SALLY: (puts her hands up and feels her hair, laughs) I guess I'll have to let it grow. No. Yuck. I couldn't stand it.
M: And you watch *Baywatch*.
SALLY: Yeah. *Baywatch*. Great show.
M: Tom and John know you're gay.
SALLY: Nooo. How could they?
M: Well, for one thing, Saturday night a carload of lesbians came by and took you out for the evening.

Sally is pensive for a moment. Then she says, "I read once

that when you're nine you can see your true spirit. So I went to the photo album and looked at pictures of me when I was nine. I saw these pictures of myself, and in every one I looked like a wild boy. There was one of me in my coonskin cap, I loved that cap, and I looked like a ragtag boy. And my birthday party. All my girlfriends looked clean and pretty in sundresses and little shorts and tops, and there I was, grinning over the cake, in an old T-shirt and jeans.

"I had all these uniforms. I got one for Christmas every year. I had a Marine uniform. I had an astronaut uniform. A general. I was sure I would grow up to be a Marine, or a priest, or a ballplayer."

SALLY: I was thinking, maybe I should get married again. You know, for appearances sake, for the children.
M: Oh, Sally. That would be so wrong. So unfair to whomever you married. Why did you get married the first time?
SALLY: I was a good Catholic girl. I was trying to make the right choice, for a Catholic girl.

Outside the restaurant, she says, "See that Mercedes. That's just like mine. What a car. Oh, gosh. I love that car. Isn't that a great car. Parts are expensive, but what a car."

She says she wants to drive out to Ann's. I tell her we can't. Ann is busy, her mother is in the hospital. Sally starts to throw a tantrum. "I want to see Ann."

"Sally, you can't now. You said goodbye to Ann yesterday." She continues to protest until finally I say we'll try to phone Ann from the pay phone in the parking lot of the restaurant. The night before she had a tantrum because I put a few chopped Brussels sprout leaves in the sautéed vegetables. "I'll never eat Brussels sprouts. Once I went on a

Brussels sprouts diet for two weeks and I swore I'd never eat them again." Later she apologized. "You were right. It was good. I didn't recognize them even." Now she was going to have another tantrum.

M: I thought we'd go to a movie this afternoon. *Much Ado About Nothing* is on. It's great.
SALLY: Oh, no. That's Shakespeare. I hate Shakespeare. I won't go.

Sally comes from an educated family. She has a Master's degree. This is someone I don't know. It's as if being here in California freed her to go back to where she stopped her social development—at age nine. I knew what to do.

M: This movie has the most wonderful actress in it, Emma Thompson. Ann says it's worth going to the movie just to see Emma Thompson.
SALLY: Oh, yeah? Really? I want to go.

In the theater, Sally slouches way down in her seat. The top of her head is even with the top of the seat back. Her knees are propped against the top of the seat back in front of her. Only a nine-year-old boy can slouch in that position. She's a tall woman, I can't imagine what kind of curvature her back is in. I'm embarrassed to look at her. Her lap is full of candy boxes. I'm glad the matinee showing has few people in it.

After the movie, in the lobby, I say, "Wasn't Emma Thompson great?"

"Yeah, great, just great," she says, still chewing candies. "She was beautiful. I loved her. I could sit through it again just to look at her." She pants and bats her eyes, as if we share a lecherous thought.

"Such an amazing actress," I say.

"Yeah," Sally says. A few minutes later she says. "Who was that old woman?"

"Old woman? The gray-haired one, married to the older man?"

"No. Reddish hair. She played Beatrice."

"That," I say, in shock, "was Emma Thompson. Who was it you liked?"

"That young girl. She was gorgeous. I'd like to have her."

"But she was just a child."

She'd been attracted to the young actress who looked about fourteen years old. Sally is aware I am shocked. I remembered that she'd gotten a crush on the young waitress we'd had at dinner Monday night. She'd said, "I was so excited I kept asking her what the specials were but I couldn't listen, I couldn't remember. I don't remember what I ate. I kept getting coffee so she'd come by. Oh, that Lisa." And that Lisa, the supercilious waitress, who would never have guessed that the silly, middle-aged woman batting her eyes at her had a crush on her, got a very large tip.

When we got back to the house it was dark. As I drove up I saw Ann's silver truck parked across the street in front of Ted's house. Ann was sitting in the truck waiting for us. "Look," I said, "Ann came to say good-bye to you. It's a long trip for her."

"Oh boy, oh boy. Ann's here," Sally said.

In the house I told Ann I'd been trying to talk seriously to Sally in the afternoon about how she felt about herself before she left for home. I told Ann Sally was talking about getting married for appearances sake and Ann's eyes rolled just perceptibly.

Sally said, "Martha said people know I'm a lesbian."

ANN: What do you think?
SALLY: Well, I remember after the gay pride parade in Washington D.C., some people at work asked me if I'd been to D.C. for the weekend. They were real nice. Matter-of-fact. I said no. I didn't know what they meant. Gee, I wanted to go, just to see. Do you think they know?
ANN: Well, I think that's a clue.
SALLY: Maybe that's why my friend Millie in Texas keeps sending me articles about church groups for lesbians. I never thought about it. I wondered why she kept sending me that stuff.
ANN: She's trying to tell you something.
SALLY: Uumhmm. Hummm. I see . . . I see. Ummm. Hmmmmm.
SALLY: I've always wondered if my cousin Kay is a lesbian. She lives on a ranch with her friend Jane.
ANN: (smiling) That's a clue.
SALLY: Once when I was about nine Kay and I were playing cowboys and I said, "Let's ride into town and look for women." She was so mad at me. She screamed, "Don't you ever say that again." I didn't know why she was so mad.
ANN: Who's your favorite actress?
SALLY: (now suddenly bright and happy, eager to talk) Catherine Deneuve. The YOUNG Catherine Deneuve. I've seen all her movies.

Ann asks her about movie titles—evidently well-known lesbian films I've never heard of. Sally has seen them all.

I'm surprised, because she kept telling me she wasn't sure

she was a lesbian.

I ask her, "When do you watch those movies, with your mother and girls around?"

SALLY: Oh. Ha, ha. I'm real careful. I wait until I'm sure everyone is asleep. My favorite actress now is Jacqueline Smith. Yup. She's my ideal woman.
ANN: Yes. She's attractive all right.
SALLY: (turns to me) Remember that time back in Santa Fe when I phoned you and asked you if you'd seen *Personal Best*?

(This is a film about young women athletes at the Olympics and had Mariel Hemingway in it. I was shocked when I got it on video and discovered the two main characters were lesbians.)

M: I remember. I told you it had made me sick.
SALLY: (grinning) Yeah. You can imagine my disappointment. (she winks at Ann)

I feel a sick shock realizing that all those years ago she was lusting after me and I didn't have any idea—I was always dropping by—no wonder her mother made me feel unwelcome.

Sally is enjoying the openly male talk with Ann. Guy talk.

SALLY: Yeah, my ideal woman. She'll be beautiful, and so feminine. No one will ever suspect she's a lesbian. Like Liz. (pause) Yeah. The trip to San Diego would have been worth it just to see Lisa.

The next morning is Thursday morning and I am relieved

that all I have to do is get Sally to the airport and on the plane. It turns out not to be that easy. She has a terrible time packing all her bags. I think I'll never get her out of the house. She's wearing one the dresses her mother or sister picked out for her. A plaid cotton skirt with a bolero jacket top. The jacket just reaches the top of the skirt waistband. Sally keeps trying to tuck the jacket into the skirt but it's too short. She keeps repeating this ritual of bending forward, tucking the jacket into the skirt, then standing up and the jacket pops out and then bending over and tucking the jacket in, and straightening up and the jacket flies out. Over and over. I say, "Sally, that's a bolero jacket, it's not meant to be tucked in, it's too short."

"Yeah," she says, "It's a hard one." Laughs. Keeps on tucking it in until the moment she gets on the plane.

In the car there's an awkward silence until we get in view of the harbor. We're almost to the airport when suddenly she starts talking, fast. I'm concentrating on the traffic and the time. I'm listening, but not responding. Only later does the full impact of what she said arrive to me.

SALLY: I don't want you to think I'm lecherous—these young girls. I wouldn't try to corrupt them. (pause) It's a sin. Can't have a woman on earth.

Oh boy. As soon as I get to heaven I'm going to run as fast as I can to where the women are. In heaven you can have anything you want.

Boy if I ever get a woman I'm going to take such good care of her. She'll never have to worry about anything.

Last year when I was in the Yucatan I went into this little Catholic church and I made three wishes. On the first one I asked for good health. For the second I asked for a long life for my family. Then for the third one I said,

> "Oh, God, I'm going to ask for what I want. I want a woman to love. If I get one I'll take such good care of her."

(as I hear this I'm thinking of the nine-year-old asking for an astronaut suit)

> I told God, "And if you give her to me, I promise I'll bring her back here and thank you."
> I really just want a woman to love. If I don't get one on earth then when I get to heaven, where you can have anything you want, I'll run right to where the women are and ask God for one. (laughs) Or maybe I should ask him to make this (desire) go away. (laughs nervously) When I get a woman I'm going to take such good care of her.

At the airport the time is short. I want to get her into the terminal, but now she starts rummaging through her bags in the trunk. "Here it is. Gotta have some of this." She takes out a large bottle of Pepto-Bismol and drinks from the little cup that comes with it. Then she runs around saying, "Oh, what can I do with this (the little cup)?" She's wearing her backpack over her dress and it's hanging open with things falling out.

"Sally, please. We've got to go."

Inside she has trouble checking in. The soft bags she wants to check through are full of glass bottles of perfumes and lotions and cosmetics. The airline woman checking in her bags tells her she can't check those bottles through, they'll break.

"Whooops," Sally says. "Gotta repack."

She spreads her bags out on the floor and starts repacking the bottles in carry-on luggage and her backpack. Somehow she gets checked in. Now she wants coffee before she gets on the plane. I tell her she can get coffee on the plane. "Gotta have it." We go into the cafeteria. She buys a banana and two different kinds of coffee which she mixes. She overfills her cup and it's running on her and on the floor. She can't get her money out at the cash register. She gets to a table and sets the coffee down then runs off and comes back with her two hands cupped full of ice which she dumps into the cup. Now the coffee is running off the table in a stream onto the floor. "Love it cold. Ha, ha. Don't worry, I'll clean it up."

Somehow, in spite of all her bobbing, baggage, banana and coffee and tucking in of her jacket I get her on the plane.

I was relieved, then sad. My best friend came to visit but I couldn't find her. I didn't know the person who was here, and I missed my friend, the one I used to talk and laugh with on the phone before the days of her frantic depression and confession. For if I could not have a conversation with Sally when she was here with me, how could I ever have a serious conversation with her on the phone again—now that I'd seen her true character? Ann said, "Sexual repression causes seriously strange behavior." Tom and John said, "She was never any different—you created the friendship." All I knew was I grieved for a lost friendship. That night Sally phoned from Santa Fe. "I want to come back. I know what I did wrong now. Oh, I did it all wrong. Let me come back—now. I know what to do now. Oh, I behaved all wrong. I was crazy! I don't know what got into me. Please, please, let me come back and do it over. Do it all differently."

M: No. You were okay. You were fine. You can't come back. But you have to change your life in Santa Fe. Start somewhere. Start with that church group for Catholic lesbians. You'll feel better. You'll meet a friend. You have to be

who you are.
SALLY: Yeah. (pause) I don't think I can do that.

So Sally went back into the closet. The door slammed firmly shut. I wondered what she meant by "do it all differently" if she could fly right back. I didn't ask. I felt I'd seen the quintessential Sally. I thought her wanting to come back was like when she wanted to fly right back to Kansas after her high school reunion to try to convince the woman who said she didn't want her to change her mind. I wondered if she'd ever really been my friend or only had a crush on me as a possible "woman." Maybe she was incapable of being an adult friend. After all, her personality was nine years old.

I phoned her a few times over the next year to ask how she was. The conversations were awkward—she didn't say much except her life hadn't changed.

SALLY: "Still crazy!! Maybe, someday."

The last I heard from her was at Christmas. She sent me a Christmas card. It was a child's Christmas card. A little cut-out figure card—a teddy bear with a candycane.

Poor Sally. All her wires are crossed. She wants a woman, a young woman, but who would want her? She looks like a wiry old spinster, fussing over her makeup and smelly cosmetics, her cloying "baby powder" scent, who can't choose her own clothes—because they're the wrong clothes.

I remember back in Santa Fe years ago when I phoned her and she said she was taking apart a new bra, cutting sections in the back and adding extension pieces "otherwise it won't meet. It's so hard to do because I can't sew. But I can't buy one that fits. I have a flat chest and a broad back and they just don't make a bra for me. So I buy the largest size AA I can and then I cut the back and add to it. Of course it never fits. It's always uncomfortable."

I asked her, "Why wear a bra if you don't need one?"

"Oh, I have to wear a bra."

"No, you don't. You can wear an undershirt or a camisole if you feel you need an undergarment."

She did stop wearing her torturous, unneeded brassieres and repeatedly thanked me for telling her she didn't have to.

"Oh, God. No bra. It's just great."

She used to tell me her dream was to go on an archaeological expedition. A "dig." Say in the Middle East. I told her I could picture her doing that. Wearing overalls and "being herself." The image fit, even though I didn't know then she was a lesbian I knew something was wrong, in her clothes.

Her mother and sister trapped her in an image that wasn't her — sometime after nine and the coonskin cap. Like her mother and sister she married a doctor and joined the Junior League. I used to say, "Sally, I just can't picture you in Junior League."

"Oh, I like it. Great women. Really great women."

I didn't understand. When she was here visiting me she always wore her single strand of pearls, even with the favored jeans shorts. Her favorite around-the-house outfit was a pair of extra-large men's extra-baggy gym shorts that hung low on her hip bones. After she went back to Santa Fe she sent Tom and John each a pair. I hate it when they wear them, hung low on their hips — I get the creepy feeling she's back in the house.

That creepy feeling. I only get it with closet lesbians. Not with people like Jill and Ann. I look at Jill and Ann and they are so normal. Such good, intelligent friends. So much fun to be with. They are comfortable with who they are and how they dress. They know who they are. They have no secret designs on me. It's the lesbians-in-the-closet who have made me uncomfortable, their turbulent, secret inner life, their secret agenda.

Once I thought I didn't know any lesbians. Now I think of all the people in my life who were probably lesbians. The teachers, the secretaries—all those wiry, lanky spinsters awkward in their dresses and oversized flat shoes. (And some who were plump and feminine.) Probably they were lesbians—lonely, confused, unhappy, frustrated. *They* must know. Just like Sally knows. Or maybe like Sally they tell themselves, "Yes. Maybe. I'm not sure. No." What I've seen is that repression of one's natural sexuality cripples or stops social development. To be a lesbian is not freaky. It's normal and natural to women who are born lesbians. It's denial of self and nature, it's living in a closet that breeds socially stunted, bizarre, crazy women.

5

Mother Superior

Mother Superior is a pretty daunting title, even to me and I'm not a Roman Catholic. The very words "Mother Superior" sound very close to "God" to me, even in a non-religious sense. A "Superior" mother certainly is an authority figure to my psyche—a figure of some distance, coolness, and austerity—someone who can size you up and therefore requires your best manners and most careful, formal speech.

That Saturday at Jill's house when we were in the kitchen waiting for Jordan and George to get ready I told Jill how good it is to have her in the book. I said, "You're so special."

She was kneeling down filling the dog dishes and she cocked her head up me and said with astonishment (something I'd never seen on her), "But I'm nothing, compared to Elizabeth. My God. She's a Mother Superior."

So even my tough little, cocky, assured, Butch Cassidy, New York Jewish, corporate-legend Jill was awed by Mother Superior. I'm amazed at the cachet a title carries.

M: Yes. She's amazing and wonderful. She was a contemplative. I asked her if she still prayed all the time. She said yes, constant prayer.
Jill: Of course. People don't change. They're who they are.

Maybe that's another way to phrase the meaning I want

to get across in this book. Jill was wearing two little circus-blue barrettes to keep her straight hair, parted in the middle, out of her eyes. It didn't matter that she had been tough enough to build a corporation in a male world, what I saw was the four-year-old little girl she'd told me about who was tough enough to play with the boys. We are all still these children we once were. We are who we are. Elizabeth must have been born to be holy as surely as Jill was born to be strong.

I first heard of Elizabeth, of course, from Ann. One day she told me that her partner, Elizabeth, had been a Mother Superior of a contemplative monastery and I was surprised. I couldn't quite imagine that. I couldn't whip up any visual picture that made sense.

In my provincial mind I tend to doubt the amazing until I encounter it. I remember my Bedouin Arab friend in graduate school who told me he was married to a beautiful blond American doctor. I had that moment of "oh, sure" doubt. It seemed so incongruous. I was used to Ali sitting with his Bedouin friends, wearing robes and headdresses and speaking in heavily accented English about taking papers from the Reader's Digest. But one day he invited me to a party to celebrate his wife's graduation from medical school. And there she was, blond, beautiful, American, and a hard-working doctor who was crazy about Ali who'd cooked all the Middle Eastern food for the party and was very proud of her. Her mother was there and she loved Ali too. She was the one who made all his headdresses that he couldn't buy in the States. She was the one who when her daughter said "I want to be a nurse like you" told her daughter, "No. You can be a doctor." Why wouldn't she also say, "Marry whom you love"? It was my first lesson in expectations and how important they are to children. I learned later I wasn't awed by titles or power because I saw the person's nature only, good or bad, and the child he or she once was (and still is), loved or not loved.

Another time Ann had said to me, "You'll have to meet Elizabeth sometime. I think you'll be surprised. She's sixty-one years old, but you'd never know it."

I knew I'd be surprised. I had no idea what kind of a picture to form. Then one day I was at Ann's house and I did meet Elizabeth, whom Ann calls "Liz." "She likes 'Liz.' Her family calls her Liza and she hates that."

Ann and I were in the kitchen making iced tea when Elizabeth breezed in from work, her arms full of grocery bags. I was stunned. It was as if Leslie Caron as Gigi had swept into the room. She looked French, she had that energy, although it was peaceful energy. Her hair was red, reddish, auburn, and cut short but with French style and pixie unevenness. She was wearing an haute style red jersey dress with an uneven hemline and a dangerously high split in the skirt. She had rings on every finger, pearls on the left, rubies on the right. And her shoes were open-heeled sandals with $3^{1}/_{2}$-inch heels. She looked very glamorous. She waltzed around the kitchen putting the groceries away. Ann was right. I was surprised. Nothing would have prepared me, and yes, Ann was right, she doesn't look sixty. I don't know what age to say she does look. Maybe if you look closely for little lines you could say 50, but her carriage and manner and movement speak of youth.

Her manner is sweet and thoughtful and kind and witty and quiet. I was charmed. The second time I saw her at the house was a Saturday when John was helping Ann pour cement. This day she was wearing skinny, red pants, a red top heavily embroidered with gold, and a different set of "rings on her fingers." Today they were sapphires and gold bands.

She was so colorfully dressed and prettily made-up that it was hard for me to see her as a nun. Ann said, "Tell her about Halloween." One Halloween when she was Mother Superior Liz went to the bank for the monastery. When she walked in in her heavy brown habit and coarse, thick, rope sandals, the tellers all squealed, "What a great *costume.*" Liz had to tell them, "This is not a costume."

At the end of the summer when I decided to work again on the book I asked Ann if Liz would be in it. She said, "I'll see." I knew Liz did not like to talk about lesbians. Ann is the political, let's-not-keep-it-a-secret one. Once when I mentioned to Liz an article in the newspaper about two lesbians in the South, she crisply said, "I didn't see that." Then quickly asked, "What about Dan Jansen? Did you read that?" Another time when Ann was talking about the mineral springs where lesbians like to go, Liz said, "I hate it. All those lesbians. All they think about is sex." So I was worried.

But Ann called and said, "It's okay. Come on Saturday." When I arrived on Saturday though Liz was pacing and anxious. She said, "I can't do this."

Ann said, "See you. I'll be upstairs or somewhere."

Liz and I sat down facing each other at the tiny kitchen table for two. Liz said again, "I can't do it." I'd never seen her nervous or uncomfortable. She'd always seemed unselfconscious, unlike other lesbians I'd met who had an air of defensive nervousness.

I told her, "The book is not about sex. It's about who you are. You're special and important as a human being, and I want to write about that."

"You won't ask me about sex?"

"No."

"And no tape recorder."

"All right." And I put the tape recorder aside.

Then began a fascinating conversation. She warmed to telling her story and I listened, feeling privileged to have it shared with me. Hours went by. It was getting dark. Normally good-natured Ann was appearing in the kitchen from time to time, looking in the refrigerator and grumbling about being hungry. We both saw her and heard her but we both ignored her. Liz was liking telling her story and I was as spellbound as the wedding guest listening to the ancient mariner.

Elizabeth's family emigrated from Europe. She grew up in a large, busy family. She is the third of six children—five girls and one boy.

"My mother was a strong woman. Our family had a country store and my mother really was the one who ran it. I loved and admired her. She was my role model. My father was not interested in the business. He was charitable, he always wanted to help people. Just before I entered junior high school he had a conversion and became a devout Catholic. He had been a Catholic before, but he hadn't attended church. But he had bleeding stomach ulcers and they seemed incurable. Somehow he met this priest and got permission to spend the night in the church praying. In the morning he was well. That was when he became devout. He began to read about St. Teresa and other saints. She founded, reformed, the Carmelite nuns. I had to go to catechism and I hated it.

"My father started to visit a monastery near our home. He took food from our grocery store for the nuns and gave them "alms"—it was an alms house. That means they depended on charity for their survival.

"My mother used to get upset because he gave so much away, both money which we didn't have much of, and the food from our small grocery store. She worked so hard to feed the family and she saw him as giving it away.

"I began Catholic school in junior high. I had to pay for my tuition, uniforms, and books. The tuition was $100 a month. That was a lot of money in the forties. I earned it working in our store. Soon I began to read my father's St. Teresa books and go to church to pray for long hours."

M: Did you decide on your own to go to church to pray?
Liz: Not at first. My father went to church to pray and I first decided to pray and went with him. Soon I found I was praying for hours at a time.
M: Did you feel God's presence when you prayed?
Liz: Yes.
M: Was it bliss?
Liz: Yes.

"Then we were invited to see a clothing ceremony at the monastery. That's where the postulants get their robes and become novice nuns. I was impressed by the joy I saw on all their faces. They were truly happy.

"That was the only time I actually saw the nuns before I entered the monastery.

"I began to think I had a calling to be a nun. But I couldn't figure out what kind of nun to be. I turned away from teaching because all my teachers were mean. I didn't care for the sisters of social work. So finally I decided on the contemplative order. I didn't tell anyone or talk to anyone about this.

"I used to get upset that my mother and aunts planned marriages for the girls in the family. Once I heard them plotting for my older sister's. 'He would be good—or that one,' they'd say. I walked by and said, 'Don't plan one for me!'"

M: Did you ever date?

"Oh, yes. A lot. It was part of my plan. When I told them I was going to be a nun, I didn't want them to say, 'You don't know what you're doing. You don't have any experience.' So I dated. Not too long any one. First one, a short time, then another. I didn't want to hurt anyone.

"At graduation time one of the nuns asked me what I was going to do, and I told her I was going to be a nun. She said, 'I always knew you had a vocation.' Then she announced it at graduation. I was very upset."

Liz is a very private person. She's friendly and warm, but she's private. Maybe that's why she so dreaded talking to me, because it was about herself. Most people who talk to her find her friendly but don't notice it's because she's interested in them and they're talking about themselves.

I look at her. Her French gamine haircut. The gold dangle earrings. The intelligent eyes. The sweet expression always on her face. Her rings are gold and jewels. Her clothes are pretty and colorful.

M: Did you always love pretty clothes?
LIZ: (laughing) Oh. Yes. In the monastery I used to *dream* of being among racks and racks of pretty clothes.

"I finally chose the monastery near our home. I'd found nothing else. I never saw the inside of it until the day I entered. The life was harsh. We slept on straw mats. They were unsanitary and uncomfortable. We had a wooden bowl and a wooden fork and spoon. Everything was made by hand. We had long napkins. One part of the napkin was on the table as a mat, then it hung down onto your lap, then another third reached up to your face.

"The food was awful the first few years—oatmeal and soup—and then it got better. We got a plate and bowl made of heavy stoneware. The food was measured. One ounce of coffee. No cream or sugar. One piece of bread. Or sometimes a terrible cookie thing made without butter or sugar. For Lent we were vegetarians. Only sometimes fish was allowed. No dairy products. We had good bread and on feast days we had sweet rolls. After Vatican II the food got better.

"The habit we wore was uncomfortable—heavy wool. It was brown, like the clothes of the poor in the time when our order began. We were supposed to dress like the poor. We sewed them by hand. The hem was deep to let down as it shrunk with washings, or wore from dragging on the ground. We were allowed to tie them up and roll up the sleeves when we were gardening."

M: Were you ever allowed to wear anything else?
Liz: No. Only the habit.

"We could only meet visitors at the 'turn.' The turn is a door that turns completely around so that packages can be received. But the nun never sees the guest. You talk to them through the door. Sometimes a child tried to sneak in by getting into the turn basket—it was large enough for a child, (she smiles) but you could always feel the weight. Our families were allowed to visit us once a month. They came into a parlor and we spoke to them through a window with dowels and a wrought iron grid. We had one hour.

And there was always someone near who could hear the conversation. Our mail, coming and going, was censored. We never left the monastery.

"Recreation was twice a day for one hour. Novices were not allowed to talk at recreation but the nuns could. So the novices learned what was acceptable speech by listening. At recreation we sat together and the prioress talked to us about news we should know, particularly whom to pray for. At that time we were praying about Vietnam. We kept our hands busy, with sewing or some kind of work.

"We had no newspapers and no television.

"When Vatican II came there were changes. I was called to the Mother Superior and told I was going to be allowed to read the news of Vatican II and discuss it with the senior nuns. There were five of them who ran the monastery: the Mother Superior (also called prioress), the sub-prioress, and a council of three. I don't know why I was chosen, but I enjoyed the scholarship immensely. The idea was to examine the original tenets of our order and get rid of rules that had been added. We were surprised how much of the way we lived had nothing to do with the original rules and purpose of the order. For example, nothing in the original rules said anything about sleeping on straw. Someone added that later.

"I felt very happy. Much happier. Vatican II was a breath of fresh air—it promised to make our way of living make more sense.

"One new idea that came with Vatican II was that we could be allowed to support ourselves. A woman came to the monastery and talked to us about our doing lab work. I was at the meeting. For some reason, after the meeting, she spoke to Mother and said 'I want her.' Me. She wanted me. I don't know why. But it was providential. A few of us were trained, and we worked in the monastery. But what it eventually meant to me was that I had a profession which I used to support myself when I left.

"Then, when I was thirty-eight, a new rule was made. You could be a Mother Superior under the age of forty. Always there had been power struggles and backbiting and jealousy, but always the same Mother Superior was reelected. When her eligibility was up, after two three-year terms, then the sub-prioress was elected until the same Mother Superior could be elected again. The power stayed always with the same five people. To my surprise, this time I was elected. The Mother Superior was furious. She refused to give up her title and insisted she still be called Mother. That's the way it stayed. I requested to be called 'Sister.'

"For a long time she wouldn't hand over the account books to me which made it impossible for me to run things. But I ran things anyway and she would complain that I'd overdrawn the account. I told her I couldn't *not* overdraw if I didn't have the books, and finally I got them. I knew nothing about bookkeeping and I had to learn.

"I started changing things. First I ordered plastic placemats and china dishes. The mats were colorful and sanitary, but many nuns were upset. This was change—and change was not welcome.

"So I learned to ask first. Who would like to have a bed? Those who want to can have a bed. About one-third chose to have a bed. So I moved to bring change in stages, not by fiat.

"I ordered a television for the Pope's visit to the U.S., so the nuns could see him. That was okay. He was the Pope. But after the visit we kept the TV and the nuns were occasionally allowed to watch a program they'd chosen as a group. This *wasn't* okay. The nuns who objected said I was 'giving them *ideas.*'

"I also changed where nuns could meet guests. But they

had a choice. They could do it the old way in a room with a covered window where the parties could not see each other. The old windows had a wood shutter, then a black curtain, then wooden dowels, then a wrought iron grate. It could be none of the parts were opened. But the dowels and iron grate were permanent and did not open.

"Now I gave them also a second room where the windows had slats or dowels to bar the window. The parties could see each other but not touch. The third room had open windows, large open windows.

"I spent time as a spiritual guide. All of us did. People in need or trouble would come to the turn and talk to us and ask for prayers. I was often criticized for staying too long at the turn. The 'Mother' Sister (who was no longer Mother) would come out and ring the prayer bell right in my ear.

"But I couldn't walk away from these people. They were so desperate. So I learned to sew habits while I talked with them, so no one could say I was 'wasting time.'

"The women who came to the turn would tell me how their husbands beat them and their children. I would say, 'You have to *leave* him.'

" 'Oh, Sister,' they'd say, 'I couldn't. I'm a Catholic.'

"I would tell them 'God doesn't want you to be unhappy.'

" 'Oh, Sister,' they'd say, 'How can you say that? You're a Catholic.'

"The titular head of our order was a man, because a woman is not allowed to head a Catholic order. Of course he did not live in an order. I saw him when I went as Mother Superior to conferences.

"There was a lot of envy for my position. I was criticized. They were angry because I spoke to my father when he brought vegetables to the back gate. They said I spoke to him 'too long.' How silly—I spoke for just a few minutes.

They could hear every word.

"I was criticized for speaking to workmen in the yard. They said I was being 'provocative.' They said I was 'giving them ideas.' MY. (This is the strongest expletive Liz ever uses.) How silly. It was an open courtyard, and small. Everyone could hear every word.

"After my three years I wasn't reelected. They said I left because I wasn't reelected. That's not true. I'd planned to leave. The spirit of Vatican II, the breath of fresh air, was gone, and the life was drying up again. I waited six months, until I passed the State examinations in my field, then I left."

M: Maybe you were meant to bring fresh air and change to the monastery. Maybe your job there was done. Who was elected Mother Superior after you left?

Liz: The former Mother Superior.

M: Did your changes last?

Liz: About half of them. In recent years there've been new Mother Superiors, people who were postulants when I was there. There is a modified habit that can be worn now.

M: Do you keep in touch?

Liz: I visit, maybe twice a year. And I help if they need me. I drove a sister to the hospital when she was dying of cancer. I also took her out for lunch—which isn't allowed—but they didn't need to know that.

"When I left the monastery, a woman named Barbara found an apartment for me. She was a woman who used to come to the turn for prayers and counseling. People would come to the gate. People came to tell us—just a faceless voice behind the door to them—what they could tell no other.

"She was suffering terribly. One day she told me she felt

she was a lesbian and hated herself for it. The first time I ever heard the word lesbian was at the turn. A woman told me she feared her daughter was a lesbian. I didn't know what it meant. After she left I had to go to the dictionary to find out what it meant. I'd never heard of such a thing.

"Barbara lived with a woman. After that she came to live with me."

M: Did you think you were a lesbian?
LIZ: Oh, no. I had no feelings like that for her. It sounded very strange to me. I couldn't imagine it.
M: Did you ever feel any attraction to women?
LIZ: No.
M: To men?
LIZ: Oh, yes. I was always attracted to men.

"Then one day we embraced—there was a kiss—it felt natural. It didn't feel wrong. We lived together until she died."

M: Were you—lovers?
LIZ: Oh, no. She didn't feel right about being a lesbian. There was nothing. Except an occasional embrace, an occasional kiss.

"She'd had a very abusive mother. The mother was crazy and she made Barbara feel responsible for her. Once when Barbara was a child the mother said she would set herself on fire if she didn't get a new dress. The child felt she had to fix things for her mother. Barbara never recovered from her mother.

"When we were nuns there was no affection allowed. We could not talk to another nun unless there was a third nun present. 'No special friends,' that's what they always said. 'No particular friend.' I'd never thought what it meant. I'd never heard of lesbians.

"I get so angry when people say, 'Oh, you were a nun—there must be a lot of lesbian nuns.' There aren't."

M: Maybe they think women can't do without sex. Like men in prison. Without women many go after other men.
LIZ: And like priests. That's sad—what they do. It makes me angry.
M: That the church covers it up?
LIZ: Yes. That.

"After Barbara died, Ann phoned to see why our dog hadn't been in to the vet. She worked for the vet. I told her about Barbara. She was very kind. She asked me to some parties. They were mixed parties. The doctor was there with his wife.

"Ann kept calling me, asking me places. Finally I asked her, 'Why are you so interested in me? I'm so much older.'

"She said, 'That doesn't matter.'"

And it doesn't. I've noticed in the times I've spent with Ann's friends that age and physical looks seem of little or no importance in the couples.

Now Ann comes into the kitchen. She's disgruntled because we've talked so long.

ANN: I'm hungry. We didn't have lunch.

She bangs through the cupboards—finds an apple and a bag of chips. She's stomping around—keeps glowering over at us. The whole scene reminds me of my boys, and husband—the hungry male, testy because not fed.

Liz and I glance at her vacantly. Liz, the female, though sweet does not give in to guilt, but appears oblivious to that very clear message. (I remember now too Jill's boyish announcements of "I'm hungry," which meant we ate quick.)

"I don't like the lesbian community. They're too wrapped up in sex—like an angry protest. And I think gays go too far, with the parades and protests. I understand, of course, but there's a lot I don't like. I think they should live quietly, with dignity.

"And the lesbians who hate men—yet they imitate them. They hate them, but they act just like them.

"They sit like this!" (she throws her legs apart)

She glances at the door and says, "If anything happened to Ann—there wouldn't be another."

M: Would you leave the lesbian life completely?
Liz: Yes.
M: Would you consider marrying a man?
Liz: Oh, yes. That's all I'd consider.
M: Are you still attracted to men?
Liz: Oh, yes. (she smiles) Very.

Liz: Two gay men I know dress up. They showed us their dresses. They don't go out. They just wear them at home. (She shudders slightly.)
  It feels wrong to me. I can't understand it.
  I didn't ask them why. They showed us the dresses. Beautiful, sequined.

M: Do you still pray?
Liz: Yes.

M: All the time?

Liz: Yes.

M: Do the others know that?

Liz: They must—they're always apologizing for telling dirty stories—"Oh, excuse me, Liz. I didn't know you were there."

M: I don't think they know. I don't think they have any idea what your spiritual life is. I think they apologize for their rough language because you're a "lady," because you don't talk rough.

M: What did you enjoy most in the monastery?

Liz: (she smiles) The prayer—yes—also the nuns. They were witty and fun. They laughed freely—really they had a wonderful spirit when they were together.

M: This was only at recreation?

Liz: Yes—only then.

M: Do you still live a life of contemplative prayer?

Liz: Oh, yes.

M: Is the prayer any less frequent or less special than it was in the monastery?

Liz: Oh, no. You can pray anywhere—anytime—in the midst of busyness. You don't need quiet, or a special place.

M: I'm learning that. Ceaseless prayer. Do you miss church?—the Mass?

Liz: Yes. I've tried to go a couple of places—but the priests—they weren't good—and so I'd stop. I'd like to have a place to go.

M: Is your faith still strong?

Liz: Yes. It is always strengthened as I grow older. Life is planned—you can see it looking back.

I needed to talk to Liz again, to check details and accuracy. I phoned and left a message. Ann phoned me back. I always talked to Liz through Ann to arrange things. Liz seemed to prefer that—Ann both protects Liz and pushes her more into the world. I had a feeling that Liz wouldn't come without Ann.

On Sunday afternoon they came to my house and I knew I was right. Liz said, "I'm sorry I did this." I said, "I know, but it's important. What you say carries a lot of moral weight." I asked her if I could record her voice. "It helps me to get the meaning right to hear your voice—it brings you back to me." I play a little of the tape I made at Jill's house—Jill blow-drying her hair and me shouting questions. She started to laugh. "See," I said, "you hear Jill's voice, and she's in the room." Liz said okay to the tape recorder and I put in a ninety-minute tape and began.

We talked first of her father's conversion experience and we talked about the daily life in the monastery. The nuns rose at 5:00 a.m. to begin praying. One hour of mental prayer and then an "office" (formal prayer) and at 7:00 the Mass. After that breakfast and then duties (work) from 8:00 to 11:00. After lunch was recreation for one hour (sitting together as a group). The prioress would talk to them about what to pray for. The idea was to pray constantly. Always in prayer. That is why there was no talking except at recreation. Only a few necessary words to accomplish a work detail were allowed. Otherwise it was pray as you work. At 2:00 p.m. were Vespers. At 5:00 p.m. another hour of mental prayer. Then dinner, recreation, an "office" (prayer as a community), then time in one's room, then an office again and the day ended at 10:00. The mental and community prayer were done in the chapel room on one's knees on a stone floor.

LIZ: You could sit back on your heels but that was hard for me to do.

People think nothing goes on in the monastery. They haven't experienced the power of prayer. Once you've experienced the power of prayer, you can do all kinds of things. We prayed for the people who asked for prayers at the turn and we prayed for people in the world. The contemplative nun's life is the life of Mary, a life of spirituality and prayer.

(as opposed to the life of Martha, one of duty)

M: I wanted to ask you about "the discipline" you mentioned once. Was that a bundle of switches you were supposed to strike yourselves with?
LIZ: Uhh-ugh. It's so repugnant to me that I can't even tell you. (but in a moment she did) It was a symbol of obedience that came out of sixteenth-century Spain. The switches were only given to nuns after a number of years, around three. I didn't use them. During Lent we were required to on certain days.
M: Then did you?
LIZ: I had to be obedient.
M: (I smile) Then did you do it very lightly in a symbolic manner?
LIZ: (laughs too) Yes. Very lightly. There were other, public, disciplines too—too terrible to tell you.

(She looks at me and knows now she must.)

One was going around on your knees begging for bread. That's terrible. It wasn't done at our monastery. Some nuns liked the disciplines. But Vatican II put an end to them.

Actually I was one of a very few that wanted to give them up, and it took a couple of years to fully get rid of them.

At some point in our conversation, the tape reached its end and I turned it over and continued.

M: How did you keep your temper among the envy, back-biting, and criticism of you that was so silly?
Liz: (laughs) It wasn't easy.
M: As Mother Superior couldn't you talk to the people who were doing it, counsel them to stop?
Liz: (she sighs) I could change their behavior by a talk, but only for a few days. So I decided to not pay any attention to it.
M: When were you first aware of God? I've met two people who talked of knowing God's presence as a child. Was it like that for you?
Liz: Yes. It was very early. I didn't know it was God. I didn't have a name for it. Rather it was a presence I felt and later I knew it was God.
M: Did you like life at the monastery?
Liz: (smiles, her face is deeply peaceful with the memory) Yes. I loved it.
M: I would think people would throw up their hands and scream "I can't pray anymore."

(now she laughs at me)

Liz: Many left. It was a confining life—only three acres and you never went out.
M: You had gardens?
Liz: Lovely gardens. It was beautiful. I was so happy. When I left they said, "You of all people had the truest voca-

tion." I could have knuckled under to the ruling powers—joined them—let them run things when I was Mother Superior—*but I couldn't do that.*

She says this quietly, firmly—there never was a question. I wonder what they thought afterwards, those who drove her out, even admitting she was their priceless jewel.

M: Did you know how you felt about the moral question of lesbianism immediately?
LIZ: Not immediately, but very soon. So many people who came to the turn to talk were tortured. They were Catholics and it was a sin to have these feelings. They suffered terribly—so many suicides.
   I knew God did not want them to suffer.
   I knew that for sure.
   There were so many parents who said, "I love my child, *but* . . ."

I tell her about Sally's family. How one night at a large family dinner one of the nieces, in her twenties, asked her mother, "We were wondering, is cousin Kay a lesbian?" There was a long silence around the table. Cousin Kay is a lesbian, and everyone of the older adults knows it. Sally is a lesbian, firmly in the closet. The girl's mother, Sally's sister, said, "We don't know, dear." The strong, matriarchal grandmother nodded. The older people looked at their plates and began eating. The questions had been silenced.
   I asked Liz, "What do you think about that?"
   Ann had walked into the room and she smiled. Liz's response would be different than hers.

LIZ: Let them live quietly and in dignity.

M: I just thought they should say "yes" and go on. I thought it would let Sally go if they accepted it. But you're saying their approach is all right?

Liz: My closest niece recently called me to tell me several of my nieces had come to her and asked her if I am a lesbian. I said to her, "What people say always gets back to me." Then she changed the subject.

M: So you avoid it.

Liz: Yes. When I first left the monastery the Mother Superior phoned my brother and told him to "watch Liz." She said, "That Barbara is a bad influence."

My brother phoned me and said, "We think she may be a lesbian." I remained quiet. Soon he hurriedly went on, "but she has so many wonderful qualities." And he began to list them.

She did. She gave him money when he needed it. She was kind and generous.

M: Do you consider yourself a lesbian?

Liz: (quiet, a little uncomfortable) There are all kinds of lesbians—radical, bizarre.

M: You're uncomfortable with the term—it's too broad.

Liz: Yes. It's a label.

M: You don't want to be labeled.

Liz: That's right.

M: Are you attracted to women?

Liz: I never was—until Barbara. I was attracted to her . . . as a person. She was a beautiful human being. It was not a sexual attraction.

M: And Ann? She is a beautiful human being too—that goes without saying. But is your attraction to her sexual as well?

(she looks at me, directly, honestly, thinking—she does not speak)

Let's look at it another way. Say we're at a party—a very large party, a big social event. There are lots of attractive people there, both men and women. Who would you be looking at?
Liz: (smiles at me, suddenly happy and relaxed) The men. For sure the men. (pause) The men first.

Ann called from the next room. "Twenty minutes." They had to leave in twenty minutes.
"Yes," I said. "I'm watching the clock. We're almost finished."
I asked Liz a last few questions, the Barbara Walters' questions.

M: If you could change the past, what if anything would you change?

She looked at me and with only a moment of thought said, "Nothing."

M: If you could change anything in the present, what would you change?
Liz: Nothing.
M: Are you comfortable with who you are and where you are now?
Liz: Yes.
M: Have you always been comfortable with yourself.
Liz: Yes.

Liz is always quiet and sure. When she pauses before

answering a question it is only for a moment. The answer comes almost immediately, and calmly and surely. She is so attuned to God in prayer that she never doubts or is self-conscious. She is sure of God's presence and guidance in her life and she accepts it. She left the monastery without guilt or doubt. She doesn't attend the Mass regularly because she hasn't found a good priest. Although she loves the Church, she knows God is with her—the Church is not necessary for her to be with God.

She knew for sure when she told the tortured lesbians and gay men who came to the turn to get help, "God doesn't want you to suffer." She knew for sure when Barbara kissed her, "It felt natural. It didn't feel wrong."

Her eyes have a deep sure peace when I mention God. They have a look of looking "beyond." Even though she is looking directly at me, she is seeing something else.

Now a shocking realization comes over me. Like a veil of ignorance being lifted I am suddenly aware that to record Liz's voice on tape I pushed the play button, not the record button. The tape was humming and turning the whole afternoon and I knew for sure now that I had nothing on it.

I say to Liz, "Oh my god. I just realized I pushed play and not record. I did it twice. How could I be so stupid."

Ann comes in from the next room. She is amazed and not amazed that I have been so stupid.

Liz is laughing. I start to laugh too.

"I was so happy to be recording your voice, and now it just 'dawned on me,' I actually *remembered* pushing play not *record*. You didn't want your voice recorded and it wasn't."

Liz is still laughing. "It was meant to be."

M: God is protecting you.

Liz always says, "It was meant to be."

Right now in her life she has lost the very good job she had in the lab where she'd been all the years since leaving the monastery. The lab was bought by a large chain of labs and the working conditions are bad and she took a huge salary cut. She knows the methods are wrong at the lab and the manager is a tyrant. She has done what she can to make both the work and the atmosphere better but to no avail. So she goes to work and does the best she can.

I say to her, "Oh, Liz. That's terrible."

She says, "It's okay. It's meant to be."

She is at peace. She doesn't understand why this is happening but she knows a plan is working. She looks at me steadily. Her eyes are lavender. She waits peacefully and faithfully for God's plan to unfold. She is calm and sure because she knows God's love and she knows she's in his care.

She said before that you can see God's plan looking back over your life. So, one-third of her life was given to the monastery. She was their breath of fresh air, the brightest flower in their garden. Now another third has been given to another group of women where she has spread her influence in her quiet way. To this other group of women who live in their own kind of silence she has brought the message, "God doesn't want you to be unhappy." To those who criticize them she says, "Let them live quietly and in dignity."

I wonder if God has other work for her to do for the last third of her life.

This much I know for sure. If I turned around suddenly and saw her, in the room or on the edge of a roof, wearing a large pair of beautiful wings, I would not be surprised.

This may sound childlike to some people, but I've actually thought of asking her, "If you die before me, please fly down and show me your wings."

6

TED AND FRED

TED LIVED ACROSS the street from me. His house and yard were neat and pretty. The house had been his mother's and then his sister lived in it when I first moved here. When she had personal troubles and moved out, Ted bought the house from his mother. I watched him start to fix it up. He painted the outside, white with pale blue trim, shutters and door, and put in a new yard. He planted shrubs and flowers and lined the short drive with flowering trees. Then he began redoing the inside of the house. He had large table saws and tools in the garage. I saw him carrying out major portions of the interior, from the bathroom, from the kitchen, and new items going in.

He looked like a tall man from across the street. He had a thick head of black hair. His little black dog was always with him. Sometimes on a summer Saturday night the front windows and door of his house were open and I could hear voices in pleasant and animated conversation and piano music or opera. The house gave off a warm glow from perfect interior lighting. People were having a lovely time. I'd sigh and feel a bit envious. I never noticed that all the party voices were male.

One summer night I stepped out barefoot in the dark to enjoy the stars and night air and there was Ted on the sidewalk walking his little dog. He had on short short little jersey red shorts and talked a mile a minute about something that was making the dog, Max, bark. I liked him immediately and immediately I knew he was gay.

The next day when I saw Ted working in the garage I went over to see him and he gave me a tour of his house remodeling. It was beautiful, all new kitchen and bathroom, indirect and track lighting, tables he made himself out of beautiful shades of light woods inlaid and bonded and fastened with wooden pegs. The kitchen was white with black accent tiles and special cutting boards and an island and hanging pans and plants. Ted was a busy bee—from one project to the next—the complete homemaker.

His favorite room was the guest bedroom, done like a ship captain's cabin with a large, raised, built-in bed done up in red and green plaids. The walls of the room were dark red and green.

I met Denny who lived with him. Denny was short, dark-skinned and muscular. Maybe of island heritage. Ted proudly told me Denny was a Marine. Denny was in awe of Ted's literal "homemaking"—"Can you believe this guy? He made the furniture!" Ted beamed proudly. I envied his gorgeous kitchen.

Ted was a vice president, in charge of data, of a city bank and at Christmas time he took Carrie, the woman next door to him with four children, to the bank Christmas party with him and Denny so people wouldn't suspect he was gay. She was supposed to be his date. I looked at Carrie when she told me. "Don't you think people at work know he's gay?"

She laughed, "Oh, I would think so. But we had fun. I bought a new green satin dress, and, you know, I don't get out much. And Jim (her husband) didn't mind."

Time passed and I didn't see Denny around anymore. The next year at Christmas Ted came over and asked if Tom, who must have been about fourteen that year, would help him carry in a Christmas tree. Tom whispered to me, "Do I have to?" He'd just recently learned about gay people and didn't like the idea. "Yes," I whispered, "You have to." Ten minutes later he came back laughing. "He's a nice guy. So funny. (pause) Really nice. He talked a mile a minute. I didn't have to say anything. *Really* gay." He laughed. He wasn't uncomfortable.

Sometime in the spring I saw a new man at Ted's a lot. I never saw him in the yard with Ted the way I used to see Denny, but I saw him behind the screen door or at the window. Ted was busy and I didn't see him to talk. We mostly just waved and shouted "hi" across the street. His mother came to visit often and I would see her with Ted in the garage, watching him work.

One winter morning I heard an ambulance wail up our street. I always react strongly to the sound because of the ambulance wails from the emergency area of the hospital the night my father died when I was eighteen. It seemed to stop right outside our house and I pulled the curtains back and looked out. It was in front of Ted's house. I ran out the front door. At Ted's the ambulance paramedics were already running out with a stretcher. The man on it was dark-haired and tall. His face was covered with an oxygen mask and tubes. "Ted, Ted?" I said, but to my relief Ted walked out the door behind the stretcher. Thank God that wasn't Ted. "Ted is there anything I can do?"

"Oh, Jack should have gone to the hospital long before this. I tried to make him but he wouldn't listen. This is the second time this has happened."

Later Ted came home and we talked. Jack had AIDS. Ted had been caring for him a long time. I didn't ask any questions. I just let Ted talk. But it explained why this man was always just at the window. Ted seemed to handle all this well. He was very matter-of-fact, not emotional, as he explained about Jack's condition. The perfect nurse.

I looked around Ted's house. It was different. The beautiful light wood furniture was gone. It was *Roman*. Roman arches over the doorways and in the tiny pretend-vestibule area, and over the mantle, and Roman *columns* in the living room! The whole inside was totally different, except for the treasured ship's captain room and the kitchen.

"Jack *didn't* like modern," Ted said. I had to redo *everything* for him."

He took me to the master bedroom and showed me photographs on the walls and dresser of Jack's family. He was particularly proud of one taken in Arabia at the turn of the century. Two people in Arab robes and headdresses. "That's Jack's great grandparents. They were missionaries. The grandmother dressed like a man. Everyone thought she was a man. Isn't that something?"

After that I occasionally went over and had a chat with Ted. Jack was always in the living room, wrapped in a blanket, always cold, always cranky and complaining, always thinner. Ted always looked at Jack, and then at me with that, "Isn't he great?" look on his face, waiting for me to confirm it with my smile. On Sundays Ted's mother would be with them. They ate in the living room on TV trays and watched football. Jack was never pleasant—he was grumpy and whiny and demanding. Ted was always smiling and saying soothing things while he bustled about chatting and smoothing and filling the room with his particular cheer. It seemed like these were just their personalities, not related to Jack's AIDS. After Christmas that year I went over to see Ted and found out Jack had died. Ted collapsed in my arms in tears. "I'm so sorry. I just can't help it." On New Year's Day I knew he was in the house alone. The evening grew dark and no lights came on in the house. I was making New Year's cabbage rolls for good luck and I took some over for Ted. He was grieving.

In the spring and the following year Ted threw himself into water sports. He bought a speedboat and spent his weekends on the water with his mother and sister. We didn't see much of him. He was waterskiing and diving and fishing and he kept his boat at the marina.

The next spring the bank Ted worked at was sold to a large out-of-town bank. Ted was panicky. He knew the local people would be fired. I tried to reassure him. "Ted, you're head of data. You're too necessary for them to let you go."

But he couldn't be consoled. "I've been with them for twenty-two years. I don't know what I'll do."

All I could say was, "It'll be okay, Ted. I just know it." And it felt true, as if I really did know it.

When Sally decided to come to visit and Ann planned a party I asked Ann if I could bring Ted. Of course. I went over to see Ted and explained that my friend Ann was having a party on Sunday and would he like to go with me and Sally. I explained to him that everyone there would be gay except me and I thought he might enjoy meeting some new friends seeing as he'd been so lonely since Jack's death. He had a brief moment of astonishment and immediately said he'd love to go. Nearly a year later he told me he'd had no idea I knew he was gay. He said, "I was so surprised."

On Sally's first night here, Saturday night, Ann and Liz came by with some friends to pick up Sally. They were taking her to a gay and lesbian country western bar and dance club. When they arrived and were waiting in the living room for Sally they looked so festive and happy in their cowboy boots and Liz in white jeans with gold sequins. I said, "Let me phone Ted so he can meet you." Ted ran across the street and a moment later I could see Ann was as fond of him as I was.

"Jack and I used to go dancing a lot. We loved to dance," he said.

"Why don't you come with us," Ann said.

"Give me five minutes. I'll go get my boots," Ted said and ran back across the street. In less than ten minutes he was back. In full western regalia. What a costume he had. Boots and western pants and a well-worn, good-looking straw western hat and the most beautiful western shirt I've ever seen. Red with elaborate gold embroidery.

Ann was telling me how confusing it is when gay people dance together. "It's sort of . . . do you lead or follow?"

Ted laughed. "Oh, yes. When I met Jack, at a dance club, he asked me, and I said, 'Oh, I lead.'"

"Jack said, 'No. *I* lead. You'll have to learn to follow.' And I did."

Jack sounded so authoritarian and severe and Ted so anxious to please and acquiesce that we all thought we knew who the dominant one was.

Then I looked more closely at the beautiful gold embroidery on Ted's shirt and said, "Ted, what beautiful, intricate needlework."

TED: Oh, yes. Jack made this for me.
M: He did embroidery?

Ann quickly looked to catch my reaction. She never misses anything. She saw my stunned face and started to laugh with me.

"Yeah, and I pour cement," she said to me laughing.

She moved her hands in spiral motions. "It's all mixed up."

Ted was still talking. "Jack could do a very rare Turkish knot," he was explaining to the others in the room.

I spoke softly to Ann, in wonder, "That why it's so beautiful—it's all a marvelous mix—full of surprises—like rare species. We must preserve them."

Ann looked at me, her eyebrows slightly raised.

I said, "Tennessee Williams—no one else could have written the plays. Oscar Wilde. If we just had testosterone men and estrogen women we'd lose all these wonderful, surprising blends of what's the best of both. We must not let them become endangered species."

They went out the door, all of them talking and laughing.

John called out to Ann, "Have fun preserving your species."

Ann turned and laughed again.

Through the summer Ted continued to fret and worry about losing his job at the bank. "I've been there twenty-two years. I don't know what I'll do," he said. Then, "I know I'll find another job." He said this bravely but he continued to worry. He said he wasn't able to sleep at night. Near the end of the summer two things happened. First the bank negotiated a severance package for any of their executives that might be terminated. The severance pay would cushion the shock if a termination notice came. That helped Ted's state of mind. The second thing that happened was the bank sent Ted to Chicago for a three-day seminar on bank data processing. What happened in Chicago put Ted into a new state of mind.

Whenever I begin to doubt miracles, one happens. Ted fell in love. There is nothing like love to change one's state of mind.

Ted waved for me to come over the first day after his trip

to Chicago. He had just come from work and he always looked so handsome in his business suits and expensive ties that my heart always involuntarily skipped a beat until I reminded myself he's gay. He is mostly bald too.

I never knew all that black hair he had was a toupee until the last spring. Then I kept seeing a tall bald man about his yard and house. I thought he had a new friend and I stayed away. I never seemed to see Ted. Then one Saturday the bald man and Ted's mother were in the driveway getting a garage sale ready. With an awakening realization I cautiously went across the street and saw the bald man was Ted.

"Ted," I said, "all spring I didn't know where you were and who the bald man was. Didn't you wonder why I didn't speak to you?" He laughed and hugged me.

"The toupee just didn't seem worth the trouble anymore. Boy, were people at the bank surprised. You know, I just didn't need it anymore. I realized I was okay without hair. It's such a relief." Now he told me, "You will not believe what happened in Chicago. The last night of the seminar I went into the city and asked where there was a gay bar. I spent the evening there and I met the most wonderful man. I really think I'm in love. Can you believe it?"

I couldn't believe it. I'd been waiting ten years and I hadn't met a wonderful man. "It's amazing Ted. You go to Chicago for a three-day meeting and you fall in love with a man in Chicago." I was worried for Ted. His heart was fragile and I was afraid he was setting himself up to be hurt.

"He's just wonderful," Ted said. "He's from that upper part of Michigan and he flew his own plane into Chicago for the weekend. He had three priests with him."

I had just gone from flabbergasted to more flabbergasted.

"He's a surgeon. He has seven children and has been married twenty-four years, but he's in the process of getting a divorce and coming out."

"Wait, wait, Ted. He's from the U.P.? The Upper Peninsula? My brother lives there. There are hardly any people there at all, let alone three gay priests flying around in a plane."

Later when I told Ann I couldn't believe there were three gay priests in the Upper Peninsula, Ann laughed. "Yes, Ted told me," she said. "We thought maybe that's where they send gay priests as punishment."

Ted's new love was named Fred. I said to Ann, "Isn't it amazing how their names rhyme?"

Ann said, "Let me tell you the other gay couples I know, just off the top of my head. There's Ben and Buck, Bob and Bob, Ron and Rob, and Rick and Dick."

I said, "Ann, Ted's in love."

She laughed. "I've talked with him. Sounds like lust to me. But . . . hey."

Lust or love, Ted's life had new excitement. He was on a diet. I thought he looked just fine, but now he was counting fat grams and calories. When I saw him at the grocery store he had nothing in his little plastic basket except low-fat turkey patties, non-fat margarine and raw vegetables. I'd forgotten how easy it is to lose weight when you're in love (sexually excited?). The weight just falls off. Who has an appetite if you're mooning over, or getting ready to meet a possible lover? I'd put on weight in the last four years and constantly struggled, without success, to take it off. Sally used to lament with me on the phone and we'd exchange diet ideas and share our confessions as to our failures to give up a donut or a dish of ice cream. I was puzzled when she came that summer and she was pencil thin, her jeans and other shorts falling off her hips. Now I knew why, just like Ted she had been lovesick with anticipation and dieting had been easy.

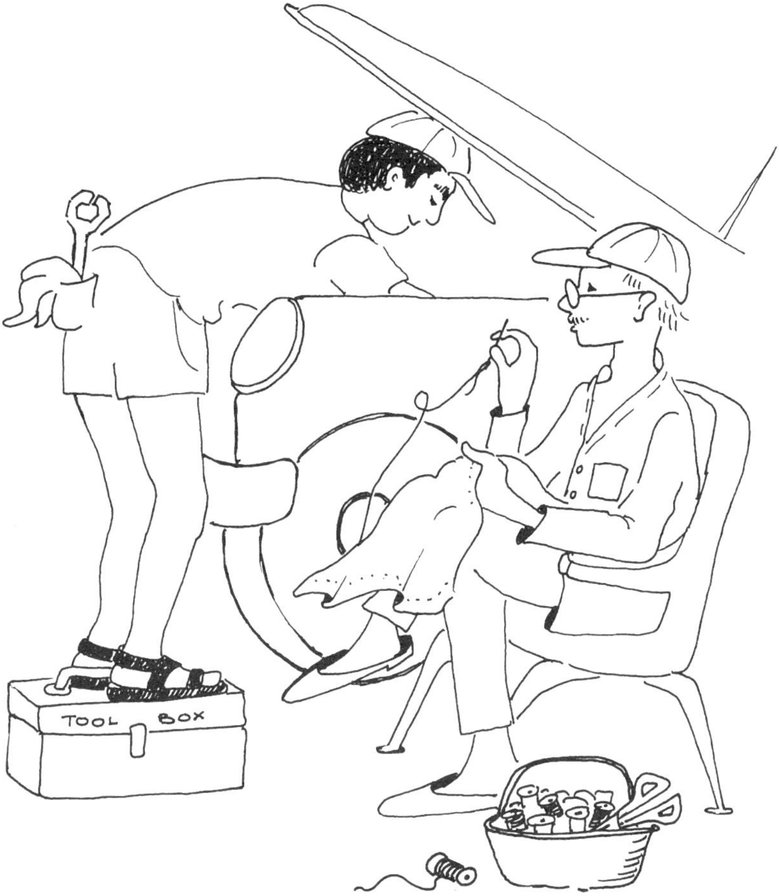
TOOL BOX

Now when Ted came home he waved me over to tell me about Fred's latest phone call. He'd say, "Wait," while he went to get out of his suit. Then when he came out he'd say, "I just had to change into something more comfortable." He'd be in his skimpy little red jersey shorts. He was so thin now. He somehow reminded me of a leggy twelve-year-old girl.

The big news this night was that Fred had invited Ted to come to Michigan for a visit.

"Oh, this is so scary," Ted said. "He's going to introduce me to his friends. They'll be looking me over. Oh, what if they don't like me?"

"They'll like you, Ted. There's no way they're not going to like you."

"Oh-my-god. I've got so much to do before Friday. I've got to buy a new pair of dress slacks. We'll probably go out to one of the clubs to meet more of his friends."

"*One* of the clubs?" I said. "I didn't think there would even be one gay club in Perry, Michigan."

"Oh, Fred says they have very nice clubs, three I think he said. And I'm copying down some of my best recipes. I'll cook for them. Oh, I hope I make a good impression."

Like a girlfriend, Ted rushed over to my house with every detail too wonderful to keep to himself. "Fred called this morning. It was six here. He said, 'This is your wake-up call.' He'd just come in from the hospital. He's so romantic. He said, 'I can't wait to cuddle up to that hairy chest of yours.'" Ted giggled. "I said, 'I can't wait to hold your hard body next to mine.'"

These details of their intimate conversations left me stunned, and uncomfortable. Writing this two years later, I smile, but at the time I was sure my face was saying, "Please I don't want to hear this." But Ted didn't notice. I was his girlfriend. "Fred was married for twenty-four years," he said. "Seven children! I asked him, 'Yuck, how could you *do* it?'"

(Here Ted never thought about *my* being a woman.)

"Fred said, 'I had to fantasize about a man.'"
Ted looked mortified. His hand flew to his cheek, "Well, I told him, 'I could *never.*'"
The trip was a great success and next Ted began to worry about commitment. Would Fred make a commitment? Months went by. Ted would come over and ask me about men's behavior.
"I just have to ask you about men. Do they have trouble showing their emotions? I tell Fred how much I care for him, but he really doesn't express that back to me. I mean he doesn't say, 'I love you.' Does that mean he doesn't care?"
Ted wrings his hands. "He says he misses me. What does that mean? Why can't he say he loves me?"

M: Well, that's very typical male behavior.
TED: Oh, is it? I just don't understand. It seems like it should be so easy. It's easy for me.
   I had surgery last week to have a hernia repaired, and Fred kept calling the hospital. He said, "I should be there. I should be overseeing this."
M: Ted, he cares. That's his way of showing his love. Lots of men just don't say "I love you."

I told him stories about my brother, my husband, and my son—men I knew from experience.

M: Even Tom (my oldest son) says to me, "Tell John (my younger son) I love him." I say, "Why don't you tell him yourself?" He says, "Oh, I can't say it—yet." Meaning what? He'll do it when he's older? I don't think so. You have to ask Fred to say it. Tell him it's important to you to hear him say it.

TED: He told me his friends say, "You'd better grab that one," meaning me. And he says he tells them, "Oh, I have." I ask him, "Does that mean we're in a relationship?" He just laughs. I say, "If we're in a relationship, you haven't told me."

He talks about the house we'll buy when we move to Atlanta. But he doesn't say he loves me. He won't make a commitment. Are men like that?

M: Buying a house in Atlanta with you sounds like a commitment to me. Probably he thinks it's understood. I know men who've just shown up with a ring or a marriage plan and just expect that the woman knows he planned to marry her. He never actually asks or even says "I love you." Ted, you're just in the age-old position of the female.

TED: I am so relieved to hear all this. I've been so worried. I just don't understand men. I don't know what I'd do if I didn't have you to talk to.

I marvel at the gender confusion. Ted doesn't know I'm more disoriented than he is. If I view Ted totally as the woman in his role with Fred, I can keep things straight.

One day when Ted and I were talking I asked Ted when he knew he was gay.

TED: I always knew I was different from other people. But I didn't know anything about homosexuality. I had no idea *how* I was different. I only knew I was different. Then when I was eighteen I joined the Navy. My first time to ship out I was leaving from San Francisco. I had never been there but I had a sort of distant aunt there and I stayed with her one night. She was going to see me off. The night before I shipped out, she took me out on the town. One of the places she took me into was a gay bar. She took me there to show me what I should avoid. That there were these kind of people in the world and that I should stay away from them.

Well, let me tell you, the minute we stepped inside, I knew. There were people in the world just like me. I recognized it immmediately. I didn't know what we were, but I knew we were alike. I was thrilled. My aunt couldn't get me out of there. I was so happy . . . to know I wasn't alone in the world.

He said this all with such gay, good cheer (gay in the classic sense of the word—is that why it came to be used for homosexuals?), with such *courage*, that my eyes teared. I was so happy for him that he had found Fred. I said a little prayer that Fred was a good guy.

I asked Ted. "Do you ever have any problems from being gay?"

TED: Well, when anyone says anything I just say, "You ought to live in my shoes."

(he gives a loud sigh of exasperation)

I remember he told me once his neighbor, a college professor, a psychologist, used to shoot a gun over the fence at his little dog Max, and yell, "Faggot."

Christmas came and Ted went to visit Fred. He said he

loved the snow in Michigan. Max loved the snow too. Ted said he loved to leap at it and bark at it. February came and Ted and Fred met for a vacation. April came and Ted put his house on the market. May came and Ted got a pink slip at the bank. He didn't care. He was jubilant. Fred was coming to get him. He was moving to Michigan, far away for a San Diego boy.

I told John. He said, "Ted's getting married."

The next day I told Ted. I thought he'd be amused. "John said, 'Ted's getting married.'"

TED: Yes. I'm so happy. I just love being married.

In June Fred came to get Ted, and to help him move. He'd flown his plane into Palm Springs and left his two passengers there for a vacation, two priests from the Upper Peninsula. Ted and Fred would pick them up on the flight back.

It sounded romantic to me. I would like a man to fly in in his plane and carry me off to a new life. It's the twentieth century version of the knight-on-a-white-horse.

The movers were there all day with Ted. That evening he came over about six and asked if he could borrow some paper plates and plastic forks and knives. He said, "I've already packed the dishes and I'm doing chicken and corn on the grill for dinner." He invited me to walk back with him and meet Fred.

I liked Fred immediately. He looked just like Ted to me except he was a little heavier. He is a tall, good-looking man. He also had a lot of black hair, which Ted later told me was a toupee. He looked like Ted except, where one knows immediately that Ted is gay, Fred did not look or act gay in any way. He is totally masculine and I had the instant feeling of being attracted to him. I'm sure most women do. He's intelligent and he listens intently to whomever is speaking, and he's fun to talk to. He is strong and gentle. Great husband material. Ted would do the cooking and many feminine roles, but he could also rebuild an engine or remodel a house.

Theirs was a topsy-turvy, Alice-in-Wonderland world to me. Fred, like Ann, watched me and picked up every nuance of my reactions and smiled at me. He had just recently come out, for Ted, and I could see he was enjoying just being himself without being guarded.

Ted was running in and out from the grill cooking the supper and chatting a mile-a-minute the way he does. He told Fred, "I was so surprised when Martha came over after Jack's death and invited me to Ann's party and said 'It's a gay party.'" He turned to me, "How did you know I'm gay?"

Fred looked at Ted and put his hands on his hips and said, "Did you go out of the house in your pink pumps again?" And Ted giggled.

Ted insisted I stay and talk while they ate their dinner on TV trays in the living room. I noticed that Fred often nervously made old, familiar, male, disparaging-to-gays cracks. So newly out of the closet, and from Michigan, he wasn't used to the idea that gay is okay. He was still unsure about how to act. But I witnessed one moment at that dinner where it was as if they were alone. Ted suddenly became frantic about the move and the overwhelming number of things yet to be done. He began chattering wildly about his worries. Fred reached across the TV trays and covered Ted's hand with his. He looked calmly into Ted's eyes and waited for him to be quiet. Then he said, "It'll be okay, hon. I'm here."

The next day was Saturday. The last day. Ted was running back and forth from his house to mine, giving me plants, giving John sports equipment. I spent time keeping Fred company while he stood by and helped Ted make last minute decisions about what to take and what to get rid of.

Fred told me about his life. He'd always wanted to be a doctor but was too poor he thought. So after college he taught high school for two years. Then he knew he had to go to medical school. He held down two jobs all through medical school—one was working in a lab on campus, the other was working weekends in an emergency room in a city a four-hour drive from Chicago where he went to school. I asked him what he did in the emergency room.

FRED: Well, I wasn't a doctor so I wasn't supposed to be doing the things I did. But sometimes there was no one else to do it, so I ended up doing real doctor work, like suturing. After medical school I was in general practice. At that time, in the U.P., that meant you did everything—delivered babies, did appendectomies . . .
M: Did you love it?
FRED: I loved it. But eventually the malpractice insurance for everything became too high and I had to stop being a G.P.

Fred talked easily and comfortably. I was impressed by his drive and his accomplishments and his humble, quiet way of talking about them.

M: Why did you get married?
FRED: (smiles) It was the sixties. It was a romantic idea—getting married—and I was romantic. I had a romance with her. Besides, I wanted children. I wanted to be a family.

Fred and his wife had seven children. Ted had told me how devoted Fred is to his family. He'd waited to come out, to have the life he knew he needed for himself, until his children were grown and established in their lives, until, he felt, they could not be hurt or derailed in their lives by his coming out. Ted had also told me Fred cared about the welfare of his wife, and would see she was well taken care of. He is a responsible man—a man who feels responsible for his family.

M: How is your wife about all this?
FRED: She's very angry. (he says this quietly, sadly)

I tell him about the Washington D.C. writer I recently heard being interviewed on NPR. He used to work for Jerry Falwell, now he's discovered he's gay and that that cannot be changed. (For years he'd tried various "cures," including electric shock treatments, in his efforts to be a "good Christian.")

M: His wife wrote a preface to his book, saying "This is a good man."
FRED: I wish my wife felt like that.

I asked him when he knew he was attracted to men. His gentle smile came back.

FRED: When I was little boy. My father was a farmer. I remember I loved the threshing time on the farm when all the men came to help with the harvest. I was a really little boy, but it was hot and I liked seeing the men work with their shirts off. At the end of the day they'd go down to the river and strip and swim nude to cool off. I liked to sit on the bank and watch.
   I thought they were beautiful.

(pause)

I just came out to my father, just before I left to come to get Ted.
M: How did he take it?
FRED: Great. He was okay.
M: Had he suspected?
FRED: He said he hadn't.

I went into Ted's kitchen, now empty. I was looking at the work he'd done and how beautiful it was. I was touching the cutting boards and looking at the tile floor with white/black pattern.

M: I wish I had a beautiful kitchen like this.
FRED: (laughing) Well, make one.
M: I can't make one.
FRED: Why not? (still smiling)
M: (sputter, sputter) Well. I don't know how. I don't have the tools. I mean, I don't have the skills.

(I mean, I'm a woman. Don't you understand?)
(But they do understand. They're both laughing.)
(I try hard to explain what I'm feeling.)

Men do remodeling.
FRED: (gently and seriously, as if to a child) *You* can remodel a kitchen too.
TED: (proud and matter-of-factly) I can tear down an engine in the morning and sew a pair drapes at night— *you can too.*

Now they're both smiling at me, in the kindest way. Like

two fathers. Or two good brothers. Like good parents. Good friends. I think how much we can learn from these gender-bending gay people.

I am the one who's trapped in a sex role.

In the gay world men can be soft and caring (my best friend) and still be *men.* Women, like Ann, can pour cement then do their ironing and still be "soft" women.

I think how endlessly our potential expands when we don't feel trapped by gender roles—I can buy power tools and start tearing the kitchen apart—a man can say, "Gee, I have to stay home today. My baby is sick. I'm going to nurse his fever and make him some chicken soup."

When we think about gay people, we have to forget about sex. It's not important. It's a tiny portion of what we are, and it's private. We have to think about people—their talents and potential.

It was getting dark when the moving van left. The last items to throw away were in the back of Ted's big pickup. Ted had already sold his Mazda sports car. His voice cracked and his eyes teared when he said, "I rebuilt that car for Jack—he loved that car." Fred put his arm around Ted's shoulders. Ted and Fred would take the junk to the dump and then go out to eat, then drive to the airport where they'd leave the truck for the new owner and get in Fred's plane and fly to Palm Springs to pick up the two priests and then on to Michigan for their new life.

It was time to say good-bye. I was sad. I was losing my friend Ted.

Ted climbed into the truck behind the wheel. Fred climbed in on the passenger side. He was holding his unfinished beer and Ted's low and out of sight.

I look at them. A little enviously. They are so perfectly matched. They look like twins or brothers, except for Fred's toupee. Ted told me, "I'm trying to get him to give up the toupee—he will someday—when his self-esteem is higher—when he really knows I love him just as much without it."

They are best friends. They can share the other's every interest. They are perfect companions. Guys doing guy things and having a terrific lot of fun.

Ted fires the engine and they wheel out of the drive. They're smiling and laughing. Ted's old life is behind him. The new one has begun, and for Fred too. I'm the only one who's crying. Because I'm happy for them, and sad, maybe, for me.

Before I ran across the street the last time, I told John, "I must go say good-bye to Ted."

John said, "I'm going to miss that big, happy guy."

But Ted wasn't always happy. He'd nursed his friend and watched him die of AIDS. He'd suffered two years of fighting depression. Now he'd been brought to life by love and friendship. I told my brother in Michigan that my good friend Ted was moving very close to his town. My brother was very sweet.

He paused and said, "I try to understand. But the thought of those people makes me feel creepy. You know, what they do."

M: That's okay. (I think of Ted.) They don't like to think about what we do either.

He went on. "Well. They won't do well here. We don't have those kind of people up here."

M: You do. You just don't know it.

And I tell him about when Ted met Fred in Chicago. How Fred had flown his plane in from Perry with three gay priests.

My brother was stunned. "There aren't that many priests in the whole U.P."

I know if Ted ever called or met my brother, my brother would treat him well. That's where we all begin. Fred for his part, insisted that the next time I come to Michigan, I stay with Ted and him at their house. Fred seemed so happy to be accepted in his new life.

Ted had been gone for four months and fall was here. I looked across at his house and missed him. I hadn't heard from him. I'd been expecting an "at home" card. I phoned Ann. Have you heard from Ted?

ANN: No. But I'm not worried. He's probably still in his nesting phase.

Good, calm Ann. I knew I would have been hurt if Ann had heard and I hadn't. I didn't want to think he felt closer to her because she's gay. See how paranoid I am? No wonder gay people laugh at us.

At Christmas I finally heard from Ted. The card was a child's card, a teddy bear in a Santa hat, jumping out of a gift box. Ted was happy. He's learning to fly Fred's plane. He's already passed his ground courses for his pilot's license and Fred was looking for a flight instructor. Flying, one more thing they'll do together. Perfect companions. I remember their smiles and laughter as they drove out in the truck that last night. I wish them this happiness forever.

7

ANNIVERSARY WALTZ

ANN WANTED RUTH ANN and Stella to be in the book. "God, they're an historical monument. You should have seen their 20th anniversary party. It was at a small jazz club and restaurant—and when they took their anniversary dance, everyone applauded. All evening people just kept going up to them and saying, 'Can I touch you?' They're an institution in the community. It's hard for people to stay together, with all the pressures, so couples like Ruth Ann and Stella are looked up to. It's what we all want."

Ann had never been wrong about who was worth talking to. So a few weeks later on a Monday night I was driving north to visit with Ruth Ann and Stella. I remembered them slightly from the summer party Ann had given for Sally. I remembered Ruth Ann as a slim woman, about fifty, with iron gray hair, short hair, wearing slim jeans and boots and patiently giving Western dance lessons all evening to everyone who wanted to learn. She danced and gave instructions out of the side of her mouth while smoking a cigarette. Stella was small and bright-faced with dark, short curls. She sat at a table smoking a cigarillo in a holder. I hadn't talked to them except to be introduced.

Now I was at their home. They have two large, beautiful cats, as pampered as children. A large screen TV was on in the background and a grandfather clock was ticking and chiming. The house is up for sale. Stella wants a two-story house—that's the only kind that feels like a home: "I want to go upstairs to bed."

Ruth Ann is a gracious hostess, wanting me to be comfortable, offering a drink. She's slim and masculine as I remembered her. Her voice is gravelly—maybe naturally, maybe from the years of smoking. They're trying to give up smoking. They no longer smoke in the house. Ruth leans forward to listen intently when I talk. I think of her as a female Jimmy Stewart—a long, cool drink—her slimness gives the impression she's taller than she is. She's wiry and strong looking.

We decide Ruth Ann will talk about herself first. We sit at a round table and turn on the tape recorder. Stella talks about going into the next room but soon she's back, sitting a little ways away on the sofa. Curled up with a big cat on her lap. I soon learn this is a couple that's comfortable together. Stella doesn't like to be away from Ruth Ann.

RUTH: I was born and grew up in a small town in the central valley of California. I have three sisters, two older and one younger. My dad and all my male relatives worked in the oil fields. We had a big extended family—lots of cousins. My grandmother was one of ten children and most of them lived there. My grandfather was the town judge. I had a happy childhood. I was surrounded by salt-of-the-earth people. My mom was wonderful—to her we were "precious" children. I went to community college and then to Fresno State. I met a young man who was just out of the Navy and fell in love with him. I married him when I was nineteen and he was twenty-four. He'd been married before. We were happy. I finished my A.A. degree then I worked for Standard Oil. I was the ditto girl.

M: How did you like this young man?

RUTH: He was wonderful.

M: Were you very much in love?

RUTH: I guess, as much as I could have been. I never gave any serious thought to being a homosexual.

M: You had no idea?

RUTH: No.

M: Did you know what homosexuality was?

RUTH: Yeah.

M: Did you date in high school?

RUTH: Yeah. A few guys. I went steady with two. I was not popular as a date, but for being a leader, and a serious student and an athlete. I played every sport I could, but I loved softball.

M: Do you have gay people in your family?

RUTH: Not that I know of, in the older generations. There is one boy cousin. I think he is gay.

After two years my husband wanted to move to the island in Alaska where his family lived. That was all right with me. It sounded like an adventure. The island had 5,000 people. The town had recently burned. The Russian church burned down and the movie theater and the bowling alley. Everything that was entertainment. The only thing left was the bars. What I didn't know when I moved there was my husband, his mother, her five brothers, the whole family, were alcoholics. So every night, after work, they walked from work across the street to a bar and started drinking. I didn't drink, but I went with my husband. By eleven o'clock I wanted to go home. He didn't. It was always the same old fight. Finally we'd leave together. But it was wearing—and eventually I just didn't love him anymore. I told him that if he wanted to go back to California with me and work on our marriage, I'd stay with him, but otherwise I had to go. I told him,

"There's nothing for me here." He said he wanted to spend the rest of his life on that island. So I left. Eventually he left too. So he didn't spend the rest of his life there. He phones me from time to time. We have respect for each other.

M: You were strong to leave so easily. Many women couldn't. They can't stop caring even when they're getting nothing back.

RUTH: Not me. I knew I needed something back. And, well, I had a strong sense of my own worth from my happy childhood. When I was in the airport in Seattle, on my way home, it was Christmas. I saw a woman in an Army uniform and I remembered I used to think I'd like the military. The discipline, the order, the logic — it all appealed to me. When I got home I enlisted in the Marines. In March, I was twenty-three years old, I was sent to Parris Island, South Carolina, for my eight weeks of basic training.

M: I didn't know you were a Marine.

RUTH: Oh, yeah. That's where I met my Stella.

M: What color was your hair then?

RUTH: I don't know. I think I was blond.

M: You *think* you were blond?

RUTH: (turns toward Stella) Was I blond, Momma?
  Yeah. I was blond.

M: Was the training rough?

RUTH: Oh, yeah. They say the Marines are the toughest. I don't have anything to compare. I had a real tough DI. A little mean. She got a big kick out of being ornery as hell. I was recruit leader. Toward the end of boot camp I was sick and tired of her and I don't think she was too pleased with me. Next I went to San Diego to Electronics School and then back to Quantico, Virginia, to Officers Training

School. That's where I met Stella.

We were in the same platoon, about fifty women. About nine or ten of us were smokers and went to the laundry room to have a smoke. That's how I got to know Stella. We were both smokers.

M: Were you special friends right away?

STELLA: (from the sofa) I wanted her time. I wanted to talk to her, but she was always talking to someone else. Ruth Ann is a great communicator. She was always in another room trying to help somebody out with a problem.

M: Did you know you were a lesbian at this time?

STELLA: No.

M: You just liked Ruth Ann? You wanted to be her special friend?

STELLA: Yes.

RUTH: But I knew I was—oh, I forgot to tell you about Jackie.

M: Right. The last I heard you were happily married but the guy was drunk. Then you were in boot camp.

RUTH: (is laughing) Yeah. We skipped right over my coming out.

M: I guess so.

RUTH: Now after boot camp, but before OCS, that was where Jackie came in. I was a Lance Corporal in San Diego and one day along came Jacqueline. She was carrying a pool cue. Not just a pool cue but it was in a case. At first I didn't know what she had. I'd never seen anyone carry around a pool cue in a case. So I asked her what was in that case.

I said, "Gol, dang. I never saw such a thing. Let's go play pool."

Well, we became really good friends. We had a lot in common. We both played good pool and we both loved to play poker. In the Marine Corps it's not hard to get up a group for a game. On Friday night a group of us would rent a motel room across the street to have a poker game. We weren't allowed to play poker on base. The game would go until midnight or one or two, whenever it was over, then we'd go back to the barracks. A couple people usually stayed in the room, after all, we'd paid for it.

M: Was the group mostly women?

RUTH: Oh, no. Guys. It was guys that played poker. And Jackie and me.

Then I moved off base to my grandparents' house. After a few months we decided Jackie should move in. My grandparents liked her a lot and she was always there. My grandparents each had a room and my grandmother had her sewing room. I had the extra bedroom, so Jackie moved in with me. We slept in the same bed.

M: Right. Girls do that.

RUTH: Right. Girls do that. I never thought anything untoward would happen. We were really good friends, but there was never anything—no suggestion of anything, physical contact, lesbianism—no flirtation—no—nothing.

We both came out at the same time. It was just a sexual encounter that happened—at, I would say, three o'clock in the morning. We'd gone to bed and gone to sleep, and at three o'clock in the morning—it was like somebody left the window open and the gay bug flew in, the window closed, and that was it.

And I was just *sickened* and *appalled*. I said, "This cannot be—this will not happen again."

It had been a compelling need. But the next morning I said, "I don't know what that was, but we're not doing that again." I was sickened and appalled.

Three or four days later it happened again. She wasn't as upset as I was. She just accepted it. I felt terrible. She was only nineteen, and I was twenty-four.

I said to myself, "This can't be *me* doing this. I can't be homosexual—I've been married." I bought into that. I knew so little about homosexuality.

Our relationship went on for about six months.

M: Did there come a point where you decided it wasn't wrong?

RUTH: Yes. I said, "I guess this is me." And when I reached that point—then I never looked back—I never regretted. Now when I got to OCS, I had just been there a day, I phoned Jackie and said, "I need to break this relationship off. I'm not going to be straight—nor am I going to be gay—I'm going to be nothing." I thought, "Well, I can just go through my life being asexual." I knew I wouldn't get married again, but nor did I think I was a homosexual. I thought, "Well, this will be easy. I'll be nothin'."

That was before I met my Toots.

I was in OCS, and I was just going to be a Marine.

I became best friends with Stella in Basic (OCS). We spent all our free time on weekends together. Shopping at the PX, or shopping at a mall—going to movies—stuff. I wasn't looking for a sex partner. I didn't allow myself to think in terms of a sexual relationship. That wasn't an issue. After Basic Stella was sent to Albany, Georgia, and I was sent to Parris Island, South Carolina, as a second Lieutenant for six weeks of advanced training.

When Stella went home to New Jersey on leave she wrote me a letter saying she loved me. It wasn't sexual—it said, "You're my dearest friend and I love you."

I thought, "How can this be?" So I suggested to her

she stop and see me on her way back to Georgia, and she did. And that's where I claim we had a sexual experience. (She laughs, heartily.)

But Stella says, "Oh, no. We didn't."

M: So you have different memories of when your relationship changed? Tell me how you remember it.

RUTH: We had *one* bed. And it was *this* wide.

(She holds up her hands—a very narrow barracks bed.)

Now I don't know where she thinks she slept that night—but she was in that bed with me. I will grant Stella that it wasn't a full-fledged . . . but it was a sexual encounter. But she blocked it out.

The reason I'm so positive is, not only do I remember the encounter, but we made arrangements to meet the next week in between Parris Island and Albany, and I remember constantly worrying and wondering what she was going to say. Would she break off our friendship? Would she change her mind and say "This cannot be"? Had I done something to really turn her off and make her not want to see me? But then I saw her. She was totally fine with it—like "This is where I belong—I like this—I want to stay with you. I love you. This is it for me."

So, I said, "Okay."

M: You never discussed sexuality?

RUTH: No. We just lived our life. Day by day. That's what we wanted.

RUTH: Then I was sent to my duty assignment, Camp LeJeune, North Carolina. Once a month we would meet half way in between, five hours of travel for each of us.

Then Stella was sent to, of all places, Camp LeJeune for her Advanced School.

M: That was, sort of, Kismet? (I laugh with delight. They do too.)

STELLA: Our whole life . . . truly . . . it was almost like . . .

RUTH: The Marine Corps threw us together.

STELLA: Then later she was transferred to Washington, D.C. In April. In May someone came down and asked me if I'd go to D.C.—a change of orders. The same Candidate School, the same Basic School—

M: Does it make you think God wanted you together?

STELLA: Yes. Something wanted us together.

RUTH: We're supposed to be together.

RUTH: After a year and a half in Washington, we knew we'd have to get out of the Marine Corps when our three year obligation was up if we wanted to be together. We knew before much longer one of us was going to get transferred.

STELLA: She could have been sent to California and me to Japan—and at that point in time I knew that Ruth Ann was going to be my life. And I didn't want to take that chance.

RUTH: By that time we'd had enough exposure to the gay life to realize we wouldn't have much of a chance of a long relationship if they separated us.

M: You couldn't ask to be together?

(everyone laughs hard at what had popped out as a normal question)

STELLA: Ooooooooooh—no!

RUTH: Hardly!

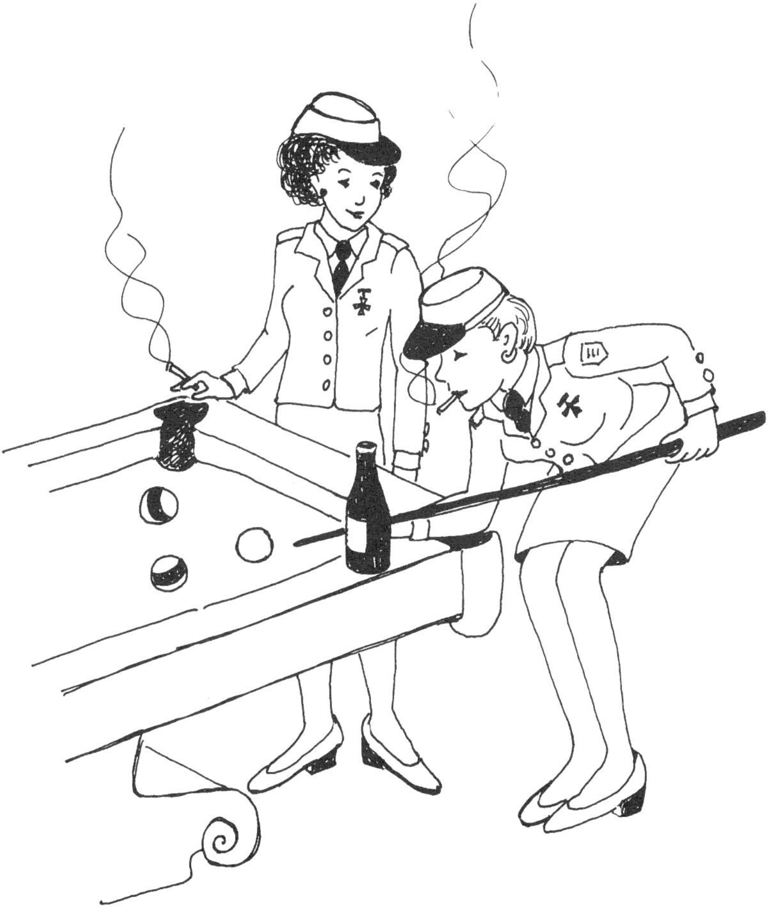

STELLA: That was the other thing—we had to be on our best behavior because of all the witch hunts that they had back then.

M: Were they going on where you were?

RUTH: Oh yeah. Um-hmmm. Right in my own home. The gal I was living with when Stella was in Georgia (pause)... we were lucky we weren't caught.

M: You knew this woman was a lesbian?

RUTH: Actually, I didn't—I suspected, but we never talked about it. People didn't. Fortunately, she didn't get caught—she didn't get put out. Investigators asked me if my roommate was gay. I said, "I have no reason to think she is. I've not seen anything."

M: Did they question her directly?

RUTH: Oh, I'm sure they did.

M: She never said anything to you about it?

RUTH: No. We didn't discuss it.

STELLA: It was scary.

RUTH: Oh, it was scary—yeah, this was your career—this was your job. You didn't want to get fired.

STELLA: And the fact of getting a dishonorable discharge—no one wanted that.

M: How unfair.

RUTH: I know, huh?

STELLA: When Ruth Ann and I went out to a couple of bars, when we were in Washington, we went clear to Baltimore—you just didn't want to do it in the area you're in. We went every couple of months. Oh, you had to watch, who you were with, what you did.

M: Tell me about your first experience in a gay club.

STELLA: Oh, it was scary.

M: Why so?

STELLA: We opened the door—all these heads turned to

look at us.

RUTH: You wondered who was there—if it was someone who knew you, would they turn you in?

STELLA: I didn't know what to expect. I was apprehensive. My feeling was—Ruth Ann and I at home, we'd hold hands or snuggle—but here we were in public. Granted it's a gay bar—but we're out with other people.

RUTH: We didn't find the way anyone else acted frightening at all.

M: You were just worried they were looking at you.

RUTH AND STELLA: (they both laugh)
Yeah . . . yeah.

STELLA: Right—that we'd be doing something we weren't supposed to be doing.

M: The good thing about going out and socializing with other lesbians is that you get to be free, and be yourself?

STELLA: Yes.

M: So you really need a place to go out socially where you can be who you are.

STELLA: Yes.

RUTH: Yeah . . . Yup. You can dance—you can . . .

M: I would think you don't even know who you are until you can go out and let yourself go.

STELLA: It's that time outside the confines of your own home that you're doing things to show the other one that you love and care for them—as heterosexuals do all the time out in public—but we, being who we are, we just don't do those things outside. But when we go to a place where we're all the same, we can just feel like we're all the same. We can just feel like we're at home, and do relax.

M: That must be a relief.

STELLA: Yes. Yes. It is.

RUTH: Yeah. Yeah. It's comfortable. We can feel free.

(pause) We can find our identity . . . We have our own sense of humor, our community, traditions . . . our own culture.

M: Can you tell me what that culture is?

RUTH: To me a big part of it is we hug one another upon greeting, and I know even in the straight world, nowadays, they hug more than they used to, but gays have always done that.

M: True straight people hug now, but it's often some guy trying to get a feel.

RUTH: Oh, yeah?

(Stella and I are laughing)

STELLA: I believe it.

M: People take a lot of advantage of that—men do, I find.

RUTH: (shaking her head—gently amazed) Huhh. We hug almost for tradition—that's not the word I want—custom—it's a custom. Some people are more into it than others—some people don't care much for it.

STELLA: There are certain of our friends that will really give you a big *bear* hug—then there are others that give what we call the A-frame hug—stiff, leaning in.

M: But you only hug people you know? Like, here's my friend, I give her a hug.

RUTH: Yah, yah. When we go into the bars we hug everyone we know—men and women alike—but you've probably been to gay bars.

M: I have not.

RUTH: Gay bars are FUN. There are no pretenses. Oh, there are a few little games going on here and there, because this one or that one is flirting—but for the most part, the women are not afraid of the men—the men are not afraid of the women—because there are no ulterior motives.

STELLA: (still over on the sofa with the big cat, laughs) Right.

RUTH: It's right out there. If you go up and ask some guy to dance, or if some guy comes up and asks you to dance, you know he's not trying to get you into bed—it's just he loves to dance and he's seen you dance and he thinks you're a good dancer—it's just so relaxed.

There's so much laughter; and there's so much just—friends—friendliness.

STELLA: In the straight world, the guys come over and try to impress you, to be a big ol' John Wayne—but in the gay bars it's not that way. They're not there to impress you—they're there for conversation and a good time, laughter. You don't have to worry about anything.

There are different kinds of gay bars—some we wouldn't want to go into either.

RUTH: The ones we go to are mixed, men and women, and for dancing—usually we do country western dancing.

STELLA: Men have different kinds of bars. Some we wouldn't go into without men.

M: What is the particular sense of humor you talked about?

RUTH: Oh, we have our own vocabulary. We say we "go to the same church." We refer to each other as "family."

M: Like "She's a member of the family"?

RUTH: Yeah. "She's family."

STELLA: I think the term is used so much because for a lot of people their family is their gay friends, because their family has disowned them—one way or another. So that term is used in that context.

M: I want straight people to read the book. I want those

parents who disowned children to read the book.

When I asked Elizabeth to be in the book, she said, "I don't want to be in it if there's any sex in it."

(Ruth Ann and Stella chuckle, because they know Elizabeth.)

I told her it's not about that. It's about wonderful people who are like every other person. Because the reason people are hateful is because they don't know—they're scared.

RUTH: That's what I think. It's ignorance.

M: What I want to do is bring real people to life. It's not about your sex. It's about how you don't choose it. It chose you. And why should you have to give up loving a person because someone else says you should?

RUTH: Especially when we have so many other things to worry about in this damn life you know—child abuse, and drug abuse, and crime.

M: Rob Eichberg, whom I'll talk about in the book, he wrote the book *Coming Out: An Act of Love,* said you cannot be who you are until you come out—you don't know who you are.

RUTH: Except I'm not out to my parents, and I'm not out at work. Most people will look at that and laugh and say, "You mean you've been with Stella for almost twenty-six years and your parents don't know?"

And I have to say, I'm pretty sure my parents don't know. You have to remember where we're from. There may have been me and one other queer in our town in all these years. So what they get, they get from sitcoms on TV. I know they don't read about it.

I am out to my sisters—two years ago Thanksgiving.

The older ones took it just fine, there was no issue at all. The younger one, it took a while to adjust, but she's there now, and she thinks I'm just fine.

M: Because you're the same person.

RUTH: Yeah. Yeah.

STELLA: (from the sofa, not very loudly and with a certain bitterness) I like the way you say she's there and she thinks you're fine. I don't know that she thinks you're fine.

RUTH: She does. (firmly, it's an old argument) But you won't listen to me when I tell you.

(It was the only time I ever heard irritation over anything in Stella's voice, and it was because she thought someone was not kind to Ruth Ann.)

M: I don't know how anyone could not think you're fine.

RUTH: (laughs) Yeah. Huhhh? What's not to love?

Now on vocabulary, we can call each other dykes. Or we might say "You've got a big ol' butt. Uh-huhhh." And that means, as long as you put on the "Uh-huhhh!"—it's just a friendship thing.

STELLA: It's like the boys say, "You go, girl" and they're referring to another guy.

M: And that means they like their looks?

RUTH: No. It could mean anything. It's a comment you make. Like if a guy is telling a story about what happened in the grocery store: "And the clerk said this and I said this" sort of story and the guy listening says "You go, girl," like "you tell 'em."

M: What does it mean when you say to someone "You've got a big ol' butt"? Does it mean something, or does it just mean they've got a big butt?

RUTH: It just means they've got a big butt. (we're all laughing) But it doesn't have to mean they've got a big butt—but it could.

(we're laughing uncontrollably)

M: What else could it mean? "You've got a big ol' butt."
RUTH: "Uh-huhhh!"
M: "Uh-huhhh!"
RUTH: It's just being humorous—being friendly.
STELLA: Right. It has nothing to do with having a big butt. It's a humorous response.
M: Like if someone is telling a story and getting a lot of attention, you could say it?
STELLA: Right.
M: So when you say you have your own sense of humor, you mean that you're kidding a lot.
RUTH: We do a lot of kidding.
M: I want to let people know what to call gays and lesbians. Now I know "gay" and "lesbian" are politically correct but I have to put the other words in the glossary. Like "bull dyke"—you shouldn't call a lesbian a bull dyke.
RUTH AND STELLA: RIGHT.
RUTH: We really don't want straights to call us that.
STELLA: I don't like the connotation in that.
M: Because it sounds like an insult when they say it?
RUTH: And they mean it as an insult.
M: Like nigger or fag is insulting?
RUTH: Yeah. But when we say it, it's not an insult.
M: Last week on C-Span I saw the National Association of Lesbian and Gay Journalists and the women kept getting up and saying to the speakers, "We want to see the 'L'

word in the media. You talk about gay men and homosexuals, but until we see the word lesbian, we don't feel included."

I told Ann and she said, "Oh, lord. They just talk too much. Just call us queers and be done with it."

(Ruth Ann and Stella laugh again)

M: And I said, "Queer is not all right, is it?" And she said, "Yeah, it is with me."
RUTH: Yeah. It's a good one.
M: I know the group Queer Nation is trying to detoxify it. So—you don't think either of your parents know—or do you think they just don't want to talk about it?
RUTH: The reason I think they don't know is some years back, when Stella and I were visiting my family, and my grandmother lived with them, I asked, "Mom, what do you and grandma do during the day?" And she said: Well, we get up in the morning and have breakfast, and then settle in and start watching our soap operas. And we watch this one, and that one, and we used to watch, and I'm gonna say *Days of Our Lives* because I can't remember which one she said for sure, then they got those lesbians on there and we quit watchin'.

(Ruth Ann and Stella start a spasm of heavy coughing and choking)

STELLA: And Ruth Ann and I (cough, cough, choke) . . .
RUTH: Stella and I go (cough, choke, giggle, cough) . . .
And I knew from that point on that there was a certain distaste for lesbians with Mom—and I know my mom well enough to know that if she knew, or thought, I was

a lesbian, wild horses couldn't draw a statement like that out of her mouth. She would have considered that hateful—and she would *not* intentionally hurt one of her kids; she would just not have said anything.

That was fifteen years ago. They may have figured it out. They may have discussed it and said, "Let's not touch it. Let's not talk about it."

M: And they love you both.

STELLA: Yes. And I have never noticed any difference from year two to the present day in how they react to me—it's the same it's always been.

M: Then they might very well know.

RUTH: They're very accepting.

M: Elizabeth said that's how it should be. People should just accept people without discussing it. She said, "I don't want to tell anyone. It's not their business and it shouldn't matter."

STELLA: That's how I feel. How some people feel about me has nothing to do with how I react to them, or how I do my job, but has strictly to do with what goes on in the bedroom, which drives them crazy. And as far as I'm concerned that's less than 5% of who I am. Ninety-five percent of me I'm just like you. I sit, I watch sports, I go to work. I'm just like you. And I don't care what other people do in the bedroom either.

At work I have no pretenses. Some people at work know. I don't really care anymore. I don't pretend I have a boyfriend. I'll say a guy is good-looking, because he is good-looking, but I always talk about Ruth Ann. I don't care anymore.

M: I hope I see in my lifetime a time when, even if people hold these feelings from the past, gay people don't have to give it a thought.

The next week I went back on Monday night—this time to talk to Stella. But before we started I wanted to ask Ruth Ann a couple of questions that had come up in my mind in the last week. The first question was the sex question.

M: Was sex any different, better, with Jackie or Stella than with your husband?
RUTH: Emotionally it's better with a woman. I wouldn't want a man again. I can remember looking at women when I was very young. In sixth grade I kissed "Skinny Judy" in the water tank we swam in. She was the first woman I kissed.

As a child I played cowboys and Indians. I didn't like dolls. I remember at five or six I was given a doll for Christmas, I didn't want it, I wanted tools. I handed it to an uncle and said, "Here, you can find something to do with this," and I went on to the tool kit.

I always wore jeans and shirts and guns and holsters. In my work life I've been a drafter, a reliability engineer, and a production engineer—always in manufacturing.

I had friends on the softball team at home that I knew were lesbians—two women doctors—I wondered how they lived. But I didn't give them much thought—after all, I wasn't one. People used to ask me about my softball playing friend Barbie, is she a lesbian? I said, "I wouldn't know." Now, looking back, I realize she probably was.

I liked working on the car with my dad. And we went fishing, went to the car races—we buddied around. I was his companion. My mother didn't like those things.
M: Did people call you a tomboy?
RD: (in her gravelly voice) Oh, yeah.

Stella is petite with dark, short, curly hair and a constant smile that crinkles up her eyes. Her smile is infectious. She has a tiny gap between her front teeth that gives her a childlike look. You see her smile and she is the most lovable person imaginable—you have to smile back. When she speaks about Ruth Ann, after almost twenty-six years together, her face lights up as if she's newly fallen in love, "Oh, I knew she was the one." Ruth Ann, more serious and reserved, looks a little shyly embarrassed at Stella's open expressions of adoring love. Ann says she always says to Stella, "Let's you and me run away together—leave ol' Ruth Ann behind." I can imagine the response that brings from Stella. I remember last week how wide her eyes grew when she said, "A dishonorable discharge! . . . that would be horrible."

Stella grew up in a quintessential Italian-American family in Brooklyn, in the Bedford Stuyvesant area—not a good area she says. The family moved to "Jersey" when she was thirteen. Her father "yelled a lot and threw things." Stella attended parochial schools—kindergarten through college.

STELLA: I was so shy and introverted then. I wanted to be a nun. I probably would have fit right in. But then I decided to go to college and I got a B.A. in Sociology. I wanted to be a probation officer because I wanted to work with teenagers. But when I went to work I was given child support cases instead. So I decided to become a Marine. It was time to leave home, and I liked parades and the uniforms.

She has two sisters. Both now suffer from agorophobia so she thinks it may be genetic.

I asked her what her childhood was like.

STELLA: There was lots of arguing in the house—and no hugging or kissing. There was love, it just was not expressed like it is in Ruth Ann's family. In fact my sisters said I was spoiled because I was the youngest.

I liked playing with the boys, not the girls. I liked the games they played—stickball in the street, stoopball, bottlecaps—that's like marbles for kids who don't have marbles. I didn't want dolls.

In high school I dated boys and we had fun. When I was sixteen and seventeen I had an older boyfriend, he was twenty-two. There was no sex. I thought he was the one, then I found out he was going out on me and I broke up with him. I told him, "It's either me or . . ."

M: Did you ever think you were a lesbian?

STELLA: No. Looking back, I can see I found women attractive, in high school and in college. I'd rather be with women than with the men. So when I look back at it in that regard I can say yes I always was, but never knew. But I didn't think of women sexually. I'd had no encounter. I didn't know what that was anyway. I like their mannerisms—they're very sure of themselves. I guess I found them better companions. They aren't trying to impress you. It seemed to me in high school and college that all men ever wanted to do was to get you into bed. Women don't do that. When I met Ruth Ann, there was nothing sexual about our relationship. When we went out we just thoroughly enjoyed each other's company.

That's what I like about women. There's no macho thing. No playing a role. No wondering if they want something from you. You just relate to each other—as friends.

I've never had sex with a man. So I don't know what's to like or not to like about it.

I was twenty-two when I joined the Marines. I went right to Quantico to OCS where I met Ruth Ann. The first time I saw her I was interested in her. But this wasn't sexual. The sexual aspect never, ever came into play in my feelings towards her, or even later when I wrote her that letter and told her I loved her.

M: Then it was a spiritual thing?

STELLA: It was just a feeling I had. When we left each other, when she left for her new duty station in South Carolina, and I went home on leave before going to Georgia, it was like something was being torn away from me when I had to leave her. I went home and thought about her and thought about her. And that's what prompted me to write the letter. But again I did not think about it in terms of a lesbian or sexual relationship. All I knew was (her voice cracks with the memory) *I needed her in my life* . . . somehow, or other . . . (teary eyes, and a sigh)

I don't know why I didn't know . . . it was my naivete?

M: Yes. You had no words or thought of it.

STELLA: Uh-uh.

M: It was just the heart. It was the heart.

STELLA: Yes . . . totally. That probably sounds weird to a lot of people.

M: I don't think so.

STELLA: I met her the first day, smoking. I knew I'd like her as a friend. I liked her mannerisms, her confidence. She was so "squared away." That's military talk. Her uniform was perfect, her shoes had a high shine. She'd come through enlisted and knew all the tricks of the trade. I was brand new. I'd just been given a pair of shoes and told to "make them shine."

M: So when you wrote Ruth Ann and told her you loved her it was because your heart was hurting?

STELLA: Um-hmm. It was. I told her I loved her and I missed her. Now that I think about it, it was so stupid... that I didn't know what it meant or even how she'd respond to it.

M: You said what came out of your heart, a need—an emotional need. I don't think that's stupid. It just shows how natural it is when you respond with your heart.

Then you stopped to see her on your way back to Georgia?

STELLA: (laughing) And that's where (we say this in unison) SHE SAYS SOMETHING HAPPENED AND I SAY NOTHING HAPPENED.

M: What did happen?

STELLA: As far as I'm concerned all that happened was that we were in the same bed together.

M: So you shared the bed. You just went there and slept. You didn't touch, nothing happened.

STELLA: (laughs) As far as I'm concerned it didn't.

M: You went to sleep and woke up in the morning.

STELLA: Yes. Whatever happened for her was totally different. Then we started meeting, once a month. We'd pick a town in South Carolina, somewhere half way in between our bases. And in my mind, that's the first time something happened. She had got a room—and again, I didn't know how to react. And when I went into the room she kissed me. That's the first time I remember anything happening.

M: Were you surprised? Because you said you hadn't thought . . . or by this time . . . ?

STELLA: By this time . . . I guess I hadn't thought about it in those terms exactly, but when it happened . . . it was like . . . WOW.

M: So you never thought about your relationhip sexually until that time in the room when she kissed you? Until then you were just friends?

STELLA: Yeah.

M: Now you had kissed the boy you were serious about many times, and that wasn't WOW?

STELLA: Yeah, it just wasn't the same. I mean my whole body . . . for lack of a better word . . . tingled. It was totally different, way different.

M: I've been talking to these women, and so many of them, like you, say they've had no sexual feelings and then they meet one person and all of a sudden all this sexuality just comes.

STELLA: And when Ruth Ann and I would part, my whole body would just . . . *ache* for her—I mean, it was a weird sensation. And that did wear off, later, when we got to be with each other, over a long time, but initially... yeah... I had never, ever had that sensation with anybody.

Now a lot of people ask me, because of my Catholic background, how I felt after. A lot of people go into denial. Remember how Ruth Ann felt? She said she was going to be nothing. But my relationship with Ruth Ann I never questioned. It was nothing I felt bad about.

Now that's not to say I haven't felt guilt—but when it did happen I never questioned it. I never said, "Oh my god what is this? From the very first moment, it was what I wanted.

M: Then where did the guilt come in?

STELLA: Well, over the years it has, because the church doesn't accept homosexuality, and I had thought about becoming a nun. I go to church every Sunday. I pray—I don't know that I feel God's presence, but I feel I can talk to him. So over the years I've struggled with do I go to church and still . . . well, the Catholic church has confession, and you're not supposed to receive communion if you don't confess your sins. So I confess I'm a homosexual. So what happens if two days later we have sex? Now I've sinned again. This is ridiculous. I am who I am — that can't change. I don't want to change that.

So I struggle. Do I go to church and receive communion in a state of sin? Then I went to confession once and went face-to-face with the priest and told him. He said, "Oh, sure, you can be a lesbian. You just can't have sex together." Well, no — that doesn't work. I said, "You don't tell that to the heterosexuals." My love . . . well, that is part of it. Like we talked about last week, whether that is 2% or 5% that is a necessary part of the relationship. It's normal — natural.

When Ruth Ann and I were first together, I didn't go to church. But I missed the church. I really enjoy the Mass. I don't go because I have to go — I go because I want to go. When the priest told me that, about fifteen years ago, I didn't go back to church for another year or two . . . at all.

M: How did you feel?

STELLA: I felt angry. I thought, "Who is he? He doesn't understand." I came to the conclusion on my own: screw 'em — I only have to answer to one person when I die. And if I did wrong in this lifetime, He'll tell me, and I'll just have to take my consequences, but I'm not going to go on what this priest says. Now I realize he supposedly represents Christ, but . . . he's human just like I am. He doesn't have all the answers.

I think I'm a good person. Ruth Ann and I have a

loving relationship—which a lot of people would like to have, and there's nothing wrong in my mind with that. So why can they deprive me of something I want to do? It just doesn't make sense to me.
M: I'll tell you, there are a lot of gay Catholic priests, and most of them are not depriving themselves.
STELLA: I'm sure not.

(she bursts into giggles—relief from the intensity of her feelings on this subject)

M: And some who deprive themselves for many years end up molesting little boys. The Catholic church is going to have to deal with this.
STELLA: That's what I figure. Now once a month I go with this fellow and we open up the church and get it ready for the services. And I think the people there like me. But they don't know who I am. And I think if they did, how would that change them? But I don't feel a need to tell them.
  If they'd ask me, I might tell them. But they don't know who I am, and that bothers me sometimes. Because I can't be honest with them. For fear of how they'd react to me.
M: So you're hiding what's an important part of you?
STELLA: As far as the church is concerned. We have a new priest now. He's been there a couple years, and I've been tempted to tell him. And he's younger.
M: And he might be gay?
STELLA: (laughs) He could well be. My feeling is—if he isn't, he ought to be.
M: It might be interesting to tell him.
STELLA: For his reaction. (she shows me her necklace) He

asked me one day about my necklace, "Does it mean something special?" And there were people nearby, so I just said, "No, it's just pretty stones." But the jewels are the rainbow of the gay pride flag. Now that bothers me to be dishonest. I don't like deceitful or dishonest people, but the church has forced me to be dishonest in that regard.

M: Do you go to confession now?

STELLA: I go maybe twice a year. But I no longer confess that part of me, because I don't feel it's a sin. Why would I want to confess that? Because I'd have to confess it the next day. I'd have to go to confession 365 days a year, and that doesn't make sense in my mind. Now if I'm cruel to someone, or rude, or curse, then I've been un-Christian, and I shouldn't be that way. But I can't change who I am. And I *don't* want to change who I am, and I think I'm a good enough person.

M: If you're born a way, and God makes you that way . . . I mean I see all this misery and harm from gay people having to lead totally repressed lives, and I understand why they do it, but in the people I've talked to I've seen tremendous damage from it.

STELLA: We've seen our friends in the Marine Corps suffer, always having to look over their shoulder, and worry. That's why we couldn't do it. We're out... but not out-out.

M: You don't wear lesbian T-shirts like Ann?

STELLA: (laughs) She cracks me up. No, I draw the line there. But this (the necklace) is not obvious. But those who do know, know what this is. But, yeah, the church issue does bother me a lot. And obviously I haven't completely resolved it—the fact that they don't know who I am.

M: You're not sure they care enough about you personally to accept you if they knew?

STELLA: People can totally change once they find something out. I used to wear jeans to church, but now, the once a month when I open the church, I wear a skirt. And on Christmas and Easter. I used to wonder what they thought of me in jeans every week.

M: Lots of women wear jeans all the time now. I lived with two women when our husbands were in Vietnam in '69, and we went everywhere together. I didn't really know what lesbians were but we used to laugh thinking people probably thought we were lesbians, and I used to say, "and they must think I'm the 'guy'" because I wore corduroy pants all the time. I like pants because they're comfortable, but I like to dress up too.

STELLA: For a long time I wore only slacks, but now I wear skirts too. I like to dress up—I feel kind of neat dressed up. I don't like the term all that much, but I'm a "lipstick" lesbian because I like dressing up. I like to make up.

M: And Ruth Ann doesn't ever want to put on makeup?

STELLA: (giggles) No. Ruth Ann looks like a clown if she puts on makeup.

M: It looks all wrong?

STELLA: Very much so. We've laughed about it for twenty-five years, because in the Marines we had a makeup class. And I literally told her back then she looked like a damn clown. I don't know whether she put it on too heavy or what—but it was horrible. (she's laughing hard)

M: They didn't require you to wear makeup, did they?

STELLA: You had to wear lipstick—to match the red cord on your cap. "Harmonize" was the word they used. Your lips had to "harmonize" with the cap.

When I had begun talking to Stella, Ruth Ann had left the room to do work she'd brought home from the office. I told her if she thought of anything she wanted to say to let me know. Now she returned with a thoughtful look on her face. "I have something I want to put in the book." This is what she said:

RUTH: Stella and I have talked about this a lot. Because people ask us: What does it take to have a long-term relationship? You probably know that most gay relationships don't last very long. So we've given it a lot of thought and this is what we came up with. Most couples lack the ability to stay together and this is tied to SELFISHNESS. We live in a "me" time. Everyone is thinking me-me-me. "This isn't working for me." My idea is we-we-we. First, we believe you need a GIVE attitude: I'm going to give YOU as much as I can—and I know you're going to do the same for me.

Second, is RESPECT. You have to respect that other person. You can't have a long-term relationship without respect. Now to get respect, you have to act "respectably." We hear about people who lie and cheat and steal. So if you find a person you can respect, grab that person and hold on tight.

FAIR PLAY. Don't ever take advantage of the other person. This is related to SELFISHNESS.

Four. Be KINDER to your partner than you are to anyone else. We always say please and thank you.

STELLA: I was going to say that. No arguing. No demanding. No yelling.

When I get home, I can't wait to get in the door—I know it's going to be a peaceful evening.

RUTH: If she's feeling upset, I let her go off. She goes off in the car. Then she comes around. I step back.

We make our home our safe haven.

Ruth Ann gets up and walks into the kitchen. For her bowl of ice cream with chocolate sauce. Hershey's. This is a ritual for this time of night. I saw it last week.

M: What sort of roles do you have? Who does what?
RUTH: (moaning loudly from the kitchen) Oooh, my god. I do everything. She doesn't lift a finger.

(Stella is sitting there calmly smiling. I've been had. This is Ruth Ann's dry, teasing humor.)

STELLA: No. We share. Dishes—she washes, I dry. We both cook. We alternate cleaning tasks. One week I vacuum, she does the bathrooms. The next week we switch—you see, she's a better cleaner than I am. I don't clean to her standards. This way every other week things get clean.
RUTH: I mow and water the lawn—take care of the car. She'll do some trimming.
STELLA: She takes care of the car because I don't have the strength—or the interest.

(I'm not sure what not having the "strength" means. It sounds like the reasons I gave Ted about why I couldn't remodel a kitchen. He couldn't understand why I couldn't. To him my reasons were an illogical, silly mind-set.)

M: Have you ever talked with Elizabeth about the church?
STELLA: Not really, not alone—she being in twenty-five years and all. She doesn't go at all now.
M: She misses the Mass though. She's gone various times and then stopped. She said she didn't like the priests. I got the impression she didn't like what they said.

STELLA: Dull. Dry. Old fashioned. There have been times I have to bite my tongue. I think, should I sit here or should I walk out?
M: Did you ever talk to her about this sin and guilt thing?
STELLA: Um-um. (no)
M: Because she has no guilt. That's the beautiful thing about her always. Her relationship with God is so personal—that it doesn't matter if the Pope comes and . . . I mean, she has a sense, from her prayer, of what's right and what's wrong. And I think that caused her some problems in the monastery.
STELLA: Oh, I'm sure it did.
M: Because she would not say something against her conscience. If they told her, you have to tell people "this and such" . . . She would think about it, and she would pray, and she would say "no . . . that's not right."

(Stella laughs gently)

Can you see her?
STELLA: Yeah. Oh, yeah.
M: I mean she seems very feminine . . . almost fragile, but she's got a very strong will. She'd say, "No. No. I couldn't possibly do that. That's wrong."

I mean they are telling her to do this, and she's saying, no that's wrong.

So, I think... it makes me feel bad that you've suffered.
STELLA: I've gotten past that . . . they're not going to deprive me.
M: Of something that feels right?
STELLA: I will deal with that when the time comes. If it's wrong, He'll let me know it's wrong.
M: I think you can deal with it now, in prayer, like you say

you do. If God doesn't tell you it's wrong . . .

STELLA: How can twenty-five years be wrong? In my mind it can't be. We have such a strong relationship with each other. And Annie talks about the "historical" . . . but hopefully we are a good influence on some people.

M: That's why Ruth Ann wanted to come out and tell me the rules for a good relationship. And those are not just the rules for gay people, those are the rules for any two people. That's what I just keep hoping, that if I can say it so many ways in the book, that somewhere people will say, "Oh, they're not any different. Gay people and straight people are just the same." It's human. It's about human beings.

STELLA: I want to say, forget the bedroom. GET TO THE PERSON.

M: Do you have any little rituals in your relationship?

They both think. In a moment Ruth Ann says, "Well, there is one that's a mystery to me—but it happens over and over, over the years."

(Stella starts to giggle. She knows what's coming.)

RUTH: It goes like this. We're in bed. And she says, "I wonder if I should take an aspirin . . . I might get a headache."
    And I look at her and say, "Do you need an aspirin?"
    And she says, "I don't know . . . I might."
    Then I say, "Why don't I go get you an aspirin."
    And she says, "That would be really nice."
    So, I jump out of bed, bare feet on the cold floor—shivering in just my skivies—and I go to the kitchen and get her a glass of water and an aspirin.

(Stella is smiling very sweetly)

RUTH: I just don't understand. (she chuckles) If she wants an aspirin, why doesn't she just ask me?
M: How often does this happen?
RUTH: Oh, two to three times a year. Not often. But it's always the same. It never changes—for twenty-four years.
M: Well, it's sweet . . . I guess she's just checking to see if you'll still get up in the night and get her an aspirin.
RUTH: (laughs) I guess so.

(It's as old as Adam and Eve.)

STELLA: Our relationship lasted because of her. She's very calm, a calming individual. We had some rough times in our early years. But she wanted to communicate. She'd say, "Let's talk this over." She doesn't get riled. Since those early years I've changed. I try not to get moody. I try to communicate. But she definitely is our solid foundation.
M: The rock.
STELLA: Yeah. The rock.
M: That's what a relationship should ideally be—a place where you can grow.
STELLA: I've grown over the years—really, really changed.
M: Yeah. You couldn't always have been *this* nice.
STELLA: (laughs) She's brought me out of my shyness, my introversion. I used to get angry and hold it in. She wouldn't know what was wrong. I think I held it in because my family used to yell and argue and I was reacting against that.
M: What sort of things caused these rough patches?
STELLA: Always the same thing. My shyness and her self-

confidence. It happened recently again. To celebrate our anniversary we took a cruise to Alaska, a lesbian cruise.

M: A lesbian cruise?

STELLA: Yes. Every passenger was a lesbian. It was wonderful. It felt so free. You can be completely comfortable. There were 750 women aboard. You see people holding hands—being who they wanted to be—being able to dance, with who you wanted to dance with—it was just wonderful. We're going to take another lesbian trip. Of course, you pay more.

M: You pay more? Why?

STELLA: I don't know. But you pay a lot more than for the regular cruise. I guess it's because we don't have that many choices. What happened was Ruth Ann wanted to dance and she pulled me up to go to the dance floor. No one else was dancing yet and I felt shy—I didn't want to be the first ones out. That doesn't bother Ruth Ann—she says they'll follow us out, there'll be other people in a minute. But it bothers me. So I pulled back and sat down. She was hanging onto my hand and was embarrassed. She felt I'd humiliated her in front of other people.

Ruth Ann brought over the photo album to show me their Alaska cruise. The pictures fascinated me. It seemed one-half of each couple was a boy-like woman. Boy haircuts. Dressed in tuxedos, suits, or pants. They had a distinctive body shape—like stocky young men.

One photo caught my eye. A very striking, attractive woman wearing a military uniform jacket, lush with medals and ribbons, hung over her shoulders. Even in a casual photo, a commanding presence. She was sitting at a dining table with an attractive, middle-aged woman in a colorful dress.

STELLA: That's Colonel Cammermeyer. She was the special guest on the cruise. She gave talks for us. She was wonderful. That lady is her lover.

The next set of pictures were the "Victorian box-picnic" Ann gives every year. Everyone comes in Victorian costume. Ann was wearing a vest and a moustache and looked like a riverboat gambler. I was startled to see her dressed as a man.

Then came the photos of the sit-down, formal dinner at Ann and Elizabeth's house for Ruth Ann and Stella's 25th Anniversary. The guests were women and men and a baby. The photos of the men with the baby who looked about ten months old caught my eye. In all the photos but one she was being held by one of two men who are her parents. In that one she is sitting in her highchair, pulled up to the dinner table. She has a blue ribbon in her hair which is still sparse and baby-bird feathery. She has tiny silver hoop earrings. She is determinedly eating cake with a spoon. One knows there is no way this child would be left home from a party.

M: Who are the men with the baby?
STELLA: Oh, that's Jim and Bill. That's their little girl. They adopted her.

I often thought photo albums—other people's photo albums—were not interesting. But now I would look up the case of Col. Margarethe Cammermeyer, about to be promoted to general when she is put on trial for admitting she is a lesbian. And I would ask to meet the two men with baby.

We talk about homophobia. I tell them about my visit to a Marine base on Friday for a reunion with an old friend I hadn't seen for twenty years. She was in California with her daughter who was expecting a baby any day. Sherry was talking about a black couple we were friends with during the days our husbands were in the Army.

SHERRY: I never could understand prejudice. I just don't see color. How can color possibly affect what you think of a person? I don't care if they're pink, or green, or purple. (she laughs her famous all-body laugh—a big woman, full of good will and good nature)

M: Maine (her state) is voting this month on a gay discrimination bill to prevent gays from having civil rights. How do you feel about that?

SHERRY: Deport them all. I don't care. (she leans toward me) They recruit, you know. (she nods toward her two-year-old grandson, Jerry, playing energetically by us)

M: That's a myth. They're born gay. Could anyone recruit you to homosexuality?

SHERRY: No . . . of coss not. (Boston accent)

(She's thinking. She's a very kind person. This is new to her.)

(Sharon, her daughter, looks at the little boy.)

SHARON: I wouldn't love Jerry any less if he's gay.

(Sherry looks at him. She wouldn't love him any less either.)

SHARON: Oh, Mom. So many of my friends in college were gay. They don't try to "recruit."

("Mom" is surprised.)

SHARON: Oh, they might be attracted to you, but if you tell them you're not interested, well, they don't pursue that.

Ruth Ann sits quietly. Then she says, "They're our hope. The next generation."

STELLA: There is nothing wrong with our relationship. I never questioned its rightness or wrongness. From the beginning.
M: It's just that darn ol' Catholic church.
STELLA: Yeah. They have a way of gettin' to you.
M: I'm glad the two of you have had your life together.
STELLA: I'm blown away by the way our friends go from one person to another. It's like twenty minutes here—twenty minutes there. I can't understand.

(she's quiet)

Ruth Ann and I were friends *first*.
M: I wish I could find that for myself—some man who cares, who'd be my friend. A man who would bring me an aspirin.

It's time to leave. I ask Ruth Ann if there's anything she wants to say about her life with Stella.

RUTH: Misery from the moment I met her. (we laugh) No. I'm totally content. I cannot imagine being any happier.

I leave without asking the question "if you could change anything in your life . . ." I know their faces would be quizzical. What could I mean? Then Stella would say, "Well, I *would* like a house where you can go upstairs to bed."

The idea of changing their nature would not occur to them. No more than it would occur to me to say, "Oh, yes. I'd like to be gay."

They are who they are. Like Fred remembering sitting on the river bank as a very little boy, watching the threshers swimming after a day's hard work in the hot, dusty fields: "I remember thinking their bodies were so beautiful."

You don't fall in love from a book of rules. No one can tell you whom to fall in love with.

8

BISHOP'S TALE

THE LAST STORY has to be Ann Bishop's. You already know her because she appears throughout the book—like a Jiminy Cricket she's in the corners of other people's stories, as their friend, as a tiny voice of reason or wry humor or moral guidance. Ann Bishop, forced into leadership from the back of the room.

Before she comes to do her interview, I think about what I know about her already. I see femininity in her face—her hoop earrings and the soft, prettiness of her face. The last time I'd seen her, at the dinner party she gave so we could work on a glossary, she was wearing a loose, emerald green, silk shirt over black pants, and her cheeks were flushed and rosy, maybe from the cooking, and her skin was translucent ivory. I saw again her very feminine beauty. Many times when we've sat talking, I've leaned forward and squinted at her and said, "Are you wearing eye shadow?" She always laughs at me because she wears no makeup. But the lower edges of her eyelids are always delicately lavender. She says men often "hit on" her. She's considered sex with a man, has "been tempted"—but has never done it.

I've never seen her wear anything but pants. For dress up she adds a vest—the green silk blouse was rare. From a distance I've taken her for a young man, and it's startled me. It's the body movement. She doesn't enjoy clothes. She enjoys tools, and computers, and gardening, and animals.

For a while she trained attack dogs. Then she worked for a veterinarian. She used to ride a motorcycle—a big one—and still talks frequently about how much she misses it and how much she wants another one. She quit riding after a bad accident when a car made an illegal left turn into her. She talks nostalgically about her little dog Armand who rode on the back, and how she'd trained him in crash preparedness. "I could 'lay down' the bike (a skid with the bike on its side), and he would step off as neatly as if we weren't moving," she says proudly.

She also likes cooking fancy food and throwing parties. "Elizabeth doesn't cook at all," she says. "She's happy with cold food out of the refrigerator." A blend of male aptitudes and female proclivities, she phones me and tells me, "My God. Thought I should tell you. I'm standing here ironing and watching soap operas. However, I'm not wearing a housedress and pearls." She sews now on the machine if necessary, but says she conquered this feminine anathema to her only by renaming it "power stitching."

She enjoys looking at attractive women and going to Rambo movies. Her jokes are often pointedly sexual in a male way. I feel odd when I see her move protectively to Elizabeth's side to put an arm around her shoulder. The way she drives, settling deep into the seat back, foot heavy on the accelerator—then the transformation is complete and I see only a masculine toughness, and remember she is a bull dyke.

Throughout our now three-year friendship I've had glimpses of the pain of a lesbian life. Ann is so kind. Probably the most giving, reaching-out-to-any-stranger person I've ever met. Yet she talks of fearing people. She heard a guest at a neighbor's house say, "I wouldn't let a lesbian *near* my child." Ann was in the kitchen—she quickly moved away from the neighbor's child who dearly loves playing with Ann. Ann says she'll now wait until she's sure the neighbor knows she's a lesbian and *still* likes her before she plays with the child again. She told me about once when she was my student and another student, Sarah, started to cry after class.

ANN: I wanted to put my arms around her—to comfort her, but I was afraid. If she knew I was a lesbian, then I shouldn't. I'm never sure how I should react. It's like I'm off the stage and everyone else is on. I watch the players, but I can't join them. I sit in the audience watching other people's lives—like a play I'm not in.

I'm a product. I study behavior, then I put it on.

It's "the lie." I learn poses.

I stand up very straight around businessmen. I hunch lower, like this, into feminine postures, sitting sideways, sideways glances, when I need to appear feminine. I draw inward and smaller around my mother. Around female friends I can play the strutting, macho protector.

(she draws herself up very large)

I am watching her transform herself, who you think she is, again and again, before my eyes. She's learned so many "roles," she doesn't know her true posture. I think about the stress and the distress of how she has to live. When we are alone I see her true self—a confident, relaxed, "youngmannish woman." But then she's up—she putters, she paces, she smokes, she stuffs her hands into her pockets. I watch her. It's painful to see her, or anyone, not know, or not able to just be, their true self. It was from Ann that I first learned about the consideration that male-oriented lesbians have for their fem partners. I was complaining about my frustration over not being able to get Tom and John to go to bed now that they're older. I told her, "When we're watching a movie and it gets late and I'm too tired to stay awake, they won't go to bed if I ask them. They just keep on silently and intensely watching the movie, knowing I'll fall asleep in my chair and then they can stay up and watch the movie. Of course, then I've missed it."

Ann laughed. "When Ruth Ann and I watch videos with Elizabeth and Stella, Elizabeth and Stella always fall asleep. Ruth and I just get up and turn it off. Then we go outside and smoke and talk, until they've finished their nap. Then we turn it back on and finish the movie."

The sweetness and tenderness with which they look after their partners—I've seen it over and over. It comes from their mixture of male and female traits.

After I'd known Ann for more than two years, she came for her interview in October of '95. I don't remember what she wore. I never do unless she's dressed up. It's usually cotton trousers and a T-shirt. I noticed again her feminine eyes—the long lashes and the lavender shading of her eyelids.

ANN: I was "made in Japan"—my parents met and married there. My father was in the military. My mother was a civilian teacher on base. She was originally from the South—Georgia. Because my father was in the military, he was away a lot, and we moved every few years—Massachusetts, South Carolina, California.

She rattles off names of towns. Her voice is flat. She's not interested in this.

M: What do you remember from your childhood?
ANN: My childhood? (pause—no answer)

M: Was it happy? Or unhappy? (pause)—or just a childhood?

ANN: It was odd. I had health problems that isolated me from my peer group. In first through third grade I lost 75% of my hearing. My mother took me from doctor to doctor. They thought it was from scarlet fever. It's called otoscerosis—hardening of the bones in the inner ear. Older people can get this from aging. They took out the bones in my ear and put in wires that transmit sound for me.

She explains the technical aspects of a complicated surgery. Taking a vein from the wrist to cover the wire and attaching it to the eardrum. I'm saying, "Oh, no. Oh, no." She says, "I was awake during surgery. I had to tell them where the sensitive spots were. I'd say, 'I'm dizzy now.' I wanted my ear bones to take home, but they were broken. They had to break them to get them out."

M: How old were you?
ANN: That was in '67. (she figures) I was eight.
M: Then you were born in '59. Tell me how old you are so I don't have to subtract.
ANN: *I* have to subtract. I don't pay any attention to my age. I never have. I always have to figure it out. I'm 36. The next year I had to get glasses. I had those little cateye glasses, pearlized. And in third grade I started my growth spurt. By fourth grade I was 5'3". My mother was in a panic. Ladies are not tall. The males in her family were tall—6'2". She was afraid I'd get that tall. She began another round of doctors. It was a comedy of errors. First it was my ears, now again. In and out of military hospitals. All sorts of treatments. I didn't even know what they

were for. They decided to give me hormone injections to stunt my growth. I didn't find out what they did until I was in my twenties. My mother threw me a newspaper with an article about doctors in the sixties giving children hormones to stunt their growth. She said, "There—that's what they did to you." At the time I was told the injections were for hayfever. I tried to find out what I was given but the military said my records had been lost. I went for injections twice a month and they drew three vials of blood, and the injections were painful—it was a thick fluid. At first I fought it, but then I learned to go along. If I was quiet, I got to go pick out a book.

The thing is, the injections brought on an early puberty. I was menstruating by fourth grade. Yeah. I was wearing the little belts with metal shrapnel in them.

M: You poor baby. Couldn't they have just let you be.

ANN: So I was isolated from my peers. I was with adults—doctors. My mother doesn't make friends easily. So I was her friend. The phrase I remember hearing most often was "I know you're too young to understand this, but I need someone to talk to." And then we were always moving. In sixth grade my best friend was a 40-year-old woman divorcée from Europe. She would come over and I would cook meals for her and we went to the movies. I look back—and it's very odd.

M: It *is* very odd. You didn't have a childhood.

ANN: No. And when I wanted to be away from adults I went out with my dogs or rode my bike. I got ten books a week out of the library. That was the limit. Whenever we moved my mother put me in the Girl Scouts or whatever group there was. But I always ended up assisting the leader.

M: I told you when I first knew you that you're a natural leader. You may lead from the back of the room, but eventually you have to lead. I mean, how long can you sit and watch people f_ _ _ up? You want to get in there and say, "Try doing it this way." It's part of your intelligence. Intelligence can isolate you too.

ANN: In ninth grade I had my first friends my own age—a clique, so to speak. Kenny and I were the leaders. We organized riding our bikes to the beach, roller skating parties, going to the movies, going to dances, and hanging out at the mall. We had fun. Of course it wasn't until many years later that I found out—everyone in the group was gay. Yes, everyone. And not one of us knew it at the time.

M: How many of there were you?

ANN: Two Jeffs. Kenny, myself, Jean, and Cathie.

M: This was ninth grade. When did you move?

ANN: Tenth grade. It was the one time I remember moving being hard—because I was leaving friends behind for a change. We left California and went to South Carolina.

M: You told me once when you were little your mother dressed you in—(I was going to say frilly dresses and large hairbows)

ANN: POLYESTER!

M: And you had long curls. You told me you weren't dressed like other children.

ANN: After my growth spurt, I wore adult clothes. She bought me polyester pants and stitched a permanent crease down the front of the legs, as much of a crease as you can get with polyester, and scarves around the neck, held to the side with a pin (brooch) (she pauses)—very appropriate for fourth grade.

M: So *she* dressed you, really—

ANN: I did not own a pair of jeans until I left home.

M: Did you want to? Did you ask?

ANN: I probably asked and was told no—and accepted it.

Ann left home where her mother made her decisions for her to go to Pomona College, a school Ann describes as full of aggressively competitive, highly charged students who came with specific agendas to be number one in something or other.

ANN: A lot of them were children of diplomats. I didn't know what I was doing there. I ended up just going walk-about. Walking the streets of the town at night, driving to the mountains and sleeping in my car. The first semester I had A's and B's—then I quit going to classes. Then an English teacher told me I had no business being at Pomona College. "You aren't smart enough to be here," she said. To be fair I should say she probably meant I didn't want to be there. But she said I wasn't smart enough, and I believed that.

(Ann believed it still when she came to my class at 33 years old.)

I liked to walk the residential streets around the college where retired missionaries lived. They put little displays in their windows, things they'd gathered in their missionary days. They were especially beautiful at Christmas.

Pomona suggested I not return until I had my head together. After that I signed up for school almost every semester, at a junior college, but I never completed a course. I would sign up and then I wouldn't go.

I worked in L.A. for a couple of years. For a gas company first. I would work in an office all week and on weekends I'd man a gas station. Then I worked for a graphic arts company, until we lost our one client, Twentieth Century Fox movie company.

I came back to San Diego County and trained guard dogs until my father died. Then I ran his business, a bar, until my mother sold it. I'm sure it was because of the hours I was keeping, the language I was picking up, and the fact that I was carrying my custom pool cue wherever I went. I was in at 6:00 a.m. to clean and do ordering, and open until 2:00 a.m. Often I just slept in my truck. I was too tired to drive home and come back.

M: When were you aware of your sexuality? Like Ted's friend Fred remembers that at four or five he liked the threshing season because he liked seeing the men work without shirts. He had no words for it, but looking back as an adult he can say, "Yes, I always enjoyed looking at men."

ANN: In talking with gay male friends, that seems to be a recurrent theme—that they are much more aware of sexual feelings at an early age.

M: Then people like Sandy told me she had no sexual feelings at all until she was forty-six. She had thought she had no sexuality.

ANN: I have to agree with her statement—for myself. I dated Ken. I dated Bill. We tried making out—but there was nothing there. (Ken and Bill are both gay, she knows now) In my senior year of high school, there was a guy who was crazy about me. I tried to make out with him in the car—god, I didn't have any feeling for the guy.

M: For heterosexual girls it's the same. I remember guys like that too. I'd have no feeling for them. Then every once in a while one person would come along and I'd have that feeling for him.

ANN: My best friend at Pomona was a senior, an utterly heterosexual guy who was engaged. Later he found out he was homosexual and had a nervous breakdown over it. He's quite happy now.

M: A character in *Doonesbury,* the comic strip, didn't realize he was gay—other people saw it but he didn't. They said, "Didn't you know?" He said, "I never thought it at all." I guess the realization can be so different for different people.

ANN: I think Patrick, the guy I dated at the graphic arts firm in L.A., was gay.

M: Hearing you talk, one would think the figure of 1 in 10 being gay is too small a number.

ANN: I think on some level we were finding each other because it was safe for us to be couples—in a world of coupledom. That was certainly true for Ken and me, and for Bill and me in school.

M: I imagine you were good friends.

ANN: Yeah. It was nice to cuddle.

M: When did you first think—Did you even have in your knowledge that some people are gay?

ANN: I think I was blocking—so hard—I went back east to visit my grandmother and went to Charleston to see Bill. He took me to several gay bars.

M: So at that time he told you he's gay?

ANN: No. I didn't ask any questions. I just watched, danced with Bill, was amazed by the passing parade—I never questioned it.

M: You had gone to prom with Bill. You once told me you were more concerned about the car and he was more concerned about the flowers.

ANN: I remember we went through all the stages together. We picked out my dress together. We picked out his tux—it was baby blue, so we lined the eyelet lace on my white dress with matching baby blue velvet ribbon together, and he bought me blue cameo earrings. We did it all together.

M: Did you enjoy wearing those feminine clothes?

ANN: Yes. Because I had control over it and Bill and I did it together—mother wasn't involved. The dress had simple lines, and I had flat dance shoes.

M: So even though it was a dress, it was *your* dress—for the first time.

ANN: Yeah. And classic rather than frilly.

M: Of course you don't wear dresses anymore?

ANN: Occasionally. Once or twice a year. I wore one last month.

M: You did?! I didn't even know you had any.

ANN: I wore a skirt.

M: What was the occasion?

ANN: It was hot. It was hot and I had to go to work. I wore a skirt instead of shorts. I don't even mind wearing dresses. It's the shoes that are the problem. I refuse to wear crippling shoes. I have odd size feet—$7\frac{1}{2}$ which is small for my size, but very wide—so I can't get fit for espadrilles and shoes I like.

M: So you and Bill went to gay bars together and you were oblivious?

ANN: I was oblivious. I knew I was in a gay bar.

M: And that was the first time you saw gay people?

ANN: —people that I *knew* were gay. In one club there was a woman singing on a stage, then I saw an Adam's apple and said, "Oh, that's a guy."

M: How old were you?

ANN: Twenty-two. I came back to California and worked and went to school. I had a motorcycle accident and took the money and went to Europe.

When I came back I had a teacher at community college—Laura. Looking back I can see I had a crush on her. She had a cold and I took her a can of soup, a flask of whisky, lemons, tea, *National Enquirers*—things like that. We had been friends before I went to Europe. I used to visit nursing homes with her, for her study specialty. I'd entertain the old people. And I helped her move, and painted her condo.

M: You were just enjoying this woman's company, as far as you knew?

ANN: I would stay at her place when I worked late.

M: What made things change—eventually things changed—

ANN: She'd given me a book—and one night I stayed over and the couch wasn't there. She was getting a new one or something. Anyway, she said, "No big deal. We can share the bed." I said, "Okay. Fine."

We were in bed. Both reading our books and she turned and said, "Are you really reading that book?"

I said, "Yeah." And she slapped her book shut. That night was the first time we made love—and I said to myself, "Yeah. This is it. Yes! Right!"

I'd been reading. She told me later she'd been reading the same sentence over and over.

M: What did she do? Were you startled? Did she, like, just put her arms around you first, or kiss you, or what?

ANN: Yeah. We started cuddling—then it moved quickly. She'd slammed her book shut and said, "Well, I'm going to sleep," and turned off her light. So I closed my book and turned off my light. Then we were just chatting about something—

M: And she made the move? It was nothing you would have done because you didn't have the thought in your head?

ANN: No. It was the first time for both of us with another woman. But she had been married twice before. But the thought had occurred to her before.

M: Were you the first woman she'd been attracted to?

ANN: Yes. It just felt very natural to me. I just responded—yeah—yeah—this is right. She did not believe at first that it was my first time with another woman—she was a little angry with me for saying that it was.

M: Because she thought you seemed a little too knowledgeable about what to do?

ANN: Exactly. Of course, come to find out, her first husband used to hold a pillow over her head so she wouldn't make noise, so it wasn't like I had a lot of competition.

She eventually fell asleep and I stayed awake the entire night thinking, "This is right." And yet, as light was dawning I remember my thoughts changed from "This is right" to "Is she going to think this is right?" (pause) And she did—when she woke up.

M: In the morning did you talk about it? Did you say "Does this mean we're lesbians?" Had she already decided she was a lesbian, or was she in the dark?

ANN: At that time her point of view was, "I'm not really a lesbian—I'm just attracted to *you.*" And that went on for about a year. We were lovers for two years.

M: What did you talk about the next day? Did you just not talk about the whole thing, or did you talk about lesbianism?

ANN: No.

M: You just continued your relationship, and enjoyed it, and you never talked about what this meant to either of you?

ANN: (sigh) She was much more interested in defining it, analyzing it, taking it apart and labeling it.

M: So she wanted to talk about it, and you just . . .

ANN: Whatever—get on with it. Yeah. Laura had to redefine who she was. I don't think I had any definition before then, so it didn't matter to me. I thought,

"Okay. Fine."

I remember telling a woman at work. She said, "Oh, yeah? I figured that out three months ago. Didn't you?"

M: So do you think Laura's wanting to define it all the time was because she felt uncomfortable?

ANN: Oh yeah. Sure.

M: She was saying, "Does this mean I'm a lesbian?" Did she talk about whether it was good or bad?

ANN: She thought, "Well, I'm not attracted to all women—I'm just attracted to her. This is just an anomaly." But her friends were not to know, except for one she told. So she would have dinner parties and I would help clean the house, get the food ready, then I would leave and drive around so that I could arrive with the other guests.

She had very structured rules for our relationship. I could come over Friday night and stay until Sunday night, but during the week I could only come by appointment—by prior arrangement—appointment sounds too harsh.

She became more comfortable later on. Once when she'd moved into a house some of her friends came over, and I was hiding out in the bedroom as usual. And she said, "Come out. Come out and meet these people." And I was in my jammies. She made no excuse.

M: So all of a sudden it was okay? How old was she? Was she older than you by a lot?

ANN: Oh yeah. She was forty—I was twenty-four. I'm not sure what happened at the end. She had a lot of issues. She'd always made me promise that if she ever asked me to go I would, without question.

M: She said that more than once—throughout the whole relationship?

ANN: Yes.

M: Like, if I decide this is not right for me and I ask you to go, I want you to go?

ANN: Yes. It was off and on. She'd ask me to leave and then she'd ask me back.

M: This had to be very unsettling for you.

ANN: It was. She was in control of the relationship. She finally asked me to leave. Then a year later she came out publicly—very publicly. She even announced it at the school where she teaches. Yeah. She's way out there now.

I'd been upset at work after the breakup. I was working for a vet and we went out to dinner and I told him. I was worried what he'd think about my being a lesbian, but he was only angry about how she'd treated me.

Next I met Jill at the animal clinic. We took care of her dogs. I went to my first gay party at Jill's. She used to entertain a lot. That all stopped when she met Jonnie.

We were swinging singles together for a while. I moved in with her. She had the red Ferrari. We went to Palm Springs. We went to clubs.

M: Jill always says she took you under her wing. Were you coming out?

ANN: Yes, in that my relationship with Laura had been so controlled by her. She would never go to a party at Jill's. Jill never picked anyone up, but I became a Don Juanette. I picked up everyone I could—I became very social. At one point I took three women on a gay dancing cruise around the harbor. I had them all in Jill's Ferrari and I stopped at the 7/11 for cigarettes and bought them each a rose—a different color for each one.

M: What word do you have for the Don Juan lesbians, the masculine ones?

ANN: Butch, I guess.

M: Butch versus what?

ANN: Fem, I guess.

M: If you're driving the Ferrari and you have three women you're buying roses for, are you butch and they're fem?

ANN: Yeah, I guess.

M: Do most people who are lesbians think of themselves as one or the other?

ANN: NO.

M: They don't—that's what I find in talking to them. I look at them and I say "butch," "fem," "butch," "fem"—but they themselves don't.

ANN: Not to the degree it used to be. According to Patsy in the '50s there were very rigid lines for butch and fem. They're much more blurred now. Most people would look at Elizabeth and me and say I'm the butch and she's the fem, and that's probably valid most of the time. Yet I'm the one who does the cooking—and not just barbecue either. And at her niece's wedding I'm the one going around putting flowers on the bride's side and the groom's side, doing the organizing and the decorating and so forth.

I dress her. I pick out her clothes—quite a few. She gets her own too, of course. Last week at the mall at Robinsons-May I got a stack of clothes for her to try on and she'd come out and I'd say "Yes" or "No" or "Keep that one," "Get rid of that one."

M: You're considered butch, but you have blends of feminine traits.

ANN: That's more accurate. We're not locked into the roles.

M: Sandy said about when she was with Greta, "Isn't it odd that we weren't attracted to each other? We were both lesbians, we should have been."

Well, it isn't odd to me. They're both fems. To me everything is blurred as far as talents and feelings—like

Ted's dominating friend who did all the embroidery. But the erotic, that seems definitely divided in the people I know. Is Jill ever going to be attracted to you? No—because you're not feminine enough.

ANN: Right.

M: I've learned a lot about the Jill's, the Ann's, and the Linda's, you're clear to me, you have these blends—but the feminine ones—it's more cloudy. There are things I can't pin down. There's Elizabeth. She doesn't have any masculine traits at all, does she?

ANN: No.

M: Sandy?

ANN: No.

M: Joanna?

ANN: No.

M: And the ones who are butch have all these really exotic blends.

ANN: The only thing I'd say is masculine about them is that they all are strong. Sometimes feminine means "pushover"—and that's definitely not true about any of them, and put Stella in that category too.

M: Include Carol too. She looks fragile but you said, "Don't be fooled, she's strong."

ANN: Also, they're not manipulative. Some people might say fems would manipulate—they don't. They come right out and say what they want. They speak out.

M: They're not dominated.

ANN: Right. They're just as likely to take the initiative in the relationship—there's not a division of labor there.

M: I've noticed in the couples I know the relationships are very equal—there're no abused women.

ANN: I've heard of it happening.

M: I've heard of it too. But the eroticism—do you think

you're one or the other? Like Elizabeth is never going to be attracted to Joanna—she's going to be attracted to someone masculine.

ANN: I don't like to say never, but likely not. Although during my crazy time, two of the women I dated were more on the butch side than the fem side—that's maybe why it didn't last.

M: What about dressing—the fact that you and Jill are butch and like to wear men's clothes? Linda said she got angry as a little girl when they tried to "frou-frou" her. Jill wanted to be tough, to play with the boys, to be the *leader* of the boys.

Remember when sociologists said women are just raised to be feminine—we're raising our girls so they can't do male things. But butch lesbians from the time they're little insist on doing construction and dangerous stuff, and they want boys' clothes—it's like what we wear is not taught, it's genetic.

ANN: Is it though that we're taking men's roles, or that we want all the accoutrements that go along with wearing men's clothes? The ease. The being able to run—to not have to wear those awful shoes—I mean there are reasons men dress the way they do. They're in positions of power and they can afford to wear comfortable clothes. They're in positions of power so they can do construction and so forth. I think that's what we're after. And if you walk like a duck, and quack like a duck, maybe somebody will treat you like a duck.

M: You don't want a penis—there's no such thing as penis envy. What you want is what men have—power, control of your life. So you think the clothes are just an extension of those desires to have their power, to live your lives the way they live theirs?

ANN: Um-hmmmm.

M: Now the Elizabeth's, the Joanna's—

ANN: They're more comfortable in women's roles—

M: —less confined by it. They actually enjoy it. Elizabeth *likes* to wear those clothes, those tippy high-heeled shoes. Do you think the basis of choosing what you wear then is psychological? That it has to do with roles rather than—

ANN: Yeah.

M: When you try to express it doesn't it seem like a huge thing to get your arms around?

ANN: I think part of it is just that I'm no longer concerned so much about what other people think. Whereas Elizabeth still has part of that—so she still dresses for work. Women tend to dress to make themselves feel good. By dressing ultrafeminine she doesn't have to worry about what people at work think—so she feels good, so she gets a positive feedback—from her family, at church. I no longer care, so I dress for my own comfort.

M: But even at home she dresses in ultrafeminine clothes doesn't she?

ANN: Sweatpants.

M: She said when she was a nun she dreamed of pretty clothes. She liked the colors, and jewels. But you don't care?

ANN: Occasionally. If I dress up.

M: During your Don Juanette period—did you change in your perceptions, or your emotions?

ANN: Oh yes. I was very male during that time. I went full-out—yeah. I was not interested in a long term relationship—love 'em and leave 'em.

M: You took on the whole psychological thing of the run-around male?

ANN: Oh yes. The six times in my life I got drunk.

M: You'd been hurt so you went out and didn't care if you hurt anyone or not—that's so unlike you.

ANN: Thanks. But that's who I was then.

M: Was it a function of having been hurt, or of coming out?

ANN: Both I think. I didn't know it at the time, but I had a lot of anger about Laura.

M: So you were a guy who got drunk and did some whoring?

ANN: I think I buried my anger that way.

M: In a male way. There're some women who do it too, but not as often. What happened next?

ANN: I met Elizabeth.

M: And she changed your life?

ANN: She calmed me down. I'd found someone I wanted to be involved with long term.

M: I know you phoned her, when you were working for the vet, about her dogs after her friend died. I don't know what you were thinking. Were you just doing your helping people in need and dogs?

ANN: I had my toolbox.

M: Were there things that needed to be repaired?

ANN: Oh, yes. Her condo was falling apart.

M: Was she hurting from the loss of her friend?

ANN: (pause) Yes. But Elizabeth's faith is so solid too . . . (deep sigh)

M: Yes. I know. That's wonderful isn't it? So she was doing fine in spite of the fact she was lonely and suffering some grief.

ANN: I just fixed things at the condo for her. And we'd go out to dinner, go to the movies.

M: You were being her friend—because she was alone, and she was enjoying the company.

ANN: She told me later she wondered why I wanted to

spend time with her. She thought I was too young to be interested in her.

M: Did she know from the beginning you were a lesbian?

ANN: Oh yes. Sure.

M: Did she consider herself a lesbian?

ANN: That's a good question. I'm not sure she'd even say that today.

M: You're right. She doesn't.

ANN: We went up to Laguna Beach to see my friend Bill for dinner. I was still living at Jill's. We got back late and I remember saying I didn't want to take her home and leave her there. And I said, "Come spend the night with me," and she said, "Okay." And we've been together ever since.

M: Was that the first time there'd been any physical intimacy between you—even holding hands?

ANN: Um-hmmm.

M: So it came all at once.

ANN: Yes. In fact she moved in with me at Jill's, and we tore her condo apart—down to the concrete, and refurbished it.

M: Sandy said that when she had her first experience with a woman it was like an awakening. Carol said that too. It was like that for you. Sandy and Carol are fems. Now Jill thinks fems like Joanna are equally comfortable sexually with both men and women. I don't think so. Sandy and Carol aren't. Stella isn't. For the fems I talked with, even though they'd been with men, it had meant nothing. They didn't feel any eroticism or any awakening until they were with a woman.

ANN: I'm just thinking of the butch lesbians I know who've been married or been with men. Most of them. More than the fems. But, no—that probably doesn't mean anything.

M: Once you told me you thought sexuality was a continuum—you thought there were straights and gays on the opposite ends of the continuum and people are spread along the line.

ANN: Yeah. I think that. Because I've been attracted to men.

M: How many people have you met that you think are actually bisexual—are truly equally happy with a man or a woman?

ANN: Joanna is probably closest to that of anyone I know.

M: Politically you and Elizabeth are very different. She believes people should be left alone to live. I know you're more active. Rob Eichberg says people aren't going to be left alone until all gay people come out. He says gays have to be visible. Once people see they're all here and all these different kinds of people, then they'll be accepted. Then they won't have these problems.

ANN: Do I believe that? Yes. Do I actively do anything about it? Hardly ever. It's not the overwhelming issue for me. If I were to have time to do something in a radical movement, I'd probably be out there in the environmental movement rather than the gay rights movement. When it crosses my mind—when I'm in a film class and we see a lesbian movie, yes, I will stand up and identify myself as a lesbian before I talk about the movie, because it's important for them to know I have a point of view. But if it's not important in class I'm not going to stand up and say I'm a lesbian and I think this movie . . .

M: The reason I thought you were more active was because you go to gay parades and events.

ANN: Elizabeth goes too.

M: I thought you dragged her.

ANN: No. She wouldn't go to anything she didn't enjoy.

She might choose not to go on her own, but she goes with me. She goes more for the social aspect. I go to add one more person—so that's political.

And I understand why she doesn't like some of the bizarre costumes. When someone is walking down the street in nothing but a thong and a fairy wand in his hand, that's an image I don't like either.

M: You were twenty-two or so before you even realized this attraction to women, and because it seemed natural, you never spent a lot of time thinking about the political ramifications or whether it was acceptable or not—(she interrupts)

ANN: I was very aware it was unacceptable.

M: Okay. Where did these ideas come from?

ANN: I was actually warned by my mother about "those kinds of women." There was just one time when she said there are certain kinds of women who are attracted to other women. And she related the story of how one of them came on to her one time. She had this reproach. "She was *that kind*." I was a teenager.

M: Did anyone ever treat you as if you were a lesbian before you actually knew you were—like when you were a teenager?

ANN: If they had I probably wouldn't have noticed. Of course I've gone through most of my life fairly oblivious. And I had boyfriends, never mind we were both gay.

M: So when you came out, and you were being a Don Juan, you were very aware being a lesbian was not acceptable. You once told me a poignant story of not going too near the neighbor's child because you thought the mother might fear a lesbian. Where did you get the idea that people think that lesbians hurt children?

ANN: In that case it wasn't too long before it was apparent

to me that our neighbor understood the relationship between Elizabeth and me, and could care less. Then I was comfortable. I got the idea from a friend shortly after I realized I was lesbian. She worked in the stables of a wealthy family. One day one of the children got a bad splinter and wouldn't let the nanny or anyone touch her—but me. She sat quietly and let me take it out. She was a beautiful little child—she looked up at me with such trust—like a little angel. My friend warned me to stay away from children. And I had a vague feeling that being gay makes one vulnerable to being attacked.

M: Have you ever had any experience where people treated you badly because they thought you were gay?

ANN: Oh, I got yelled at, on occasion.

M: When you were with friends in the evening, so it was really obvious?

ANN: Yes. "Fucking dyke." People yelled that, things like that.

M: Never in work or daily life?

ANN: In my personal life I've never had a negative response.

M: That's great.

ANN: —kind of like waiting for the other shoe to drop.

M: You are feeling wary?—always?

ANN: Sometimes. Like when I brought it up with my shirttail cousin who's taking care of my mother.

M: So you still feel wary?

ANN: Oh, sure. Like when I stood up in that film class and said, "As a lesbian I . . . blah . . . blah . . . blah." I was shaking. Sure. Sure.

M: Does Elizabeth ever feel uncomfortable about your being a couple in public? Or wouldn't she tell you?

ANN: I try not to do anything that would make her

uncomfortable. I don't ask her to hold hands in the mall. We do occasionally, without thinking. It seems to me that anyone who has the least clue would figure out we're together, but if they choose not to know, we're not going to throw it in their face. Even on vacation, in casinos and so forth, the most I do is stand next to her with my arm around her waist. Although I occasionally, sort of jokingly, give her my arm to take.

I mean, I'm not thrilled with seeing a heterosexual couple making out in a casino—so why would I want— There might be one or two times when I wish I could just take her hand—but, no, I'm aware that's probably going to cause more trouble than it's worth. Unless we're just out hiking or something.

M: I'm all for that we can all just hold hands in public— and no kissing—on the lips kissing—that's what seems to bother people about other people's sexuality—then we'll all be all right.

ANN: I actually have more straight friends who want to walk arm-in-arm, or something, with me.

M: Oh, yeah. Because women do.

ANN: And they don't even think about it.

M: Yes. You're walking in the mall and talking and laughing and you lock arms. I know when I see my friend next week that I haven't seen in twenty years I'm going to feel very physical, want to hug her and take her arm. It seems everyone ought to be able to do that—why is it such a big thing?

Jill is so masculine in the way she dresses—even wearing men's shoes.

ANN: The three-piece custom-made suits.

M: Now I can't talk about this with her. I did ask her, but it's like Elizabeth and sex, there are certain lines I become aware are in their consciousness that can't be crossed, that they don't want crossed, so I don't try. Now you say you dress the way you do because you're comfortable, and I see that. But there's something about the fact she wears men's shoes—it wouldn't bother me if she wore a three-piece suit and women's shoes.

ANN: When you wear a man's suit, then men's shoes look right with the suit.

M: But you could wear any shoes with the suit though—Cindy Crawford does.

ANN: She doesn't wear the full thing—she wears it with an oversized shirt or something—so it looks like she's dressed up in a man's clothes. Jill wears men's clothes to fit her, to look like they belong on her. Crawford wears men's clothes and it looks like she's playing. Jill is not. She's doing the whole role.

M: Snakes, and snails, and puppy dog tails. How much is testosterone involved? Linda, Jill, Sally, some of John's high school friends are girls who did rough, tough, boy stuff. They talked about being rag-tag, rough, essentially little boys as children. They played rough, wanted boy toys. You weren't that way.

ANN: Uhmmmm.

M: You liked the motorcycle. You like tools.

ANN: I went back and forth. My father and I used to wrestle. My god. We broke a couple of doors. We'd wrestle. He taught me blocks and flips and things. I flipped him into a closet door and broke the door. We played war games. Then—I'd go to the library and sit quietly and read. I had different personas for different occasions.

M: So you blended in. But you didn't have the desire to go out and join the boys in the rough play on the sandlot like the others did?

ANN: Well, after third grade they wouldn't let me anyway. I was a foot and a half taller than all the boys. Our favorite game was tetherball. I could just hit the ball over their heads. I'd just—THWAACK!! Wang-ng-ng-ng-ng.

M: So you could play strong and rough. The boys didn't intimidate you. You intimidated them.

ANN: RIGHT. I was "none of the above." I was my own category. When I would first go to a school, the kids would think I was a teacher. Then they would find out I was another student. I didn't fit.

M: Because you were tall, and your mother dressed you like an adult, you looked mature enough that people thought you were an adult. Was it just the way you were dressed?

ANN: Probably not. I think my speech patterns were adult from being around adults. In the sixth grade one of my best friends was my math teacher. She was big on politics. So she got me going door-to-door passing out flyers and going to rallies. Except for band and orchestra my social life was with adults.

M: About your mother. I know she's not well now. Does she have Parkinson's?

ANN: Yes. She shakes.

M: And her other problems. She did a lot of weird stuff. Like getting a gun because she thinks people are after her.

ANN: Possible early Alzheimer's. Or she may have had one or two strokes. Or it could just be her native paranoid-schizophrenia that's being released.

M: When did she start having peculiar behavior?

ANN: I was born in '59.

M: Oh. All your life you think of her as being paranoid, schizophrenic?

ANN: She used to be able to hide it better.

M: So you think she's always been unwell?

ANN: Um-hmm.

M: When you came out as a lesbian to everyone else, I know you didn't specifically tell her, but did your behavior, or dress, or anything about you change enough so that she noticed?

ANN: She wrote me a letter. This was when I was living at home. It had a number of boxes with options next to them and I was to check off the one causing this problem in my life. Under Options I had: drug dependency, involved with a married man, pregnant, homosexual relationship. A whole list of possibilities. This was when I got involved with Laura.

M: Was this because you were away from home a lot?

ANN: Yes. But by this time Bill had come out to my mother.

M: How did she take that?

ANN: When my mother got her master's degree in counseling, homosexuality was still listed as a disease by the APA. So my mother has never admitted it should be taken off the list. To this day she still worries about Bill and thinks a good woman could cure him.

(She pauses, then bursts into laughter.)

Just two weeks ago she asked me if I was pregnant because I was having cramps.

M: So she doesn't have a clue.

ANN: On the other hand, my cousin Rick claims he talked to her about it—about her not feeling comfortable coming to Elizabeth's and my house. He brought her by for a surprise visit last week. He just said, "Look—that's a relationship you're just going to have to put up with, or not see your daughter."

M: So she really does know, but denies it. What did you do with the letter with the little boxes?
ANN: I ignored it.

Ann and Elizabeth had to leave then to go to one of the many functions they have with Liz's large family of brothers, sisters, nieces and nephews. The family Ann calls her "in-laws." That day it was a christening party. Usually Ann prepares and takes some large dishes of food. Today it was her pasta salad.

I often think what good parents they would make. Elizabeth is so loving, quiet in manner, sweet-natured, an interested listener—wise. Tender. Witty. Ann is so kind, calm, thoughtful, patient. Both of them intelligent.

They give a lot of attention to their pets. Elizabeth often has a large cat cradled on one arm as she walks through a party greeting her guests. Last year they planned their vacation so they could take their little poodles with them—resorts that accept pets. Ann said they aren't really happy leaving the dogs behind for too long. The dogs had new outfits: bomber jackets and leather caps.

M: Do they mind being dressed up?
ANN: They're poodles. They know it's expected.

On Halloween Ann and Elizabeth dress up for the neighborhood children, and carve pumpkins into elaborate jack-o-lanterns. You can bet the poodles are at the door in costume too.

They do things together, and apart. Elizabeth has her charity work, helping people who are ill, going to the monastery to drive old sisters to the doctor. Ann has her college courses—she's almost finished now, a degree in biology—and the toy shop in the garage where she and Ruth Ann refurbish old toys, and the lesbian library of 300 volumes she and Sandy built and then gave away last year to a new gay/lesbian organization. And she eats once a week with the "lesbian lunch bunch." Recently they had a car wash to raise money for a lesbian who had medical expenses. I asked, "How much money did you make?" About $78. I told Ann, "Next time put out a sign that says LESBIAN CAR WASH and watch the cars roll in." She goes to guy movies with Patsy, the Saturday matinee. She always makes time for Elizabeth, friends, any person in need, and animals.

One Friday night near the end of July, I phoned her to ask her to come over to answer a few last questions for her story. She said, "Tomorrow is the gay Pride Parade. Do you want to go with me?" Elizabeth wouldn't be going. She had a memorial service to go to at the monastery.

Yes. No. I thought I should go. How could I write a book about lesbians and miss the one-time-a-year chance to go to a gay Pride Parade? I was ill. I had some kind of virus and was weak, fatigued. I told Ann I wanted to go, but didn't know if I could. It was extremely hot in San Diego that week.

Ann said, "We're going out now, but you can leave a message on the machine." They always go out on Friday night. Dinner with friends. A play. A comedy club. I always thought on my Friday and Saturday nights home alone that lesbians were having more fun. Lesbians and gay men seem to have the aptitude of planning a fun social life. In heterosexual couples it always seemed to me the woman had to try to plan it but the man wasn't very interested in what she planned. After a while she tried less.

The gay Pride Parade. Should I go? Do I want to go? I had all these ambivalent feelings. I wanted to see it, but I was afraid. Would I feel strange and alone, left out? Would someone who knows me see me there and think I'm a lesbian? That scared me. Then I felt guilty for having that thought. I was insulting lesbians to be afraid to be labeled one. I'd been sure about not wanting to go to a gay bar. I had no need to see that, to intrude upon what I thought of as their private life. But a gay Pride Parade, that seemed a necessity—to participate and support gay people.

Should I wear my STRAIGHT BUT NOT NARROW T-shirt? So people won't approach me like I'm a lesbian? (Hit on, ever so gently.) Or if I wear my STRAIGHT BUT NOT NARROW T-shirt will it look like I don't want to be identified with them? Will it be an insult to them? Like I have to announce I'm not gay. Is that like saying I think they're a threat? Will I spoil Ann's time because I'm not a lesbian?

Panic. Felt very ill. Before I went to bed I phoned Ann and left a message. "I really want to go, but I just don't feel well enough to go out and stand in the heat. I'm sorry to miss it." The next morning at nine Ann phoned. "Do you want to go?"

M: Yes. I do. I want to go.
ANN: I'll pick you up in forty minutes.

It's always fun to go somewhere with Ann. She always drives. She always has everything planned: chairs, umbrellas, a water spray bottle with a fan. I just sit back and relax. This day turned out to be better than Disneyland.

We drove around the Hillcrest area near Sandy's house looking for a parking spot. There weren't any. There was an aura of great festivity already. Houses were decorated with balloons, rainbow flags, banners and streamers. Parties of people were out on their porches. On the sidewalks people, especially guys, were walking about in flamboyant and colorful costumes. Happy to be admired. Everyone was excited and friendly.

We parked behind a bank on the parade route and set up the chairs on the curb where Sandy's friends had saved space. Ann had a new hairdo since I'd seen her—short and curly on top, longer in back. I liked it. As we walked down the main street women who knew Ann rushed out of cafes to see her. One looked just like her, the same new hairdo. She was a strong, stocky young woman, friendly and laughing. She talked about her job transfer and how her partner wanted to have a baby (artificial insemination). I felt completely at ease as I have every time I've been among gay people. People are just people and these people are especially kind. They hug everyone they know in a sincere way.

My STRAIGHT BUT NOT NARROW T-shirt was a big hit. It brought strangers up to talk with me. "I like your attitude," (thumbs up) "I like your shirt," and "Where can I buy one for my friend?" or sister or mother. It was the right thing to wear. It was my political statement. At first I couldn't remember the name of the company that made it, and then I remembered. "DON'T PANIC," I said. "The name of the company is DON'T PANIC."

Before the parade there was one lone young man on rollerblades, wearing a red, ruffled flamenco dress over cut-off jeans, the dress tied up so as not to get caught in the skates. Behind him on a rope he dragged a skateboard piled high with objects, I couldn't tell what, and a portable stereo CD player playing music. He skated down the parade route, then would turn around and we'd see him skate by in the opposite direction. By an hour before the parade the sidewalks were filled with people socializing and laughing.

I knew the first thing in the parade would be "dykes on bikes." I'd heard from Ann before that that's how every gay

Pride Parade begins. And I'd heard about it in the movie *Jeffrey*. I was looking forward to it. It was the main reason I could think of that I wanted to see the parade. In the movie *Jeffrey* you only hear the dykes on bikes, you don't see them. I wanted to see them.

It was a terrific roar. The parade was beginning. Before we saw them we heard the noise of what sounded like a hundred big motorcycles. Then they were there. How many? I can't say for sure. Fifty? or Sixty? Big bikes. Noisy bikes. The women riding them were in slim fitting jeans or black leather pants. Nice looking girls. Girl-next-door girls. Not flamboyant. Not made up. Pretty, fresh-faced and smiling. They didn't just drive by. They roared, and popped wheelies and U-turned and came back and did it again. The noise of the engines, and the fragile looking young women man-handling those tons of machinery—what was it? the power? I don't know, but I burst into tears. It was beautiful. Ann, beside me, was saying, "Damn. I miss my bike."

The other time I couldn't hold back tears was when parents marched with their gay children. Holding signs that said, "I love my lesbian daughter," "I love my gay son." I have never seen a parade before where the people on the curb participated with the people in the parade. Calling out and being answered. There was a San Diego City Schools bus filled with lesbian teachers hanging out the windows. Someone on the curb yelled, "I don't believe it," and a lesbian teacher yelled back, "It's true. We can't believe it either. But we're out." (meaning we don't have to be afraid of losing our jobs) Gay police marched and gay fire fighters were in a fire truck. And floats of every kind with dancers and bands. And precision marchers and dancers. And the Gay Men's Chorus. And the most amazing young gay men performers, skaters, and baton twirlers who leaped into the air doing splits and, a favorite with the crowd, the gay men cheerleaders from Hollywood, dressed up in big wigs and big bosoms. And organizations like Mama's Kitchen that cooks meals for people with AIDS carried big rainbow flags held flat like a sheet and people ran out from the curbs and put money into them. The parade went on for hours. I wanted to leave and walk over to Sandy's house, I was getting a headache from the heat, but I was afraid I'd miss something. And always the same young man on the rollerblades dragging the flamenco dress and the skateboard with the stereo CD player on it. Visibly tireder every time he went by. Yet moving faster than the parade and skating back through it to do it again. On his last foray he was so exhausted he tangled in his rope and dress and fell in front

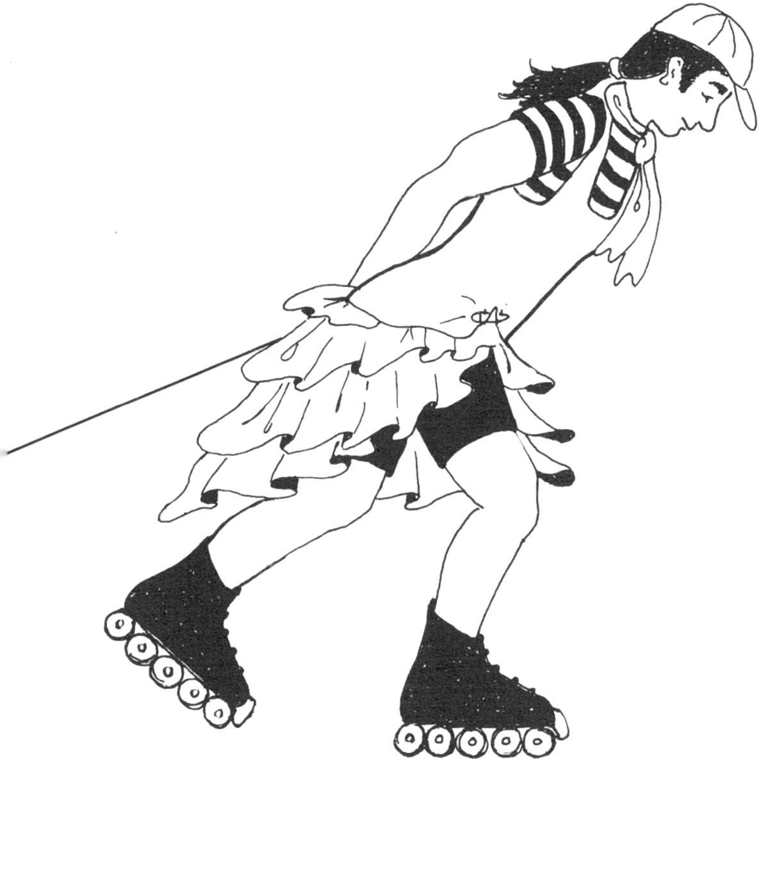

of us and lay in the street, too tired to get up. People from the curb rushed out and set him on his feet, his rollerblades, and in his exhaustion he made himself skate on, barely able to drag the burden of the laden skateboard. It began to feel like we were seeing someone from a concentration camp, pushed to near death. Ann raised her hands in the air and applauded. "I don't know what he's doing. Is it performance art? I don't know. But it's something, and I'll applaud him."

It was estimated 80,000 people lined the main street of Hillcrest to watch the parade. The night before there had been a rally. Wilson Cruz, "Ricky" on the TV series *My So-Called Life,* sang acappella "Somewhere Over the Rainbow" . . . there's a place for me, and people cried. Tonight there would be a festival and booths in Balboa Park.

On the drive home in Ann's truck I talked and asked questions. Did you ever notice how many lesbian couples look like twins—matched sets? Why is that? Ann said she didn't know. She said, "Maybe it's like people who look like their dogs—they choose dogs who look like them. Maybe lesbians are attracted to people who look like them. Then they live similar lives and dress in similar clothes." I said, "It must be odd, you face each other and it's like looking in a mirror."

I wondered silently about all the stocky young butch lesbians. Does their hormone mix make them stocky, or do they beef up unconsciously to "carry more weight"—to look strong, to look masculine? Or is it just their male lifestyle? Physical work, hearty appetites, no desire to look frail like a model. No answer, or "all of the above"?

I tell Ann, "I used to be so excited about seeing women out doing men's work, really nontraditional female work, climbing utility poles, working on underground wiring, welding, being mechanics—I thought the world was really changing for women, then I discovered all those women were lesbians. They're the women who wanted to do the guy jobs."

The dashboard on the truck has a fabric cover with Ann's button collection. About fifteen. One is the penguin Opus. One, a pretty "fifties" high school girl in a graduation cap, turns out to be Elizabeth. Ann's new favorite: "May I please see some I.Q.?" Two of them are about lesbians: "How dare you presume I'm straight" and "Heterosexualism can be cured."

I ask Ann if her nephew-in-law, who works on her truck, has seen the buttons.

ANN: I presume so. We've driven together in the truck. They come in handy sometimes. I knew this guy at work had a crush on me so when we went out to lunch I drove him in my truck. I think he got the idea. The next day I took him some of my garlic puffs, which he loves. I think that helped. We're friends now.

She sang for me. She talked about how she loves Rosie O'Donnell. "She's the only person I know who knows more songs than I do." She sang from the folk operetta *The Point* by Harry Nilsson the Rockman's song: "People just see what they wanna see . . ."

Back at my house we continued the interview we did in October.

M: Did you feel loved?
ANN: By my father. But he went away. Overseas. Vietnam. Two years in Turkey. I didn't feel unconditionally loved by my mother; I was wary—of her moods—stomping

around, slamming things.

M: Did you think it was your fault?

ANN: Sure. No one else was around. But it wasn't cause and effect. I remember my dad and me sitting outside waiting for the slamming to stop. We didn't talk about it. I couldn't relate it to anything. Afterwards she'd assuage her guilt by going out and buying me things she thought I should have—frilly dresses for example—things I didn't want—but I knew I'd better be grateful.

M: Was there ever anything said directly to you that made you feel unloved?

ANN: No, but I never stood up tall enough, or kept the frilly bows in my hair. Even praise came with a "but" at the end. Like she would walk up to me and say, "You look so lovely in that dress," and I would be expecting a hug. Then she would lean forward and whisper, "if *only* you'd stand up *straight*" and jab her thumb into my spine. Occasionally she did relax and give me affection, but I was never sure whether I was going to get affection or a poke in the ribs—so I was wary.

M: How do you feel about your life now?

ANN: I feel like I'm being dragged kicking and screaming into adulthood.

M: At 36? You're precocious.

ANN: A lot of it is becoming parent to my mother, and taking care of details—stocks, etc.

M: And being a lesbian?

ANN: Elizabeth and I are very solid—but being a lesbian is not a big part of my life. Even though I go home every night and live with a woman, I don't think it's what people think of when they look at me. Right now my main role is as daughter; I have to remember not to take Liz for granted.

M: You work on your relationship?

ANN: Oh yes. Always. I never want to become complacent about it.

M: What do you do?

ANN: Gifts. Letters when I'm away. Making an effort to have certain meals together when our schedules are different. I always make her favorite scones for Sunday breakfast. Recently I went on a business trip for a week—the first time we'd been apart in eight years, since we'd been together. I left her a box of greeting cards, a book I knew she wanted—I wrapped them up and left them, and notes here and there for her to find—and a we've-been-together-so-long gift: a twenty-five pound bag of fertilizer she'd been wanting me to pick up for her.

M: Do you ever have ambivalent feelings about being a lone lesbian in a heterosexual group—like I had about going, *before* going, to the gay Pride Parade with you today?

 I had all those feelings because I'm ignorant, because I'm not experienced being with gay groups. How do you feel as a lesbian in a heterosexual world? Driving back this afternoon you said the world is hostile every day because of the fact you're a lesbian.

ANN: It's what you're getting back—how people are treating you. Now I can choose how much that affects me. When I was younger I couldn't. I had only a vague feeling of not fitting in without knowing why. But then I'd always not fit in period. Ever.

M: Because you were raised as an adult, because you were tall, because you missed a lot of school—you never fit.

 You were 5'5" in fourth grade. We'd better say how tall you are now. Or people might think you're a giant.

ANN: (laughs) I'm 5'8". I just saw my first grade report card the other day. It put my reading level at fourth or fifth grade or something. And the comment from the teacher was: "Mindy has a wealth of experiences to share."

M: Right. In first grade you should have been pouring water into cups. Pulling toys away from other kids, instead of lecturing other kids.

ANN: Another comment was: "thrifty with school supplies."

M: But now you think it was sexuality that set you apart?

ANN: I had boyfriends that I adored. Nevermind they were gay—I didn't know it. I had a boyfriend. I went to the dances. I hadn't a clue about myself, yet I went to a gay bar and felt very comfortable, but I didn't question why. It was two or three years later before I figured out I was gay. My friends picked up on it before I did—so when I came nervously wringing my hands to tell them, they said, "Way to go Sherlock! Did you just figure that out?"

Like the Rockman says, "People see what they wanna see . . ." even to yourself. (she sings the song)

Bill took me to all those gay bars and I didn't even consider he was gay. He just said they were the best bars in town and I thought that was why we were going. Okay. Fine.

M: Why do you think you didn't—

ANN: I wasn't ready to face it—for whatever reason.

M: So you think it was really psychological—a wall—one you couldn't face?

ANN: It was for me. Most of the gay men I talk to recognize it at an earlier age. Women seem to recognize it at a later age.

M: How do you feel about heterosexual people? Do we seem alien to you in any way because your sexuality is different?

ANN: No.

M: I want to know how it feels from the other side. I

listened to Christian Coalition people on C-Span and they don't have a clue. They think there's something really weird about your sexuality and it scares them.

Today I watched the women couples—their very natural giving of affection—one in a male fashion, the other female—yet obviously natural, unconscious behavior. Yet this behavior is what scares the Christian Coalition people. Do you have any of those feelings about heterosexuals? Like Ted did. Ted found heterosexuality really creepy to think about.

ANN: No. I think part of my coming into adulthood now is recognizing that there have been times I have been attracted to men.

M: That helps you feel less that heterosexuals are alien to you. It's that continuum line graph you talked about before—with heterosexuals on one end and homosexuals on the other, and people scattered along the line. You could be here, you could be over there. It doesn't make a big difference.

ANN: Sure. I don't feel much alienness at all. Like my friends Gordon and Kay are a married couple. And I adore both of them. They have a great relationship. I encourage it. We joke. No. I don't feel uncomfortable at all. The people I feel uncomfortable with are either the ones I feel physically afraid of, or that dislike me for being a lesbian. I just try to tell them to get over it—and I stay away from them.

M: Do you know any of those people?

ANN: Not anymore. I don't put myself in their way.

M: This is a question I'm very interested in. I know about Elizabeth's faith—her constant prayer—her closeness to God. How does her faith affect you? What is your attitude toward it?

ANN: Hmmmmm—

M: You don't strike me as a particularly religious person.

ANN: No.

M: So you're living with this person who literally believes that God not only exists, but is involved in our lives constantly. How do you view her faith? Do you view it with some skepticism?

ANN: Admiration.

M: But you don't feel it?

ANN: No.

M: Does that mean you don't believe it?

ANN: I have a belief in a positive force—and an interconnectedness of the universe. But—no, I don't believe in—God on the throne.

But I do think we believe in the same basic belief. She has icons. I'm just happy with a great formless cloud. I believe there's a good energy that tries to put direction into our lives. If you want to call it God—great. That's more positive energy.

M: What about prayer? Elizabeth believes prayer makes things happen.

ANN: She calls it prayer. I call it positive energy.

M: Has her faith changed your life at all?

ANN: It's made it easier for me to have my beliefs. Previously I probably thought it was wrong to think the way I did—that it was pagan. I didn't dare tell anyone.

M: Because you didn't call it God?

ANN: Right. But Elizabeth said, "Whatever you want to call it—that's fine." And to see the realism of her faith. That people can be heroic and they can also be asses. You have to hope for the best—and plan for them to be an ass. Praise them when they do right so they keep on doing it, but expect them to do something bad, and try to mitigate it.

M: That's where Elizabeth's natural intellect and faith impressed me—she knows instinctually, or by grace I suppose she would say, that we don't all have to have the same religion or give it the same labels. She knows the force you believe in.

Now the Baba Walters' question.

ANN: Hah! The mighty oak! (laughs) By the way, it's Baba *Wawa*.

M: If you could change anything about your life, what would it be?

ANN: I'd have my mother be at peace.

M: Ah—so that's where your focus is now.

ANN: The other day—mother hasn't put two sentences together in two months—she beckoned me over to her and when I got close she looked up and said, "Help me. I've got a disease." (Ann has a sharp intake of breath and a long pause) And in spite of our love/hate relationship, that just twisted a knife in my guts—so I would like to see this end. For her to be at peace.

M: What did you do?

ANN: I said, "I know, Mom. There's nothing I can do about it. I'm very sorry. I'll just be here to help you as much as I can." I gave her a hug and I left.

M: Does she sometimes seem like she doesn't know what's happening?

ANN: Yeah. I went over for her birthday last week and gave her presents and a big hug and said "Happy Birthday," and she looked up and said, "Happy Birthday to you too."

M: You're lucky you have your cousin looking after her.

ANN: Damn lucky. He's a saint.

M: Do you sometimes wish your connection to God were more traditional like Elizabeth's? Elizabeth can pray for

God to take care of something—you've got this nebulous sixties', hippy-ish sort of thing—"ah, there's a force in the universe"—or it's New Age stuff now—(Ann laughs at me) Elizabeth's is a lot more useful, isn't it?

ANN: Joseph is her particular patron—her first to speak to—I don't know. I don't feel any real connection to the icon image of God, or Joseph, or Mary, or Jesus Christ.

M: You can't petition the force. You can't say, "Okay, God. Help me with my mother—what are you going to do here? This is a burden for me." That's a tremendous release. Of course people who don't feel it think it's something concocted for one's own comfort. But to people who believe, it's real.

ANN: I can do that—but to the universe. "Lord, give me the strength,"—and I will use words like Lord or Goddess, or whatever—to help me with imaging. In a Madeleine L'Engle sort of way. That there are forces of good and evil, and everyone has to join the fight on one side or the other—in the whole universe, right down to the atomic particle. So good and evil can be found in everything you look at, so that you tap into either. You can call upon either. People are either sappers: suck out your positive energy—or zappers: energize you.

M: I remember in a book I read a long time ago, a character believed you had to be careful whom you sat next to on a bus, that some people can suck out your energy just by sitting next to you.

ANN: Stay away from sappers!

(a long pause)

I'm always surprised when people remember my name. I'm nothing special. I just try to do right.

M: That was one of the first things you said to me when I met you. I want to know you long enough—until someday I hear you say, "I know I'm special."

(she bursts into laughter)

ANN: I'm just coming into adulthood. Before I was always responding to people—now I control relationships, at least contribute instead of just reacting.
M: That's a wonderful stage to be in.
ANN: I have strong women, and men, now to emulate.

We talk about Brenda, a constant member of the group Ann calls the "lesbian bunch," who is heterosexual.

M: I can't understand that.
ANN: I don't understand it either.
M: I need time with heterosexual girlfriends—just the climate of talking about guys—like my friend Mary who's always talking about what Kurt Russell movie is out, what guy movie star she thinks is hot. I just get a boot out of that—it's kind of—my world.
ANN: In our group Brenda can say that, and at least half of the group would be interested.
M: Which half?
ANN: I can appreciate a good-looking guy.
M: The attraction is there?
ANN: Sure. Sure. You look puzzled.
M: I am puzzled. It's a constant puzzlement. If the attraction is there—why were all your boyfriends gay guys? They were safe guys. You were never going to have the irresistible "we can't stop where this is heading" thing. That's where attraction leads—that happens to you with

women. You're attracted to guys but not to the extent that you've ever been caught in a situation where you couldn't turn back.

ANN: I've been on the brink a couple of times—but I have turned back.

M: What is the attraction?

ANN: Seventy percent women—thirty percent men.

M: That's your line graph again. The pull toward men is only 30% strength—so you can put your foot up and say "whoa"—70% and you're a goner.

   I still have a hard time dealing with bisexuality. I just can't conceive that it actually exists. Like the guys in the parade today with their bi-sexual sign saying "I'm 100% this and I'm 100% that." Gay and heterosexual. Who are they kidding? I don't believe it.

ANN: I feel a strong attraction for men—so I can understand it. If I'd found the right man, maybe I would have settled down with him. I don't know. I can admit to that possibility. But it's just more fun to— The gay community does not take bisexuality well—maybe a little better than the straight community, but not much. I think there's pressure within the community to decide whether you're one or the other.

M: Like, don't hang around here if you don't know who you are?

ANN: I can recognize that as "us" against "them." I can play into that in the gay community—and totally enjoy being—

M: Gay?

ANN: Being a lesbian.

M: But in actuality you believe people are on a continuum and we shouldn't make these big divisions.

ANN: Right.

M: So whatever you are today is okay?

ANN: Fine.

M: I heard on the radio this week the "Queer Players"—a San Diego group of young lesbians who put on plays and put out a newspaper with poetry.

ANN: I know them. They're the ones who did the "butch test" we talked about at the parade—I got 100%.

M: They were saying that one of the problems in the young lesbian community is that there is a great deal of pressure to act, look, *be* "butch," and they felt that was a shortcoming because the feminine ones are really looked down upon.

ANN: Lipstick lesbians. Big deal. Of course, I married one.

M: Yeah. Well. You're not going to marry a butch one.

ANN: Because of all the craziness in my life I find myself simplifying the tenets of my beliefs more and more, and keep coming down to the basic: if you're not hurting anyone else, do whatever you wanna do.

M: Also, these are young lesbians, so they're more radical. They're wanting to be OUT-OUT.

ANN: They have every right to be—they're coming to it at an earlier age and they're questioning it. That's great.

M: But they need more seasoned people like you to say, "Hey, the fems are the ones we fall in love with, so quit being so rough on them."

What is that button in your truck I liked—"I'm trying to find myself, if you see me, let me know"?

ANN: I think it's: "I'm trying to find myself, have you seen me anywhere?"

M: You say you're now coming into adulthood, which I find is like beginning to find an identity, not in a definitive sense, but at least being sure what you're thinking, and not easily influenced.

Did you find yourself, or weren't you trying to find yourself?

ANN: (laughs) Well, I bought that button ten years ago. I was trying to find myself—it's a project that never ends.

M: Adulthood for me has been the feeling of gaining some wisdom, or being able to see people for what they are, and not being rocked, or changed, by their behavior.

ANN: More confidence in being confrontational—as in "You are an idiot and I choose not to accept that in my life." I can do that. That's my choice.

9

A JOURNEY

AT FIRST I WAS AFRAID to write the book. I didn't know how to write it truthfully without causing possible harm to people in the book. For example, the three priests that flew down in Fred's plane from the Upper Peninsula of Michigan for gay vacations in Chicago or Palm Springs: if I mention the U.P. (not very populated) will their secret be out? ("Out"?) I finally decide that if I try too hard to disguise people I'll lose the power of truth, of accuracy. I decide to write the whole truth—changing only people's names—keeping the U.P., among other things. Now, looking back, two years later on these fears, the answer seems obvious; it didn't then when it caused me much anguish. For one thing people "see what they wanna see" and those whose eyes are fully open probably know their priests are gay.

I remember a recent article on actresses who were lesbians. Tallulah Bankhead, Barbara Stanwyck, but they're not harmed now. Present day lesbian actresses and comedians were not mentioned. Their careers would be harmed, perhaps destroyed. Are so many women actresses and comedians lesbians because they can play a role so well? I've wondered if so many of the female comedians are lesbians because it takes a lot of testosterone to do stand-up comedy. Ann and her friends know many of the lesbian comedians because they see them perform in clubs. (Roseanne is not a lesbian!) The secret—so dangerous—is kept. It shouldn't be dangerous. Did Montgomery Clift's being gay hurt his career? Rock Hudson was gay, and Raymond Burr. All those bedroom scenes in *McMillan and Wife* lose their sweetness knowing Rock Hudson was gay. Perry Mason doesn't kiss or get into bed with Della so those shows aren't damaged for me by knowing Raymond Burr was gay, but maybe they would have been for my mother who had a crush on Perry. People in or around show business know who's gay but a sense of honor, even in the media, keeps it fairly quiet. Rock Hudson movies are on TV about as often as John Wayne movies. He made a lot of movies. I watch them now—Rock always the lead male making love to the lead female, and think he was a much better actor than he was ever given credit for being.

I wonder if I will ever feel totally comfortable in the gay world. The first day John went to work for Ann she picked him up in the early morning in her truck. He didn't seem nervous. He was going to do a day's work pouring cement. She took him to a "cool" place for lunch where they had burgers and fries and people watched. That night while I interviewed Carol they played guitars and sang together. John, 14, was wearing his favorite T-shirt, Heckel and Jeckel, and his Greek fishing hat. When I came in from the backyard Ann was also wearing her Heckel and Jeckel shirt and her Greek fishing hat. They were prepared and entertained us. Later Ann told me she'd been extremely nervous in the truck in the morning, about what John would think of her. He put her at ease.

Yet I was very uncomfortable when Linda sat down outside and pulled Carol onto her lap and gave her a little kiss on the cheek. I looked nervously toward the house, hoping

John hadn't seen. I had to turn away from that small intimacy. I feel completely comfortable with Ann and Elizabeth—except occasionally when Ann throws her arm protectively around Liz's shoulders—it's the masculine movement of the gesture, the protectiveness, the "my woman" implication, and for a moment I feel discomfort, the "I don't belong here feeling." I'm Alice in Wonderland, Alice in a world where expectations are turned upside down. Things are not what they seem—as incongruous as playing croquet with birds as mallets. They are only being natural—why is it so unsettling to me? It's only its strangeness—it's the world topsy-turvy.

Over the early time I am writing the book occasionally the tolerant Tom and John become angry and suspicious of lesbians. It comes out in a mean comment. I realize they fear somehow I might become a lesbian by association. They think they are in danger of losing the mother they know. In December, 1994, Tom and John and I sit talking at the kitchen table. Will we ever feel comfortable in the homosexual world? Will we always feel a little freaked? Tom thinks so. I don't know. Ask me at the end of the book.

I see women whose beauty I admire, but I don't have any sexual feeling for them. I see men I don't know at all, one who passes me in the supermarket and some feature, the curve of a lip, makes my heart flutter. I love many women as sisters, but never one could be a lover. There are men I hate, yet still have sexual feelings toward. I am only attracted to the "other." I cannot fathom being attracted to the "same"—all those lesbian couples like matched sets of dolls—like a Star Trekian adventure in a mirror.

Sexual orientation is a complex mixture of hormones and

genetics, only partly understood. But it's not a "lifestyle" or a choice. Rats in laboratories have their sexual orientation changed by injection of hormones. Inject a female rat with testosterone and she runs around mounting females. Castrate a young male rat, depriving him of testosterone, and he behaves sexually like a female, presenting his rear end, tail up, to the males. Their brain structure changes to match their new hormones—the male brain having a different structure and size than the female brain in the area that determines sexual behavior.

All human embryos are female until the seventh week when certain gene and hormone switches determine some of the embryos will begin to turn into males. Human brains have different sized areas for sexual behavior that match their sexual orientation, and a July 1993 study, later repeated, showed a genetic link on the X chromosome for gay men. I already knew that from observing several families of gay friends. You could see the gay links through generations and cousins. Although the study was repeated for lesbians, the chromosome link for lesbians was not discovered. But I know it's there. In the families I know the homosexuality shows up in both the males and females. In Sally's family for instance (where the homosexuality is firmly in the closet) she has a lesbian first cousin and another first cousin has a gay son. Newt Gingrich's lesbian half-sister Candace announced in her autobiography that there is a gay male cousin as well.

Throughout nature there's homosexuality and through all cultures there is homosexuality in the same proportions. There is still a mystery to sexual orientation, but we get what we get and we can't change it. So we must accept it. Our sexual orientation has nothing to do with our human worth. Though it seems to have to do with our creativity.

Those wonderful male designers like Isaac Mizrahi, and those wonderful female comedians. We can't condemn people for their sexuality any more than we can condemn them for large ears or tiny feet. Neither religion, nor psychiatry, nor social stigma can change natural sexual orientation. They can only force it into hiding, into that dark closet. To force people to suppress their identity twists them and prevents their flowering—socially, sexually, creatively, or in whatever other part of themselves.

I think of Jordan standing on the porch crying out, "Hurry up—write the book. Please hurry. We need help." One cry alone is enough to write it. I don't want sweet Jordan afraid of getting beat up just walking on the street in Hillcrest some night. I don't want Jill afraid that her business will collapse and the 200 people she's employed for twenty-five years will lose their jobs. I don't want my friend Sally to remain nine years old because her mother and her sister want her in the closet. (Help! Child in the closet. Child in the closet.)

I want them to be safe. I want them to be loved for their unique beauties of character. If I feel uncomfortable seeing one woman put her arm around the shoulders of another in a protective way, well, that's my problem (created by our society). The gesture doesn't bother me if the women aren't lesbians, it shouldn't bother me if they are. I feel uncomfortable because the idea of lesbians is strange to me. I guess we have to ask their patience. They are loving enough, and have suffered enough, to have compassion for us.

The young are impatient and angry, but that's how the young have always been—that's how the world changes. Any group that's suffered being hated for their ethnicity, skin color, religion, or gender, ought to say: I won't hate any person for these reasons. The list includes Jews, blacks, women, Hispanics, Asians, white males—the group list goes on until it includes all people. The hatred begins to look pretty silly—intellectually—but we know how deadly it is. We need to do what Martin Luther King asked: judge every person on his character.

When John was eleven, he learned there were gay people. He said one day, "It's simple—there are four sexes." Or maybe more.

We can easily love people no matter what color they are—color is no different than the color of clothes. We can love people of different genders, men and women. Then we can love people of all genders.

At church I tell for the first time, a woman friend, that I am writing a book about lesbians.

"Sssshhh," she says sharply, snapping her head around to see who's near. "Don't say that word. Someone might hear you."

I laugh. "I don't care."

WOMAN: (in a low voice) Don't you know you'll be accused of being a lesbian?
M: (laughing) I don't care. I'm not worried.
WOMAN: A sympathizer then. They'll call you a sympathizer. Perhaps that's worse.

Later I tell Tom. "It will upset the Baptist cousins. I'll really be rocking the boat."

TOM: Mom, I'd be so proud. That's what I'd want to do if I could.

A year later I found out the woman is a closet lesbian. I

should have figured it out earlier. I'd seen with Jill also the fear of speaking the word "lesbian" where anyone might hear it. Straight people are not afraid of the word. Interestingly, about a year earlier when we first met this woman and gave her a ride to a concert, John asked me, "Is she a lesbian?"

M: Do you think so?
JOHN: Definitely.
M: I don't think so. She talked in the car about having sex with men.

Boy, was I naive. (See the "Fox in the Hen House" appendix.) And how many women do you know who bring up their sex experience in front of your fourteen-year-old son?

According to the theologian and writer Verna Dozier, Jesus came to teach us how to live—to show us the kingdom of heaven on earth. He expanded on the Commandments, explaining the full, interpretive meaning of each one. But he said nothing against homosexuals, although I believe he did speak of them.

I only use the four Gospels of the New Testament for instruction on how to live. I stay away from Leviticus where the oft quoted anti-gay rhetoric of the fundamentalist Christian comes from. In Leviticus, Numbers, and Deuteronomy, God, through Moses, lays down some harsh laws for the socially primitive people of that time. The killing of sons, daughters, wives, and husbands by communal stoning is required by God for a variety of offenses.

In Leviticus 20:9 the Lord orders death for anyone who "has cursed his father or his mother." In Leviticus 24:10-23 God orders death for those who curse, and disfigurement for anyone who causes a disfigurement: eye for eye, tooth for tooth.

A bride who cannot prove her virginity by a bloody sheet on the wedding night is to be stoned. "The men of her city shall stone her to death with stones . . . purge the evil from the midst of you." (Deuteronomy 22:13-21)

A rebellious son is to be stoned to death according to law. "Then his father and his mother shall take hold of him and bring him to the elders . . . and say, 'This our son is stubborn and rebellious, he will not obey our voice; he is a glutton and drunkard.' Then all the men of the city shall stone him to death with stones." (Deuteronomy 21:18-21)

And, "While the people of Israel were in the wilderness, they found a man gathering sticks on the sabbath day." They took him to Moses and Aaron because they weren't sure what the punishment was. "And the Lord said to Moses, 'The man shall be put to death; all the congregation shall stone him with stones . . .' and all the congregation brought him outside the camp, and stoned him to death with stones, as the Lord commanded Moses." (Numbers 15:32-36)

Well, you can see why I don't follow the laws of those books literally. No one does. Sexual laws are given in Leviticus 18. Incest is fully defined in verses 6-18. If a man's been with a woman, he cannot sleep with her daughter or any near kinswoman. He cannot take a woman if he's had her sister and she is still living. The other sins of the flesh that are forbidden to men (verses 19-23) are: to lie with your neighbor's wife, to lie with a male as if he is a woman, to lie with a beast, and to approach a woman during her menstrual uncleanness. For women it is forbidden only to give herself to a beast, "it is a perversion."

The proscription against lying with a male in this passage is for the heterosexual men who seemed to be "doing" everything and everyone and needing some rules as to what is natural and moral. (The sexual proscriptions are repeated in Leviticus chapter 20.)

Jesus makes no proscription against homosexuality in the New Testament.

Jesus in his teaching, according to the notes in my *Harper Study Bible* (1985), freed the law from false interpretations and its "human accretions." (Which picked up again in the later books after Jesus' death.)

He worked on the sabbath, explaining to those who criticized, that he was telling them something greater than the law of the temple: "if you had known what this means, 'I desire mercy, and not sacrifice,' (Hosea 6:6; Matt. 9:13) you would not have condemned the guiltless. . . . What man of you, if he has one sheep and it falls into a pit on the sabbath, will not lay hold of it and lift it out? Of how much more value is a man than a sheep? So it is lawful to do good on the sabbath." And the disciples were allowed to pick grain on the sabbath because they were hungry. (Matthew 12:1-12)

He explained the Sixth Commandment is more than "You shall not kill." It is also you should not get angry with your brother, or insult him. Whoever does shall be liable to the fire of hell. (Matt. 5:21-24) He explained the Seventh Commandment, "You shall not commit adultery," means more than actual adultery, it means lusting in your heart as well. (It means buying and reading pornography.) (Matt. 5:27-30)

Then he talks about marriage saying in the days of Moses divorce was allowed with a certificate, "but I say to you that every man who divorces his wife, except on the ground of unchastity, makes her an adulteress." (Matt. 5:31-32)

He changes the "eye for an eye" of Moses's time to "if anyone strikes you on the right cheek, turn to him the other also." (Matt. 5:38-42) The Old Testament "Love your neighbor and hate your enemy" Jesus changes to "love your enemies and pray for those who persecute you, so you may be sons of your Father who is in heaven." He says, "For if you love (only) those who love you, what reward have you (earned)?", i.e., what have you done that was special? (Matt. 5:43-48)

So where does Jesus perhaps refer to homosexuality? In Matthew chapter 19, the Pharisees, a particularly strict and influential Jewish sect who believed in an exact Law and were hostile to Jesus, questioned him on marriage laws to test him on Mosaic Law. They asked him, "Is it lawful to divorce one's wife for any cause?"

Jesus said, "Have you not read that he who made them from the beginning made them male and female, and said, 'For this reason a man shall leave his father and mother and be joined to his wife, and the two shall become one flesh'? So they are no longer two but one flesh. What therefore God has joined together, let not men put asunder . . . For your hardness of heart Moses allowed you to divorce your wives, but from the beginning it was not so (not God's original intention). And I say to you: whoever divorces his wife, except for unchastity, and marries another, commits adultery."

The disciples then asked if it wouldn't be smarter then not to marry. Jesus said, "Not all men can receive this saying, but only those to whom it is given. For there are those men who are not meant to marry because they are born that way; others because men made them that way; and others do not marry for the sake of the kingdom of heaven. Let him who can accept this teaching do so." (*Good News Bible* translation) (Matt. 19:3-12)

Some men cannot marry because they've been injured by men (perhaps in war). Some do not marry because they go to serve the kingdom of God (the Church). Who are the ones *born* not to marry? I know many men who are "born not to marry." They are homosexuals. And when they are forced to marry by society, their families, or their church, the natural, God created, male-female relationship Jesus spoke of does not exist, and misery ensues.

Jesus clearly says, some men are born not to marry. They will not therefore be able to keep the marriage as it was intended and thus should not marry. Only those men "who can accept" the marriage teaching, those who are born to marry, should marry.

He does not say those people born not meant to marry should be hated for how they were born.

In fact, Jesus taught only love. When a Pharisee lawyer asked him a question to trick him, "Teacher, which is the great commandment in the law?" Jesus answered, "You shall love the Lord your God with all your heart, and with all your soul, and with all your mind. This is the great and the first commandment. And a second is like it: You shall love your neighbor as yourself. On these two commandments depend all the law and the prophets." (Matt. 22:34-40)

Jesus said, "Woe to you" the Pharisees and all who tithe and follow the law but neglect "the weightier matters of the law: justice, mercy, and faith . . . you also outwardly appear righteous to men, but within you are full of hypocrisy and iniquity." (Matt. 23: 23-28) In John he says, "I do not come to judge the world but to save the world." (John 12:47) He said, "Judge not, that you be not judged. For with the judgment you pronounce you will be judged, and the measure you give will be the measure you get." (Matt. 7:1-2) "A new commandment I give to you, that you love one another; even as I have loved you, that you also love one another." (John 13:34-35)

I think all people who call themselves Christians have to follow these teachings of Christ: to love and not to judge. Thomas Merton, the writer monk, wrote "the life of a Christian has meaning and value only to the extent that it conforms to the life of Jesus." (160, *The Sign of Jonas,* Harcourt Brace)

Last summer I watched reruns of the old television series *Remington Steele*. It was a series I hadn't been interested in when it originally played. But now I was fascinated with the stylish character of Remington and the great style and physical comedic talent the actor Pierce Brosnan brought to the role. In one episode Remington's colleagues, Laura and Mildred, ask why a certain character is not married. Remington hesitates momentarily, strokes his chin in a thoughtful way, and says, "He's not the marrying kind." The two women nodded, "Oh." And the story went on without further mention. That old phrase reminds me not only of what Jesus said, that some men are not the marrying kind, but also of a gentler age.

When I was growing up in a small farmtown in Michigan the gay people in our town were accepted without much talk about it. One man, Russell, was particularly well-liked. He lived near us with his mother in a big, old farm house where he catered parties. All the women loved him—he dropped by for a bit of gossip, and he always remembered their birthdays with large, decorated, homemade layer cakes to-die-for. Not many farmer husbands had that kind of romance in them. And the men liked him too. They wouldn't go deer hunting without Russell. Russell could not only play poker with the men, his presence meant they had great food to eat. Russell loved to cook, so they had all the benefits of the male week at the cabin without the traditional bad food.

People have a true nature. Lilies of the field look pretty. Birds fly. Gay people when they are allowed to flower are more wonderful than the lilies and birds in the variety of their talents that comes from the blending of the genders. I think some recent films have helped people see gay men as people. *Four Weddings and a Funeral* had a gay male couple that you didn't realize were a couple until the funeral at the end. They're treasured in the group of friends for their very different personalities. Gareth—so free-spirited and flamboyant in his love of life. Matthew—good, fastidious, quiet, dependable, a listener, thoughtful and caring. Their sexual orientation had nothing to do with their interest to the film or to the group. Not until Matthew's speech at Gareth's funeral do you realize their coupleness and the deep love and faithfulness their "marriage" had had. The love Matthew expresses in the funeral speech is the love every marriage should ideally have, and few do. That's why there are so many tears in the audience at this part of the film.

Michael J. Fox's new sitcom *Spin City* has a gay character that you do not recognize as gay because he has no gay-stereotype behavior. He's a strong, quiet, good-looking black man. Not until episode three did I know the black man was gay. This was when Fox's character, having trouble with his live-in girlfriend, asked the man if there were fewer problems living with a man. The strong black man, arms folded, with a slight smile said, "No. It's the same."

The interesting thing was that in episode two, Michael J. Fox's character, who is Deputy Mayor of New York, was looking around the office for a gay guy to present to the press because there was a rumor the Mayor's office was not tolerant of homosexuals. Fox's character chose the speech writer, a nervous young white man, to pretend he was gay. This is good writing. The black character was there all the time, and everyone, except the viewing audience, knew he was gay but didn't choose him. The next week we find out the black guy is gay—and accepted—as if, because it doesn't, that has nothing to do with his job. I'm reminded of Stella's saying, "It's what we are—but that's not all we are." (In fact the new Fox show has too much heterosexual sex for me. I've seen the first three episodes and all three had Fox getting naked and getting into bed with his girlfriend. I find Fox getting naked for sex awkward. Naked he looks about twelve to me.)

The character Ricky in the television series *My So-Called Life* helped people understand young gay men. Ricky was tender, sweet, caring—liking eyeliner and stylish clothes—everyone's, both boys and girls, best friend, but preferring the makeup sessions and gossipy girltalk of the girls' restroom to the possible danger of the boys' restroom. When Ricky was kicked out of his house by his father at Christmas for being gay and wandered the streets in shame, I think every heart had to be touched by his pain and the unfairness that he was hated by his father for the very gentle qualities we had come to love him for. The actor Wilson Cruz who played Ricky based his performance on his similar experience of being kicked out by an angry father. They were later reconciled but the experience of a young man being kicked out of his home for being gay is not unusual.

Suicide is the third leading cause of death for young people. Up to 40% of gay youth attempt or seriously contemplate suicide. Thirty percent of gay and lesbian young people have attempted suicide. Gay youth comprise 30% of all youth who do commit suicide—and many more may be gay, but die taking their dark and unmentionable (in their home) secret with them into death. (From Gary Remafedi, M.D., MPH, *Death by Denial: Studies of Suicide in Gay and*

Lesbian Teenagers, Alyson: 1994; and other Remafedi research quoted in journals.)

These statistics are chilling to me. Parents are killing their children by refusing to love them as they are. Young men are terrified of not being a "man" as defined by their father or the male culture. They feel they must prove their manhood. But by what standard? In Randy Shilts' *Conduct Unbecoming* many young men chose military careers, or chose to fight in Vietnam, to prove they were men: Join the Army, Be All You Can Be. A few good men.

I am writing down the ideas I wrote in my journal from December 1994 on, but I'm writing in October 1996, so I add ideas from the present too (like the Michael J. Fox show). Last Friday night (9/27) I saw a story on *20/20* of a teenage girl whose mother sent her to a school in Utah for "problem children" to be cured of her "homosexual tendencies." She was shown what she considered pornographic pictures of women in sexual acts and made to sniff ammonia—"aversion therapy" she said. She said she was horrified. The school was prisonlike—named Ravenhill—Raven-something. The dark image of the raven remains in my mind. Scary stuff—the ominous black bird, ever present, with the message "Nevermore." The girl managed to run away when she was sent home for a medical appointment. For a while she was a runaway on the streets until she made her way to San Francisco where she received help. She was taken in by a lesbian foster parents family until she became independent. She now has an apartment and works as a journalist. She hopes for reconciliation with her mother. But the mother is adamant. Nevermore.

Rob Eichberg (Rob Eichberg, Ph.D., *Coming Out: An Act of Love,* New York: Dutton/Penguin, 1990) believed that coming out, acknowledging one's gayness, was necessary for a person to be happy, to be whole. A clinical psychologist, he ran weekend seminars for gay men to discover how they felt about themselves. Some "came out" to themselves for the first time, some to others, in the group, for the first time. They wrote letters to people in their families telling them for the first time that they were gay. Some of the letters were never sent, that was not required, the object was to express their feelings. Many of these letters are in Eichberg's book. One begins "This is the letter you didn't want to get. . . ." The letters are filled with suffering, forgiveness, and love. They are from grown men who want their parents' love. Many apologize for illegible sections: because "I wrote it through my tears." Letters tell of isolation: "I thought I was the only person in the world like 'that'"—and yet are generous: "You did the very best you could."

Letters tell of brutal rejection.

> The fact you didn't answer my last letter, the fact you asked me no longer to call your house . . . the fact you made a reference to me having AIDS . . . (as if it were wished upon me . . .) Well . . . I have been diagnosed with exposure to the AIDS virus . . . You are bigger than the hate and disappointment you feel . . . I think I deserve the same love and acceptance as the rest of your children . . . I love you with all of my heart. (230)

And abandonment.

> Birthdays are spent with friends . . . My bosses taking me shopping for clothes, shoes, and car tires. . . . Any special occasion . . . is spent with strangers. Strangers who show more love than you can even imagine. (236)

Another letter.

> I came to hate you for abandoning me. . . . Now I realize you were only victims of your own parents and thus carried into my life all your own values and judgments. . . . When I came out to both of you as being gay, all I was looking for was acceptance of what I was, since I could not love myself. All I got was silence, and it hurt so bad; I felt so alone. I felt so abandoned again and unloved . . . and yet now I realize that you were only doing the best you could, coming from where you came and knowing what you knew at that time. . . . I knew I had been infected with the AIDS virus as early as September 1985. . . . I have felt so guilty . . . since I'm a doctor. . . . When I found out, I wanted so much to have you hold me like you did when I was sick as a child. (238-9)

Many letters mention gay siblings.

> [to a dead father] you were ashamed of me. . . . It hurts me. . . . I do not blame you. . . . At the moment your relationship to me colors every relationship I have had and may ever have. . . . [You] lavished your affection on Becky. I think this is ironic that the one you could show love to is also gay. (216)

What affected me most in the book was the brutal treatment of (adult) gay children by parents. Typical responses to a son telling his parents he is gay were: "How could you do this to us?" "I don't want to hear about it, it's just a phase." And, "Don't tell your father, it would kill him." (136)

I think when people know that being gay is genetic the

child could reply, "No, how could you do this to me?" Just to let the parent know how it feels to be blamed for the way you are born. (Although gay people are as happy being gay as heterosexual people are being heterosexual. They're just unhappy being hated for it.)

Think of persecuting your child for his brown eyes or his blue eyes. One section of Eichberg's book shows advertisements by The Lesbian and Gay Public Awareness Project to end homophobia. One ad says: "Are you abusing your child without knowing it?" It tells of a young man who committed suicide because he was gay. He'd heard his parents say they hate gays, God hates gays. The ad says: "No one chooses his sexual identity. If you are teaching your child to hate homosexual people, you might be teaching them to hate themselves." (190)

Eichberg says that coming out is what will bring equality for gay people. When people see how many gay people there are, how many they know, then people will not fear them. He says people fear gay people will damage the values they hold dear. "I am always struck by the strong belief held by many people that homosexuality can or will destroy families. Families are strengthened when love and understanding is furthered. . . . Lesbians and gay men do not want to destroy their families, rather they want to be included in them." He quotes from the Lesbian and Gay Public Awareness Project: "It is homophobia that destroys families, not homosexuality." (184)

Parents should not dislike a child for being gay—gay is their birthright from one of the parents. Parents can only ask, or demand, a child live a lie—pretend he is heterosexual, pretend she is not a lesbian. That makes the parent feel better but destroys the child. Children, to become adult, to become happy, must reject abusive parents so they can be themselves, so they can love themselves, and find those people who will love them for themselves.

I think of the famous, very anti-homosexual political activist Phyllis Schlafly. When it came out that her son is homosexual, she refused to discuss it, but continued her political campaigning against gays.

In *The Day of the Scorpion,* book two of the Raj Quartet about the British rule in India, Paul Scott writes about the psychology of imperialism, the ruler and the ruled. There is what he calls "a situation"—the ruling class person always has contempt for the ruled person. What the Indian, Hari Kumar, who was raised in England and falsely imprisoned in India, figures out is this: the "situation"—one man's contempt for another—can only take place if both men are participating in it.

Thus if parents (or friends) abuse a child (adult child), then that child must leave the parents. This is hard to do because all people, at any age, want their parents' love.

Eichberg wrote about living powerfully and dealing with bigots.

> I am not saying that in order to function powerfully you have to love a bigot—it's much more complex than that. When you are functioning powerfully you will love yourself even when confronted by a bigot. Likewise, you will be aware that the bigot is expressing an aspect of yourself—of each of us—that is scared, defensive, ignorant, self-righteous, and petty. If you let yourself observe a bigot, you will be able to see the child and adolescent that was raised with the beliefs now being expressed. You will see a person who most likely is not very happy or satisfied with his or her own life, and is taking this out on others. You will have a

> full range of feelings toward this bigot, including compassion and love. This will open a context large enough to allow the bigot to change if he or she so desires. (136)

Amazing advice for anyone dealing with any kind of bigot. (Also, it's very Christ-like.) Eichberg says if you are in a depressed mode and shrink away, then the bigot gets what he wants. If you return his aggression, you become a mirror of him, as rude as the bigot you oppose.

One of the letters, gay man to parents, quoted above says "now I realize you were only doing the best you could, coming from where you came and knowing what you knew at that time. . . ." Now we should all know more. Yet just this week (October '96) the local movie critic again referred to the film *Thelma and Louise* as implicitly lesbian. No. No. No. In the story Thelma and Louise are two heterosexual women. Yes, they took a road trip together and became stronger, but they didn't "become" lesbians.

Personality growth has nothing to do with sexual orientation. No matter how long they drove in that car they are still heterosexual women at the end. This critic's attitude is the old Amazonian myth bubbling up again: if the women are strong, and the women stand up to abusive men, then they are a threat; and they aren't "women"—they're lesbians. It's the ancient male fear of women banding together and having strength. The threat to the patriarchy.

Huck and Jim go down the Mississippi on a raft together. No one (in her right mind) says "Oh. They must be gay." Male bonding stories are a classic American literary genre. In film they're "buddy movies." In *Lethal Weapon* one wouldn't think of calling Mel Gibson and Danny Glover gay because they're riding around together in a car or stuck in tight places together. Women can have the "sisterhood"—it doesn't *make* anyone lesbian (although one can be a lesbian).

Rob Eichberg's book was published in 1990. In the Acknowledgments at the beginning of his book he says he has been "sustained by the memory" of his close friends who died of AIDS. (xiii) I turn the page and count forty names. And he says there are "unfortunately, many, many more."

I learned of Rob Eichberg for the first time on August 14, 1995. I saw his obituary in the morning newspaper. He died of "complications from AIDS." He was fifty.

FEBRUARY 2, 1995

This morning I saw my across-the-street neighbor, Leo, in his yard. I was walking on the sidewalk in front of his house, which is next to Ted's old house. I had often spoken to him but he had always turned away without response. I had given up. But I was close to him this morning, on his side of the street, not on mine, so I thought I'd try again to be friendly. I was smiling, feeling happy. Then I came closer and saw Leo scowling as he put out his trash, and I remembered that Ted said Leo used to shoot a gun into Ted's backyard, pretending he was shooting at Ted's little dog. When Ted ran out to the yard, Leo would shout, "Faggot."

I no longer felt happy. Leo turned his head away from me and walked back up his drive. He made an ugly sound, clearing his throat, and spit into the grass. I've been told this man is a psychology professor at the university.

FEBRUARY 25, 1995

This Saturday morning I watched the *20/20* Barbara

Walters' interview with Olympic diving champion Greg Louganis. John recorded it for me because I was too tired to stay awake last night. I wept watching it. This young man, so beautiful of mind, heart, body, talent, had suffered so much—had been abused instead of loved, and thought he deserved abuse because he was unlovable. Part of the abuse when he was in elementary school was because of his brown skin color. Part of it, when he was older, was because he was gay. He said, "I always knew I was different, but I didn't know why." These were Ted's very words. And so many others'.

BARBARA: (talking about the 1976 Olympics) You came to terms with something else (your sexuality) in your life?
GREG: I don't think I came to terms with my sexuality, my sexual orientation. But I was understanding what it was.
BARBARA: You realized you were a homosexual.
GREG: Right.
BARBARA: And that you'd known this somehow or other since you were a very little boy.
GREG: Since I was a little boy—yeah—I knew I was different, and I didn't understand what that difference was.
BARBARA: Did the other people on the team know you were gay?
GREG: I didn't try and hide it—you know, I didn't try to have any false life or anything like that—but, I mean on some of the trips it was really hard.
BARBARA: Did they shun you?
GREG: Yeah. Nobody would room with me. I mean I was lucky to find one person on the team that would room with me.
BARBARA: But it wasn't publicly known.
GREG: It wasn't publicly known. No.

Greg, like many people who believe they are unlovable, had a long relationship with a person who abused him.

Fear of homosexuality has to be carefully taught. One evening in 1989 I sat in a classroom at Wangenheim Junior High School in San Diego and listened to the district sex education teacher, Roger, explain what would be taught to our eighth grade boys. There were about six fathers, one other mother, and me in the boys' group. Things were going well until one father spoke out loudly.

FATHER: You aren't going to talk about homosexuals are you? I don't want you saying it's okay.

(he looked around proudly for approval)

I don't want my boy becoming a fairy.
M: I think people are born with their sexuality—I think it's all right to say that—to try and dispel fear and cruelty toward them.
FATHER: (on his feet, angry, red-faced, pointing his finger in my face) I don't want my kid to hear nuttin'. The Bible says (blah . . . blah . . . blah . . .) it's a SIN (blah . . . blah . . .) I don't want my kid to hear nothin' about FAGGOTS.

(Now all the other parents join him in shouting. At me. At Roger.)

ROGER: It's OK. We don't mention homosexuality. That's for you to discuss at home.

I was really downhearted. Discuss at home. Like evolution. For some kids the only way they'll ever overcome their backgrounds, have any enlightenment in any field, is school. They can't get it until college. And most won't go to college and many who do won't learn understanding of homosexuality. One of the teachers at John's high school warned me about what to prepare John for at UCLA.

He said, "I graduated from UCLA. There's all sorts of evil stuff up there. Satanic cults. I saw it myself in peoples' homes. And you won't believe it, but the homosexuals actually have clubs. Right on Hollywood Boulevard. They come out of these clubs and drag you right in."

Satanic cults and homosexual clubs were the same in his mind. Perversions from decent behavior—clubs young people were enticed to join. When I left my small western Michigan town in the sixties to go away to the University of Michigan, my uncles were worried. They warned me about the communist professors that were there.

In schools today the fear of the Christian Right is that if the "word" (homosexual) is spoken, their children will choose it. So the word goes unspoken and young people who know they are "different" do not know what that difference is. Or they've been told it's hateful and a sin to be what they are. And they hate themselves. And some hate themselves enough to take their lives.

I think of the disturbing stories of ruined lives in Randy Shilts' book *Conduct Unbecoming*. Barbara Baum and other young women in the military imprisoned and careers ruined on suspicion of lesbianism, or for being friendly with a "suspected" lesbian. I was touched by Jim Dressel's story, perhaps because he was from western Michigan, my home, and I felt I knew the people who destroyed his career and life. He was from Holland, a city of Dutch heritage and religion, the Christian Reformed Church, a Calvinist Fundamentalist religion. He was a Vietnam war hero who flew more than

250 combat missions and after the war served in the Michigan Air National Guard. He knew he was "different" and he knew that was unacceptable. So he decided to not act on his sexuality and devote his life to the political career he wanted. He was elected as a Republican Representative to the Michigan legislature and had served for four years when he was asked to be a co-sponsor of a gay civil rights bill.

He was good looking, forty, and a bachelor, and people started to talk that he might be gay. That was unacceptable in his county. In the 1984 election in his constituency people started printing the slogan Anita Bryant had popularized in Florida in the late seventies: "Homosexuals do not reproduce, they recruit, and as they recruit, they corrupt." He lost the election. At the Air National Guard he was shunned by the other pilots. They were afraid people would think they were gay if they spoke with him. He had to resign. He lost everything he loved in his life.

Then there was Pete Randell. A poor boy from South Carolina he joined the Army because he couldn't afford college. He'd been told at home that homosexuals were evil, and he saw them brutally abused in the Army. He'd felt attracted to men, but didn't think of himself as a homosexual. He was very good looking and hardworking and he rose quickly to distinction as a member of the elite Old Guard serving in Washington, D.C., at the Tomb of the Unknown Soldier and at the White House. After the Army he got a job as a staffer at the Nixon White House. He was the one who actually typed the list of Nixon's critics that became known as the famous "Enemies List." He saw a lot of gays on the White House staff and a lot of gay activity was known to go on in the small offices. Most of the gays were married, for cover to get their security clearances and for their high level social obligations. Pete married too, and had two children. He'd now had a few sexual experiences with men, but forgot them right afterwards. He still didn't consider himself a homosexual. He was concerned about his career and serving the administration. By 1984 he was Executive Director of the Air Force Board for Military Corrections. He had an impressive list of awards and his own staff of twenty at the Pentagon and traveled the country to lecture at Air Force bases. He was thirty-eight and he'd begun to wonder about the gay "community" he'd heard existed. He'd heard about a gay bar in Washington, D.C., and finally went there. He expected to see bizarre and perverted people, but he saw normal people, happy, laughing and socializing in a normal way. He discovered the high level gay Republicans and the high level military gays in D.C. He discovered that these were decent people. What his parents had taught him was wrong—a lie. He decided to separate from his wife. When he told her he was gay, she asked for a divorce. She told his parents who disowned him (his father said, "You ain't nothing but a goddamn queer faggot") and she told the Pentagon. He lost his security clearance and thus his job. He was offered a job as a typist in his own division—the only job he could hold without a security clearance. He resigned, which was what the Air Force wanted. He lost everything, and his own children wouldn't speak to him.

See the Time Line appendix at the end of the book for how hatred and fear of gays began in the 1950s with the McCarthy hearings and was fanned for forty years by that most famous gay, J. Edgar Hoover, Director of the FBI. It burst into flame in the late '70s when orange juice spokeswoman Anita Bryant set out to overturn a gay civil rights bill in Dade County, Florida, and when Ronald Reagan in the 1980 presidential campaign cleverly wed the Republican party to the southern Religious Right Fundamentalists to win the vote in the South.

February 1995

There's an article in the newspaper about a very tough little girl basketball player whom John used to play rec center basketball with. Now a girls basketball star she says she liked playing on boys' teams better. Boys are more dedicated, they play harder, she said. "I just wanted to be one of them."

I thought of Jill, and Linda, wanting to be boys, playing the rough boys games as little girls, and Sally who dressed like a boy.

On Saturday (10/26/96) I went out to the ocean. We'd had a storm and the path from the cliffs down to the beach was cordoned off with "Beach Closed—DANGER" signs. Four little boys—how old could they be, eight? ten? they looked little—were in the water in wetsuits and with boogie boards, struggling helplessly against the strong currents. Testosterone, I thought. The boys insist on believing they're invincible, challenging even the sea. They take terrible risks. They thrive on it. Little girls are not innerly compelled to go down on cold days and jump into stormy seas.

I remembered Ann talking about gay marriages. "The guys have trouble. Lots of wandering, looking for new partners."

I looked surprised. She smiled.

"Imagine it," she said, "every relationship has two sets of testosterone."

February 1995

I'm in the bookstore at the local mall. I don't see a clerk

anywhere. I call out and am answered by a deep male voice. A twentyish person comes toward me—slim, dressed as a girl, skirt, mesh top, makeup, beads—I strain to look closely—definitely a beard shadow. I'm confused. I look into her eyes—definitely a male. Then I hear a high pitched voice, and a tiny, bald, fortyish man comes wiggling up to help. His hands are tossing in the air and he's talking effusively. Definitely gay.

They are who they are. They can't feign the mannerisms or the wiggle which are as much a part of their genetic makeup as a heterosexual girl's slight sway of the hips in her walk. A man I know, Harry, (who is in the closet, he thinks) cannot, no matter how he tries, hide that slight sway in his walk. He tries to control the hands that want to wave his cigarette around. The hands tremble as he holds them still. I see it in other gay men who think they are in the closet. The nervous demeanor, ill at ease, glancing around. Suspicious. The hands shaking under the strain.

How can people believe that a man's being gay had anything to do with his relationship to his mother and father? The mother was smothering, the father was absent, or the father was brutal, or the father was weak. Notice we don't have all those theories about lesbians? They are ignored as usual.

I think about family relationships. Ann loved her father, so did I. Our mothers are problematic: critical, cold. Ann's a lesbian, I'm not. It means nothing. We only loved our fathers more because they allowed love whereas our mothers did not.

Ted adores his mother and she adores him. She flew to the U.P. (Upper Peninsula Michigan) last Christmas to spend two weeks with Ted and Fred. Harry on the other hand hated his vicious and manipulative mother and loved his weak and foolish father. Ted and Harry are both gay.

Elizabeth loves and admires her mother and loves and admires her father. Jill loves both her parents.

Family relationships have no causal relationship to homosexuality, but they are an interesting subject. Lesbian daughters have wonderful relationships with fathers — they're perfect companionable, noncompetitive sons; they share love of cars, sports, Harleys, ranches and trucks, yet they're still warm and understanding daughters to their mothers. And I watch Ted and his mom, giggling, gossiping, and cooking together in the kitchen — yet he's still a strong and protective man as a son.

FEBRUARY 1995

John and I are talking about gay people's fears, since the genetic studies of homosexuality were published, of being genetically wiped out.

JOHN: But wouldn't that be good? Don't they want to be heterosexual?
M: No. They don't. They like the world through their eyes. The same as you like being a heterosexual man, or I don't want women wiped out. We like our own nature. They're only unhappy about being hated.

I'm thinking about my Chinese cooking teacher in Tokyo, Nancy Chi Ma. She used to cook with Danny Kaye. When he came to Tokyo she would close her restaurant and she and Danny would cook together for friends. She said, "I learned something from him. He was always running around, to this pot and that pot, then he'd put his head over my shoulder and watch what I was doing and say, 'Yes,

Nancy, but did you put the *love* in?'"

I think about this book I'm writing and hope I put the love in.

MARCH 1995

Newt Gingrich (conservative Republican Speaker of the House) has a lesbian half-sister. She's photographed with her famous brother; she's in Washington to support gay civil rights. Her hair is shorn in a stepped boy-cut, like Sally's. She works for the United Parcel Service (it's a cliché that lesbians like jobs with uniforms) and had to rush home from Washington, D.C., for her rugby game.

Her mother makes a statement: "We wish Candace could be . . . well . . . more *natural*."

Hello. She *is* being natural—this is her nature.

What her mother wishes is that she would conform to some norm of feminine dress and behavior. For Candace that would be unnatural.

MAY 1995

I am constantly surprised by gay people's lack of awareness of gay issues and lack of understanding of gay attractions such as butch/fem. When Ann was at the gay Pride Parade in 1993 the day after the announcement of the gay gene (a discovery Ann and I naively thought would immediately change the world) she asked a gay friend, "Did you thank your mother for your genes?"

She said he looked with surprise down at his jeans. No one was talking about the study. And they are completely surprised by who is attracted to whom and who is not. I found most gay people don't think about their sexuality.

They are just living their lives. Their major interests are elsewhere. For Ann it's the environment. For Elizabeth it's prayer and her charity work. For Ruth Ann it's helping people solve their problems. For Ted it was creative projects, of any kind, and all the sports he did. Sexuality is not a consuming life "style." It's just a part of who they are.

MAY 1995

I'm getting ready to go out and I ask John what to wear.

M: How does this look?

He looks at me with exasperation as he rushes out.

JOHN: I don't know. If I were gay I'd know, but I'm not.

I'm reading Dorothy West's new novel *The Wedding*. Generations of blacks who think constantly in terms of color, of black and white and shades in between. The mixed race black family's granddaughter was going to marry a white man and they wanted her to marry a black man. Generations of color consciousness and the pressure made her confused as to what she should do. At the end "the scales had fallen from her eyes . . . color was a false distinction, love was not" and her white grandmother finally took a black grandchild in her arms.

So it should be for any other inherited trait. Including gender, the four or more that exist. We shouldn't love our black children more than our white children, or our boy children more than our girl children, or our straight children more than our gay children. It is so painful to think of a child rejected.

August 1995

Tom and I go to see the film *Unzipped* about the designer Isaac Mizrahi. It's Isaac working and talking with friends, about the fashion business, about his favorite films. It was fun to be with him. He's so alive, so creative, witty, perceptive, and warm, and sensitive, and fun.

You realize no heterosexual man could be this person—you love who he is—his creativity is a result of his "orientation." (Could anyone but Oscar Wilde have written the wildly witty and obtuse *The Importance of Being Earnest?*)

Isaac's mother loved him and his creativity from the time he was a little boy. "He made these clothes for a wedding. The whole town was talking. They were so beautiful. He made me a straight jacket—I wore it on all the holy holidays. I was so proud. I said, 'My Isaac made this.'"

She is so proud of him, always saying things like "No one could do that but Isaac"—and she's right. And maybe Isaac is so happy and successful because his parent loved him so dearly, and let him be himself, and let him follow his talent. I wish every parent of a gay child would see this film. I wish every parent of every child would see this film.

I watch the comedy channel and see the classic gay jokes. "I hope your daughter plays softball." "I'm gay, I'm Catholic, ergo, I'm a priest, right?"

In October '96 I hear Episcopal Bishop Spong on television asked about gay priests. He says by centuries of required celibacy the Catholic Church has created the world's largest closet. Young gay men become priests because they love God and want to serve the church. They never intend to become bad priests, or do anything wrong. Yet maybe some dedicate themselves to loving God because they are not allowed to express their human love. And maybe some join the Church because they see nowhere else to go.

One can learn a lot about people from literature. Go with the author right into their minds and motivation. Right now (October '96) I'm reading Paul Scott's *Raj Quartet*—four books published in the early '70s about the British rule (raj) in India, particularly during WWII. You can get the film of the story, *The Jewel in the Crown*, at the library as well as the video store, and it's beautifully done. I think it's the best film I've ever seen. But you can still read the books—the depth of character development and motives, and analysis of colonialism in the book is fascinating in its richness. I mention these books here because of the gay characters. One, the Russian Count Bronowsky, is in his seventies and has dedicated his life to politically educating and serving an Indian ruler of one of the Provinces. When he was young he realized he was homosexual, but he also realized he was attracted only to heterosexual men who would never be interested in him. So, he put his sexuality aside and dedicated his life to service. Another homosexual character is the most chilling villain ever created. He's a man one is so instinctively repulsed by that I feel uncomfortable when other characters have to sit down at a table and eat a meal with him. The man, you discover, is a closet homosexual. Scott describes him as working outward from "the hollow center of his self-invented personality." He has the need to manipulate and control the people around him and he needs to keep, by manipulation, someone who hates him close to him, so he can watch his effect on a person, so he can see the hate he generates. I have never seen a character come off the written page (or in the film) as so genuinely evil.

His cruelty and need to control has more than one source

(e.g., class envy), but the driving one is his repressed sexual identity. I know two real, in-the-closet, gay men like this. Vicious and manipulative. Their pleasure comes from crushing whatever people they can—particularly for some reason, the most innocent—maybe the innocents are their victims only because they make easy prey, they don't expect evil. I've also seen them target people they envy or desire, sometimes at enormous risk of exposure. Paul Scott talks about this risk taking as a "death wish" and compares the pleasure feeling the destroyer gets to the one inveterate hunters have as they look into the animal's eyes just before they squeeze the trigger.

While most homosexual and lesbian people are gentle and loving, there are these few who are dangerous, angry because they are not beloved by society and twisted from thwarted desire and the dark, shameful confines of the closet. Not men by society's measuring stick, they prove their power by their ability to destroy the people who come in contact with them. Paul Scott sees their motive as unable to punish themselves, they punish others. There are two other homosexual characters in the last book of the Quartet. One is an innocent young man in the Army who knows he's attracted to men but has been told that's wrong. He doesn't know anything about homosexuality except his hidden feelings. He's very vulnerable to danger. The other is an older sergeant who is a nurse to the war wounded. He makes no secret of his homosexuality, prancing about acting out entertaining, gossipy stories in the mess hall. Yet no wounded man feels uncomfortable under his caring hands in the wards. He's a professional. And for all his silly talk in the mess hall, no one thinks he's ever acted on his homosexuality.

In the *Raj Quartet* there are four homosexual characters out of about forty well-developed characters. Ten percent.

Many gay scholars, including Rob Eichberg and sociologist Brian McNaught believe that ten percent is the correct number. Others estimate maybe 4% of the male population is gay, and only 2 to 3% of females are lesbians. (I think that's only because lesbians blend into the population more, that even fewer come out, and more are married.) In a survey done last year where surveyors went door-to-door asking people their sexuality, 1% said they were gay. The survey people knew that the number is much higher than that. People are not going to tell a stranger at the door what their husband or wife doesn't know.

No one knows for sure what the real number is. We'll get closer to knowing when gay people don't have to be afraid to be themselves, when people recognize that homosexuality is not perversion; perversion is the subversion of the natural.

Many people have a strong discomfort level with homosexuals. Tom one day got angry with me after I told him about how Martina Navratilova helped Monica Seles back to tennis after she was stabbed by a crazy man. He blew up at me. When he was calm, I asked him, "Do you hate the messenger (me), or the message?" The message being about Martina's kindness and human generosity. He said, "I don't know. Yes. I do. I just don't like bull dykes."

Men are very uncomfortable with these women they can't approach in their classic role of seducer. When the movie *To Wong Foo, Thanks for Everything! Julie Newmar* came out men didn't want to go see it. And male reviewers gave it some very strange, off-center reviews. In the film, three male actors, well-known and very hunky, play drag queens, men who dress and behave as women. The male reviewers wrote about how well the men did as women and mostly revealed their discomfort. They missed the mythic point of the movie: that these men in women's clothes made very powerful friends for women abused by men. Being saved by a powerful friend is a fiction genre. The fatherless boy in *E.T.* got a powerful friend from another planet. Aladdin had the genie rescue him. The women in *To Wong Foo* got big, tough-guy girlfriends, guys in dresses, who could fight and protect them. It was a beautiful story.

The discomfort goes both ways though. My friend Jeanne wouldn't go to see *Junior*, the picture where Arnold gets preggers, because she shuddered at the thought of Arnold Schwarzenegger in drag. I told her it was the funniest movie I could remember seeing. Tom and I saw it on video and we rolled around on the floor laughing so hard we cried at big, tough Arnold with all the sensitivities and insecurities of a pregnant woman: "Does my body disgust you?"

OCTOBER 1995

I look across the street at Ted's pretty house. The new owners are buzz-sawing down the flowering trees that line the drive. Ted made the house perfect. It makes me think of the campaigns going on in San Diego to get gays to move into certain areas of the city to rescue them and bring them to life as they did in the Hillcrest area. The campaigns say: Come and Live in Our Neighborhood—We Know Gays Make Good Neighbors.

OCTOBER 9, 1995

John reads in the newspaper that the Colorado anti-gay laws enacted by voters will go to the Supreme Court, taken there by a car dealer and a group called Family Values who are appealing the Colorado Supreme Court's ruling that anti-gay laws are not legal. John was angry, "I want to ask them, is your Family Values to destroy another person? Is that what family values means?"

The Fourteenth Amendment assures that every U.S. citizen has equal protection under the laws.

I think of James Baldwin's words in *Notes of a Native Son*.

It was necessary to hold on to the things that mattered. The dead man mattered; the new life mattered; blackness and whiteness did not matter; to believe that they did was to acquiesce in one's own destruction. Hatred which could destroy so much, never failed to destroy the man who hated and this was immutable law.

OCTOBER 10, 1995

Ann called. Patsy does not want to be in the book. "I'm sorry," Ann said. I was sorry. Patsy and her sister were both lesbians who grew up in the tough, male dominated Texas oil country. Her sister is dead.

Ann is upset. She just heard that Emma Thompson and Kenneth Branagh are divorcing.

ANN: I haven't felt so bad about a divorce since Steve Lawrence and Edie Gorme—that little sinking feeling.

I met Patsy at Ann's house in the summer of '93 when Ann gave the party for Sally's "coming out." Patsy was sitting in a small group circle on a patio area. I sat beside her. She was somewhat a shock to me. She looked like small, female John Wayne. She was wearing khakis and a white shirt. Her hair was gun metal gray, straight as a string, and hung just short of her shoulders. Her voice was deep and she looked for all the world like an old West gunfighter or Indian scout out of the nineteenth century. I couldn't be sure of her age—maybe sixty, maybe less. Her face was plain and weathered. She's an engineer.

I was a new audience. She leaned her chair dangerously back, threw her booted feet up on a chair in front of her, struck a match on the concrete patio for her cigarette, and started to tell stories. She's a born storyteller. I listened to her Texas drawl and folksy metaphors and she told stories of Texas where the men were red-necked ol' boys who were threatened by women who looked tough, walked with a swagger, and had voices as deep as their own.

"Oh, Ann," I said, "I wanted those Texas stories. Especially the one she told about her sister and her in the bar."

Ann laughed. "Oh, that one. I can tell you that one. I've heard her tell it a million times."

Patsy and her sister Pam walked into a Texas bar late one hot afternoon and ordered beers. Patsy says, "We were all dressed up in polyester pantsuits and LOOKIN' GOOD." They stood at the bar with their drinks. Some good ol' boys were sitting at a table and looking them over. Finally one of them spoke in a loud voice. "Would ja look at what just walked in! Looks like a couple of bulldykes to me."

Patsy said to Pam, "Let's just go. Let's get out of here." But Pam was in no hurry. She finished her beer and Patsy got her down to the cash register to leave. While Patsy was paying, Pam leaned her back up against the bar and looked out at the redneck men. In a loud voice she said to Patsy, "Little bitty things"—she held up her hand with her index finger and thumb measuring out about one to two inches— "jus' lil' bitty bitty things—that's what they got. That's why they act like that."

Patsy threw back her head and laughed at the memory. "Boy, I couldn't get her out of there fast enough. That Pam. She was tough. She took no shit. She was alwas' doing somethin' like that."

I don't know what Pam died of. But I know she would like the T-shirt I saw a woman wearing at the gay Pride Parade this July. She was a small, slender, but very tough looking, gray haired woman in faded (worked-in) jeans, with a cigarette hanging from her mouth as she helped people set up chairs. Her T-shirt said: "That's *Ms.* Bulldyke to you."

I said, "I like your shirt." She stood up straight and took her cigarette out of her mouth to give me a stunning, warm friendly smile. "Thanks. I like it. It works." Like Pam, bold enough to hoist them on their own insult.

November 1, 1995

In yesterday's paper there was an obituary: Nat Kelly Cole, 36. No cause of death was given but donations were asked for AIDS Project L.A. or Project Angel Food. His famous father and sister were mentioned.

Today's paper. Two large obituaries taking one-third of a page. David Haikkila, 44, "complication of AIDS"—a long list of achievements. Singer, actor, pianist. Degree from UCSD in '92, summa cum laude. Phi Beta Kappa. Jacob Bronowski Award for Academic Excellence and Creative Achievement. A long list of brothers and sisters. Donations asked for three AIDS agencies.

Jim Thompson, 53. College days as civil rights and anti-war activist. Leader in the AIDS community. Died of AIDS complications. Brought "Being Alive San Diego" support organization from six members to 1,300.

Now, in November '96, just one year later, the paper every day is not filled with men dying too young. There's help from a combination "cocktail" of AIDS drugs. But at a cost of $15,000 a year.

November 2, 1995

I saw my old friend Sherry. In from a Maine island. She tells me Maine has a pending state law on the ballot to keep gays from having civil rights.

I say, "But these people are American citizens. What will they do?"

SHERRY: They can leave the country.

It turns out Sherry has been listening to talk/hate radio and believed what she heard: they recruit. When I explained that gay people are born gay and do not recruit, she said, "Oh, no. And all those young men committing suicide—so many are gay." She told with great pain of being in Boston and seeing some young black toughs chasing a young white gay man through the streets.

SHERRY: I called for help on my car phone. But I don't know if it arrived.

Would that all people learned as fast. What she had been told didn't make sense. So when she heard the truth, all the pieces fell into place. Her naturally compassionate heart responded. She knew there was nothing to fear.

November 8, 1995

Sherry phones. Very upset. "Maine has voted to take civil rights from gays."

John was even more upset. He shook his head. "What will they do next? Separate drinking fountains?"

It turned out Sherry had it wrong. Maine voted down the anti-gay civil rights proposition.

November 11, 1995

I heard on NPR people in a New Hampshire church congregation being interviewed about the presidential election. The people were saying they were voting against Clinton because of his policy on gays in the military. One man said, "These people shouldn't *have* jobs."

December 2, 1995

In this morning's paper. A largely gay church, the Metropolitan Community Church, was not allowed to march in the annual pageant of churches in Key West, Florida. Their pastor said, "We had a wonderful float." I'll bet they did. I'll bet it was the best float.

The parade chairman, Rev. Redwine of the First Baptist Church, said, "It's not that we hate homosexuals . . . we can't condone the homosexual lifestyle." Funny he should use that word hate. And "lifestyle." They do not have a "lifestyle," only a life. Two other churches dropped out in protest, and the mayor who was going to be the grand marshal, and five city commissioners who were going to judge the floats. Local feeling was against the decision because of the

Metropolitan Community Church's long history of charitable work.

I think of Buddhist monks who go forth every day with their empty bowls—what they have each day depends on what people put in their bowls.

God cares very much what we put in people's bowls. We all go forth holding out our lives to others. Gay and lesbian people hold out the bowls of their lives and often receive hatred—their lives are spit upon.

December 5, 1995

I receive a postcard from Ted from London! I can feel his happiness. Life is an adventure, with a companion, now.

I remember Fred said he stayed with his wife until all their children were raised. And he took care of her financially. He is a good and decent man. Now he is maintaining his medical practice until his son is out of medical school and ready to take over the practice. Then he and Ted will leave Michigan and move to some new place. The South. Maybe Atlanta.

I like the word "normal" for gays. The Dutch government used it in their study of homosexuals in 1969 which pronounced homosexuals normal. Andrew Sullivan, the young (and gay) editor of *New Republic* magazine, titled his book about gays *Virtually Normal*. I heard him interviewed on the radio (NPR again).

He was asked: "What proof do you have that (homosexuality) is involuntary?"

He responded, "My life."

December 12, 1995

I am telling John about the hate campaigns against gay rights in the late '70s. Anita Bryant's: "They can't reproduce—so they must recruit."

He looks upset. "Don't they know if they don't want them to reproduce, they should treat them as normal people? Then they wouldn't get married and reproduce." [to hide]

Of course, homosexual people reproduce just fine. (Remember? They're normal people.) A common answer to being accused of choosing to be homosexual is: Of course I didn't choose to be homosexual. Why would anyone choose to be hated?

A tenet in the homosexual community has to do with the idea of more people "coming out." The idea is if every homosexual turned purple tomorrow morning you'd be stunned to see how many people you know and respect are homosexual. And you'd accept them as a normal part of the human group.

January 2, 1996

Tom is home from college on Christmas vacation and his friend Jack is here. They went to the beach but didn't go surfing because Jack didn't have his board.

M: What did you do then? Did you go for a run?
Tom: (laughs) Who? Jack and me?

(John is laughing now)

M: Yes. Why not? Do you think that's gay or something—

to run together?

TOM: Mom, you'd better do some more research.

JOHN: Real men don't jog together.

M: Billy Crystal does, in his movies. In *When Harry Met Sally* the Billy Crystal character went jogging with his friend.

TOM: You can *run*. But you can't do it spontaneously. You can't just go prancing off down the beach. I go running with Jack and Rick, but it's planned. You have to have the right *equipment*. It has to be serious exercise. It has to be *painful*.

I remember some of those friendly exercise "runs" now. They were competitive. They killed themselves to beat the other guy.

JANUARY 5, 1996

Tom gave me Mother Teresa's book, for Christmas. She says:

> It is not how much you do but how much love you put into the doing and sharing with others that is important. Try not to judge people. If you judge others then you are not giving love. Instead, try to help them by seeing their needs and acting to meet them. People often ask me what I think about homosexuals, for example, and I always answer that I don't judge people. It isn't what anyone may or may not have done, but what *you* have done that matters in God's eyes. (*Mother Teresa: A Simple Path*)

In January I'm panicky over an "illness" I have. Twice I've just passed out. No warning. Just blackness rolling over my eyes. The doctor found nothing wrong. Maybe the extreme stress I'd had in November and December with John's surgery on his leg. I tell Ann I feel panicky. "What if I keep doing this? What if I can't drive?"

She's very calm.

ANN: You don't have to let it change your life.
M: I know Jill has epilepsy and she drives. But she says she only has attacks in the night.
ANN: (coughs) Well, that's not quite true. But she has some warning—an aura—sometimes, a strange odor—I've seen her, she just lies down on the floor. She manages it—lives with it. You can too.

(pause)

She did give up flying planes.

All the women who are in this book have that kind of courage. Some said "no"—Patsy, Joanna. Ann rolled her eyes, "'No,' they said." I think of those brave ones who revealed their souls and their humanity as saints.

I'm at my friend Jeanne's house. Her six-year-old and eleven-year-old daughters are giggling together about someone—"Oh, but he's gay."

M: Do they understand that?
JEANNE: Yes. They do. They don't think much about it—they just accept it.
M: Did you explain it to them?
JEANNE: No. They just picked it up—that some people like the same sex.

My friend Susan had told me the occasion came up where she had to explain homosexuality to her eight-year-old boy.
SUSAN: Well, some people just want to marry someone of the same sex. That's how these two men are.
MICHAEL: Uhmm. That's interesting. How do they decide who wears the bride dress?

I think of Ruth Ann saying, "That's our hope—the next generation.

MARCH 22, 1996

Today I receive a letter from Ted. He and Fred have been to Tampa, Florida. Stayed in Fred's condo there and attended the NGPA convention. I thought, "GP"?— doctors? National GP Association? Then he talked about aviation, and flying, and planes. And said it was the National Gay Pilots Association convention—"which proves," he said, "that fairies really *can* fly."

I was laughing out loud. It hadn't been a very good day—now it was good. Dear Ted—I miss your cheerfulness. I miss his childlike joy in the good things in life, and his unfailing optimism and joking over the negative things.

MARCH 29, 1996

A Reform rabbi endorses the legalization of homosexual marriages but does not recommend rabbis perform the ceremonies.

APRIL 3, 1996

My Baptist sister-in-law (ex—part of the group we refer

to as "the Baptist cousins"), Janey, phones me from Oregon. She says she's "supporting" a friend who's refusing to see her brother because he's gay.

JANEY: She's rejected him and she's in such pain. I sent her a Bible verse to comfort her in her suffering. She doesn't approve of his lifestyle choice. I believe the same. He has a partner and she's afraid he'll bring him to the house— they hold hands. She doesn't want her sons to see that.
M: Maybe she could just ask them not to hold hands—if that makes her uncomfortable. And what about *his* pain? He's the one rejected.
JANEY: I know you believe differently, but I'll never change. It's a choice, the Bible says, it's a choice, the Bible says . . .

APRIL 23, 1996

There's an article in *Time* magazine (4/29/96) on the new political tactic of the Religious Right. *Time* calls it flying under the radar of the national media. Local grass roots workers create hate and fear of homosexuals in local areas, "trickle-up" hatred. In Grand Rapids, Michigan, a religious group went after a gay high school music director who they'd found out had had a commitment ceremony. Although the teacher has done nothing wrong he can be fired for, and he's talented and popular, the school board is harassing him by "monitoring" him, i.e., hoping he'll quit. And misinformation is being sent to the parents of his students.

Sow the seeds of hate. Keep the mention of homosexuality out of the classroom, build resistance to ordinances that prohibit discrimination against gays on the local level. When enough grass roots hatred is sown, the Religious

Right can challenge gay civil rights issues on a federal level.

So much hatred shouted about. I think of the Bible: "Be still, and know that I am God." (Psalm 46:10) The Lord was not in the wind, and not in the earthquake, not in the fire—he came to Elijah when there was quiet—he came as a still small voice. (I Kings 19:12)

Christ's words in saying who would go to heaven: "Whatever you did to one of the least of these my brethren, you did it to me." (Matt. 25:40)

That's pretty scary when you think of the hate some people are throwing around in the name of Christianity.

July 15, 1996

I heard General Colin Powell interviewed on NPR. He was asked about his opposition to gays in the military. The interviewer asked him about the parallel to the opposition to blacks in the military in the 1940s. (Gen. Powell is black.) The same argument was used: it will lower the morale of soldiers to have to mix with people so "different."

General Powell said, "Yes, the parallels have been pointed out to me—but the difference between blacks and whites is only *skin color* which is of no significance, whereas the difference between gays and heterosexuals is sexual preference which is of great significance."

I tell John what I heard. He disagrees with Powell.

JOHN: Often, in my experience, the difference between blacks and whites is cultural—which can be much more significant than the differences between straights and gays of the same culture.

President Jimmy Carter in a recent interview recalled the use of the Bible to defend segregation—and the arguments that integration would destroy the schools, and the white race through intermarriage.

I think of the Family Values man from Colorado. He says he fears gays because he fears for the family if gays have civil rights. He says he fears "a genderless society without a nuclear family."

Groundless fears. If gay people are accepted the only change in the nuclear family would be fewer miserable marriages where a homosexual marries to hide his homosexuality. All heterosexual men and women will still want to marry each other and have children. In February one conservative Congressman made an attempt to have all HIV infected service people expelled from the military. There were 1,049 male and female service members with the HIV virus. More than half were married.

The Family Values white heterosexual men should put all that energy into educating heterosexual men to be better family men—better husbands, and more involved fathers. That would do more to strengthen the nuclear family than chasing chimeras about gay people. Gay people aren't a threat.

The man feared a "genderless society." I say we have a multi-gender society now, and always have, and always will.

I propose a new term: GENDER BLENDS, to describe those people who fit somewhere other than on the heterosexual end of that line Ann talked about.

A rainbow has only three primary colors but blending creates infinite shades and varieties. I remember that box of eight Crayolas I had as a child. Then I saw on a classmate's desk a box of 64 colors! It became my dream to possess a box like that. I've been enchanted and enriched by the gay people I've met. They're fun and compassionate and loving and creative, and each one always a surprise in their genderblend. Remember Ted's friend who was a domineering male, but he embroidered shirts for his friends? And Ted, tearing down his car in the afternoon and then going inside to sew his new drapes? I love the lively "boys" and more quiet and stoic girls of the gay community. Once when I was struggling years ago someone said to me: Gaiety is the pose of courage. I never found out if that was a quote—it sounds 18th century—or was original, but it makes me think that "gay" is a good word for these people whose laughter and gaiety are a graceful front to the deep courage they have to keep on being loving in a world that directs so much hate at them.

Ann made a line graph with heterosexual people at one end and homosexual people at the opposite end, and with a few people scattered along the line.

I think we have to make two fans at the homosexual end of the line to indicate the genderblends homosexual men and lesbian women have. The fan for lesbians would have butch or traditional male characteristics on one edge, and fem or traditional feminine characteristics on the other edge. And gradations and shadings of the two would blend across the fan.

The fan for gay men would have a gradation of traits from traditional male (you'd never guess he's gay—like Fred) to the feminine traits—those men who waited so long to be "flight attendants," the hairdressers and designers and ice skaters who have a feminine creativity and sensitivities.

UCLA biology professor, Judith Lengyel, tells her students, "Sex, as a concept, is really quite plastic." And she's just talking about the biological causes of a fetus' sex determination.

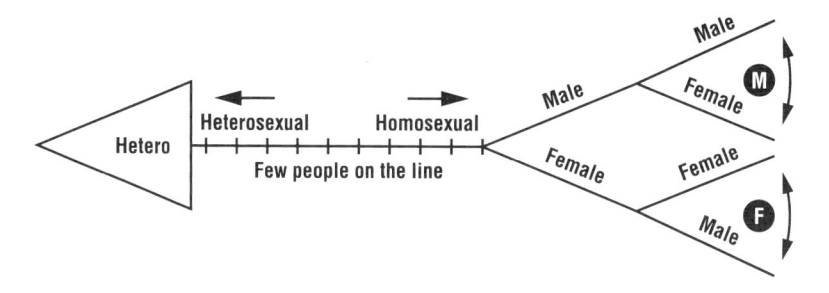

Writing this book has been a serendipitous experience. You may think I sit around the house and listen to National Public Radio all day long. I don't. I don't even turn the radio on when I'm at home. I only hear the radio if I dash out in the car on some errand. Yet I seem to have heard every gay person on NPR in the last three years. I heard Randy Shilts when his book was first published in the spring of 1993, before mine was even a dream. It's like the predestined birth of a child.

Almost every time I turned television to C-Span during the last two years I saw something about gays—two Saturday mornings I hit accidently on the National Lesbian and Gay Journalists Association meeting in Washington, D.C., and I never turn on the television on a Saturday morning. The first time I saw, among other speakers, George Stephanopoulos speaking about President Clinton's administration's policy toward gays. He wants them to have all civil rights. He changed the law that said they couldn't have security clearances (by executive order, August 1995). He does not believe in marriage (as it is now) for gays.

Stephanopoulos said, "The Bible says we are created in God's image—no one is left out in that—there are no 'excepts.'" The camera panned the audience of gay and lesbian journalists; men brushed tears from their cheeks. Anyone who has suffered mistreatment knows that feeling—a kind word in a world that's been hostile, and the tears suddenly are there.

Another time Ted Turner was on the panel and was asked if his networks are gay-friendly to their gay employees. Ted said he thought so, he meant them to be, but though there were many employees he thought probably were gay, no one had said they were, so of course he hadn't brought it up. Maybe they felt safer after hearing him.

OCTOBER 26, 1996

One of the oddest serendipitous experiences happened on this day. We had a sudden and unusually hard rainstorm in the night. It woke me up and I got up to watch it. We hadn't had any rain yet this season and I love rain in California. The rain turned to hail. When it was over I was so fully awake that I watched the end of a movie (*Short Cuts*) that I'd been watching on tape earlier but had been too sleepy to finish. The movie finished at 1:04 a.m. I turned off the tape and there on KPBS TV was this man, Brian McNaught, talking to an audience about what it's like to grow up gay. He was a fascinating man to listen to, his kindness so deep that it flowed out to everyone listening. As Randy Shilts had said, Brian said, "Hatred comes from fear, and fear comes from ignorance," so he educates people about what it is to be gay. He talked about the 1,500 gay youth suicides a year. He said that people who work with runaway, homeless children say that 50% of those kids on the streets are gay—running away from, or kicked out of, hostile homes.

Brian said, "I never met a gay person who felt they belonged in their family." He said he'd felt like an alien—

like there was no one else like him in the world. (Remember Ted, newly in the Navy, going into the gay bar in San Francisco: "I was thrilled. They were like me. I thought I was the only one.")

Brian kept his secret and was an over-achiever. He made his family proud. He tried to be interested in girls so he could be "normal" and marry and make his family proud of that too. But he couldn't. And at age 26 he tried to kill himself by drinking turpentine and taking a bottle of pills. Then he thought about how this would hurt his father and mother and he called for help, and got his stomach pumped. (His book *A Disturbed Peace: Selected Writings of an Irish Catholic Homosexual* was published in 1981.) In this seminar, *Growing Up Gay,* Brian took his heterosexual audience through a visualization exercise: what would it feel like if your family, and your teachers, and their expectations for you were homosexual, and you're heterosexual, and that's considered bad and you're afraid to tell them. How do you feel on prom night? If you're a guy, your parents expect you to go with a guy, a guy who wants to dance with his face on your neck and get a kiss goodnight. Brian takes them visually through the horrors of being an alien in one's own family. At the end many eyes were filled with tears. He asked the audience how they'd felt. They answered: lonely, frightened, isolated.

Brian said when he was growing up there were no role models for gay children. When he was older and a gay person was interviewed on TV their face was scrambled, like a criminal's, so they couldn't be identified.

There are role models for gay children today. Maybe the word homosexual cannot be mentioned in the schools by teachers, but the kids are learning what homosexuality is, and there are role models in public life. Congressmen are out. Sports. There's Martina Navratilova who's admired not only for her great athletic talent but for her intelligence, emotional grace, humor, kindness, and loyalty. And there are many people in the dreaded world of entertainment who are publicly out.

Last night (November 18) I took my dinner into the living room at seven and turned on the TV—Bravo network—I saw the career of k.d. lang profiled. Now I'm a fan. What an amazing voice and talent. She's Canada's national heroine—and she's a lesbian. She thanks her mother for pushing her and encouraging her to be as much as she could be. She's growing musically and personally. In her music she's constantly exploring musical genres and pushing her talent into new areas. Personally, she said, "I have male energy, but I'm very maternal—emotionally I'm becoming more feminine." She talks about her genderblends, honestly and openly. She is learning about herself just as she learns about what music she can create.

And TV sitcoms are full of gay characters now. Last night also I saw in the TV program guide for *Melrose Place*: "Matt and Dan have their first date." So gay youth today know they are not the only person in this world with feelings that don't fit the heterosexual mold.

This generation of young people has some role models. And this generation of parents of gay young people have some good role models: parents who loved and treasured their gay children and didn't throw them away. This generation of gay youth will know that if they don't have a family, they at least have a "community." They are not aliens, and they are not alone. And there is a life, there can be a very beautiful life, without being a heterosexual.

November 20, 1996

On the sitcom *Ellen* last night Ellen talked with her psychologist about feeling left out, ignored, when her girlfriends talk about their relationships with guys. The conversation went something like this.

DOCTOR: You feel you don't fit in—maybe we should explore this.
ELLEN: Oh, no. I'll get over it.
DOCTOR: How long have you felt this way?
ELLEN: All my life.

If *Ellen* comes out as the first show with a lesbian character as the main character, people will see she's the same Ellen they've loved—even loved *because* of her particular genderblend. And more people will understand the "Ellens" they know—and young "Ellens" won't feel as lonely and confused wondering why they don't fit in, and if there is any place they do fit in.

Back in early 1994 when Ted was "in love" and running over for advice and suffering wondering if the love he had for Fred was requited, I wrote in my journal: Ted is "in love." Why the quotation marks? At the time I didn't think, in some weird part of my ignorant mind, that two men could be "in love." Now I know better. They were and are definitely in love as much as any two human creatures can be. At first it was giddy attraction and hope (and lust, as Ann pointed out). Now the love has matured into commitment and companionship and deep and loyal friendship. Remember Stella talking about when she was young: "I knew I preferred the company of women"? She fell in love with her friend Ruth Ann, quite surprisingly and suddenly. Remember the words people used in their stories: WHOOOOSH, BOOM, it just happened, we didn't know what it was.

You don't choose whom you love; love chooses you.

Love is not sex—it's a feeling you have. One homosexual man explained in a radio interview: homosexuals can have sex with heterosexuals—but they don't fall in love with them.

Several years ago, Tom was in ninth grade, so it was spring of 1990, I sat in the back of an empty church and discussed homosexuality with a woman priest friend, Betty. In Tom's Sunday school class the head priest's daughter (these are Episcopalians), also in the ninth grade, always livened up dull classes by asking a forthright question. That Sunday her question to the male teacher was: "Is sodomy only bad for homosexual people or is it bad for heterosexual couples too?" You have to imagine her fresh and pretty, freckled little fourteen-year-old face to fully appreciate this. She asked with her usual bright smile and large innocent eyes (behind which was a great deal of mischief). The teacher, always so sure of himself, coughed (choked?) and said he'd have to think for a moment. But he soon had an authoritative answer: "No. It's only bad for homosexuals because the Bible says it's bad for homosexuals. Heterosexuals can do whatever they want if they're married." Tom couldn't wait to tell me about this exciting Sunday school session.

I told him I knew that Sunday school teacher was wrong. If something is wrong for one person, a homosexual male, it can't be right for another person, a heterosexual male. Besides, in a heterosexual couple one person is always the perpetrator and the other always the perpetratee. The act was, to my knowledge by accounts I'd heard, very painful to the woman—she feels victimized—and it seemed to me an unnatural act, something the body was not made for.

I talked with Betty about this that day sitting in the empty church. She said she felt the same. We talked about homosexuality and where we thought it fit in with Biblical scripture. We both felt that homosexuality was natural for those who are homosexuals, but we both thought homosexuals shouldn't practice anal intercourse because we thought the Bible spoke against sodomy as an unnatural use of the body. We struggled with this problem. Homosexuals should be able to love each other but not in that way. We were doing the best we could to sort out what we couldn't understand. It bothered me then, as it did her, and over the next few years. Who were we to say that some people shouldn't have "sex"? At the time we both thought the word sodomy meant "anal intercourse" and I think many people do, but I learned different when I was reading Randy Shilts' *Conduct Unbecoming*. Women were getting arrested on "suspicion of sodomy." Whoops. I'd better look it up. Sodomy is any sexual activity which is not *coital* (i.e., heterosexual intercourse which could lead to conception). Therefore all those criminal sodomy laws on the books in many states apply to heterosexual couples in any kind of oral sexual act as well as applying to homosexual oral sex, not just anal intercourse.

The Catholic Church says it's all right to be homosexual but not to have any sexual practice (it also says that married people should have sex only for procreation), almost what Betty and I thought, with some confusion, those years ago in that empty church. Now I know we were wrong. It's not my business to judge whether homosexual men have sex or what kind of sex they have; because I can't understand. Just as I think no man ought to make any kind of decision about abortion rights. The morality of what a group does has to be left to the group that understands it, and *lives* the decision. How can we as heterosexuals be so presumptuous as to say: We can have sex, but you cannot?

Brian McNaught says, "You don't have to like what I do, but don't take my job away."

I recently talked with another woman priest and asked her what she thinks. She said, "It's the privacy of the bedroom. What one wants to do for the other is not our business." I asked her her views on gay marriage. She said, "It's good to form commitments—the only difference between homosexual people and us is sexual practice—and that's personal."

While she was talking I could tell her mind was somewhere else. Suddenly she burst out, almost mid-sentence, what I've found is almost everyone's favorite question.

"What I want to know," she said, "is *what do lesbians DO?*" I looked at her earnest face and couldn't help laughing. "Not much," I said. "Not much."

The question deserves an answer.

And the answer is easy to find. Many years ago, in the mid-'80s I picked up a movie video with Mariel Hemingway in it, *Personal Best,* about young women athletes. They were lesbians and there was kissing. I was upset. I couldn't watch.

I didn't think much about it. Then when I started this book Ann occasionally told a lesbian sex joke and I learned a bit more. Then one day Ann gave me a novel by one of her favorite authors—*Confessions of a Failed Southern Lady* by Florence King. I was sure she wanted me to see what that Southern belle thing she was raised with was all about. But near the end of the book a romance between two women develops and becomes physical. The descriptions made me feel uncomfortable but left me educated. Actually the scenes were very tender. All that stuff called foreplay that heterosexual women complain men don't do—well, lesbians make an art out of it. (We know there's no anal intercourse.) Actually, knowing Ann and that she's not dumb, I think she was gradually educating me, giving me a vaccination against being uncomfortable with the idea of sex between women.

All the women whose stories are in this book talked about how it was natural for them when it happened. Over and over I heard, "I didn't know what to do, but it all came naturally." And "Neither of us knew what we were doing but it just happened naturally."

I remember when I was young wondering if someone didn't tell us about sex, would we know what to do? I know the answer now. Yes. Even lesbians who had no idea they were lesbians, and who didn't know anything about lesbians, knew, naturally, what to do. We can probably extrapolate that to gay men too. I would say they also know naturally what to do sexually. We may not understand what other genders do, but that's okay.

So I knew the answer to that question everyone but lesbians seems to ask, "What do lesbians do?" Then one day I was in the videostore browsing in the adventure movie section for a film. A video was lying on the top of a shelf and I picked it up, to see what it was, and maybe shelve it. Oh, my God—it was a lesbian video—you're going to be sorry I don't remember the name, but on the cover which was blocked off like tic-tac-toe, were nine illustrations of lesbians doing—Oh, my God, nine different things that made me almost drop the box then look around to make sure no one saw me looking at it. I think what happened was that some child had wandered into the adult video alcove, slipped right under the radar, and brought out his or her selection, about some ladies in skimpy costumes doing some very acrobatical stuff—the child probably thought they were superheroes. And the mother probably looked at the cover and said, "Oh, my God," and dropped it in the adventure section and got out of there quick. I think the film was probably made for heterosexual males who like to fantasize about what superhero-looking (Amazon) lesbians do (why?). Nevertheless, I found out there was still a lot I didn't know, until then, about what lesbians do.

While I was writing this book I was reading simultaneously the journals of Thomas Merton (*The Sign of Jonas*) and of Thomas "Tennessee" Williams (in *Tom* the biography by Lyle Leverich). Thomas Merton was a contemplative (vow of silence) monk living in the monastery Gethsemani in Kentucky. His goal was oneness with God and his writings, though nontraditional, were encouraged by the Catholic Church. Tom Tennessee Williams struggled to write plays about the earthy, destructive passions of men and women. In my mind I called them the Sacred and the Profane—two of the greatest natural writers of the twentieth century and two of the most fascinating persons.

Opposites and the same, their lives shared similarities. Thomas Merton gave up a life of heterosexual fast living to lead a spiritual life, to be with God, finding peace in communion with God. Tom Williams lived a tormented life—lonely, desiring love and never finding it. In his plays, shocking for their times, the conflict is between the sensual and spiritual.

Both men were raised by relatives. Both suffered the loss of a beloved sibling. Thomas Merton lost his brother Paul in WWII; Tom Williams lost his sister Rose (the girl in *The Glass Menagerie*) to mental illness.

Thomas Merton separated himself from the world to

become a holy man. Solitude and constant prayer were the life he wanted—writing was a burden—until he realized writing was a prayer and a way to be close to God. Tom Williams had a strong religious background. He lived with his Episcopal minister grandfather and grandmother for much of his childhood. In adulthood he separated himself from his family (mother, father, brother) and friends to hide his homosexuality. (Later when he was finally successful and could rent a house in Key West, he often had his aged and ailing grandfather stay with him and his lover.)

He wanted to be heterosexual but finally had to accept the fact that he wasn't. His plays are full of tormented passions of the flesh, desire, the physical; the characters are caught up in carnal desires yet struggle to be spiritual. Tennessee in his personal journals constantly cried out to God for a "return to my goodness." He hated the sexual life he couldn't control and yearned for the spiritual. The forties, fifties and sixties were not a time of understanding of homosexuality. It was painful for me to read of his suffering and self-hate. His old friends who found out after his death—alone in a New York hotel room, he never had a home—that he was a homosexual said they would have understood, but they didn't know—he'd pushed them away.

Merton had so much peace and joy in his life, and Williams had so much torment and pain—yet in so many ways they seem to me two sides of the same coin: these two men whose passions we see in their writing were given the same great talent by God. They both struggled with what God called them to be (writers), and I'm sure God loved them equally.

Tennessee Williams' "journals" were scraps of paper, napkins, and hotel stationery kept in boxes. Toward the end of his life he wrote that he felt his "deviation" made him a "deeper and warmer and kinder man . . . more conscious of need in others, and what power I have to express the human heart must be in some large part due to this circumstance. Someday society will take perhaps the suitable action—but I do not believe that it will or should be extermination—Oh, well." (from *Tom* by Lyle Leverich, Crown Publishers, Inc., 1995, 421)

In March (1996) I went to hear the Episcopal Bishop of San Diego speak to a small group of people after church. He spoke about family and said, "The Church represents the need to live in community and family." After he spoke I talked to him and asked him about the ecclesiastical trial of an Episcopal bishop, now retired, for making a practicing homosexual a deacon. I asked why this trial was taking place now when the event it's about was six years ago. The Bishop said, "Because the seven year statute of limitations was running out. The Church has to abide by its own rules." The rules say priests must be celibate if unmarried. Gay priests are allowed, but, like heterosexual priests, must be celibate if unmarried. We both agreed the national publicity of this church trial was bad. Then the Bishop looked at me and asked, "Where do you stand on practicing homosexuality?"

"I'm on a journey of understanding," I said. "Not where I was a few years ago. Where do you stand?"

"I'm on a journey too," he said.

I thought of his speech: "the Church represents the need to live in community and family." If only all churches would include their homosexual children in the church family, and allow homosexual people to form families, instead of driving them away.

After being seven years in the monastery, away from the

world, Thomas Merton went into town. On the drive in he was wondering how he would react "at meeting once again, face to face, the wicked world." But he met the world and found it no longer so wicked after all and wondered if perhaps the defects he'd found in the world had been defects of his own that he'd projected upon it.

> Now, on the contrary, I found that everything stirred me with a deep and mute sense of compassion. Perhaps some of the people were hard and tough . . . but I did not stop to observe it because I seemed to have lost an eye for merely exterior detail and to have discovered, instead, a deep sense of respect and love and pity for the souls that such details never fully reveal. I went through the city, realizing for the first time in my life how good are all the people in the world and how much value they have in the sight of God. (*The Sign of Jonas,* Harcourt Brace, 1953, 91)

I think of my favorite part of the Episcopal prayer book. It's in the Baptismal Covenant. We promise to "respect the dignity of every human being."

I wrote this book for people to understand gay people, not for gay people themselves who have little interest in the biology of their sexual orientation or if there's a feminine/masculine polarity in their attractions. Most of them have a mystified expression on their faces at these topics. They don't want to avoid the topics, they've just never considered them. They want to just live in their bodies, not muse on them. Ann said, "What I'm really interested in is environmental politics." Elizabeth said, "Let them live in peace and dignity."

Let them add their minds and talents and work to the

important issues in the world.

Thomas Merton wrote to convince people of "the reality of God's love for us." (*Jonas,* 90) I am writing to convince people that the reality of God's love includes lesbian and gay people. Jesus taught love not hate, acceptance not rejection. It's not too late, ever, for anyone. Merton says, "Every minute life begins all over again. Amen." (108)

I came to know the hidden people—cautiously, carefully—I learned their worth and came to love them, for their very humanity. I'm glad I took this journey.

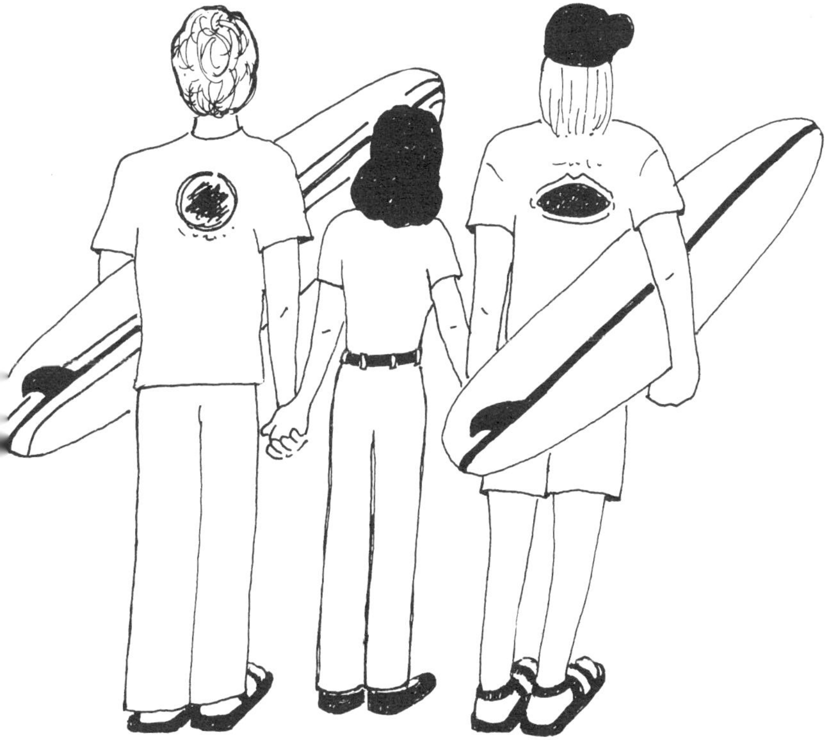

Appendices

How to tell if your best friend is a lesbian

I

FOX IN THE HEN HOUSE

IT'S NOT BAD to have lesbian friends, but it's more than merely disconcerting to discover you have a friend masquerading as a heterosexual to be near you. When I was divorced in my early forties I was happy to have women want to be my friend. I was lonely and enjoyed the companionship of getting together for a dinner with a friend or just getting a phone call for an adult conversation after a day spent with children.

Women are used to guys following us around with dopey expressions—we recognize what's going on and can ward off problems, but we don't recognize the secret lesbian in our intimate circle of friends because we don't expect it—the woman, the "bull dyke" who's spent a lifetime in hiding.

These secret lesbians disappear when they sense you're on to them and you make clear you're not interested. Like men who pursue you, they're really just interested in looking for action, not in your friendship.

The following list of "how to tell" is from my own experience with three women who arrived and sought my friendship, and from the experience of my friend, Maryann, who said to me, "Do you think my friend is a lesbian, she's always buying me expensive jewelry?" She may be married as Maryann's friend was, or divorced as one of my friends was.

1) She buys you very expensive jewelry, although she

never wears jewelry herself.
2) Every time you go to her house she wants to play one-on-one basketball. She plays rough. She almost breaks your arm.
3) She always wants you to go swimming, or to take a trip to the hot springs.
4) She gives you a book of love poems. Yes, *love poems*.
5) She sits up all night in the cold on a curb to buy tickets for a concert she thinks you might like.
6) She goes to Stallone movies alone.
7) She says, "*Everyone* is bisexual."
8) Her hobby is collecting Civil War musket balls and muskets, or tearing down cars, or riding Harleys.
9) She always dresses in pants and wears no makeup. If she does wear makeup, it looks oddly clown-like.
10) If she wears a dress she looks like Huck Finn in drag.
11) She wears khakis.
12) Her haircut is SHORT.
13) She used to be a welder.
14) She can't cook.
15) She likes tools.
16) She wears a backpack instead of carrying a purse.
17) Her body language is a clue. One I knew grabbed women with a one-armed hug from the side, pulled them over and kissed them. The woman is helpless, her arms are pinned down. (Whereas women who are going to hug or kiss in greeting, dance up toward each other face-to-face.)
18) She stands firmly on both feet with her hands jammed in her pockets. Sometimes rocks up and down.
19) She manages to mention to people she has just met that she's had sex with men. ". . . at the time I was having sex with this man."

20) She finds an excuse to take your hand in both of hers. Her touch gives you the creeps—lizard flesh. She's looking soulfully into your eyes.
21) She says, "If it's dark, what difference does it make whose hand stimulates you?"

If your instinct tells you something is wrong, it is. If you feel repulsion at her touch or presence, something is wrong. Don't worry. Once you become aware and put a little distance in the relationship, she will "disappear" from your life without ever asking why.

How to tell if your husband is gay

II

THE LAST TO KNOW

HAVE YOU HEARD the old expression "the wife is always the last to know"? I had wondered how that could be, until it happened to me. The wife is the last to know her husband is having an affair because her unconscious mind chooses to deny what she sees. Actually the wife is the first to see the clues. To admit to herself that she doesn't believe the lies (he's working late, he's out of town on business) is to admit the marriage has failed and that is something she can't accept. Later, looking back, she knows she saw all the signs through the years, then averted her glance from the truth and hid her tears.

The shock of infidelity is crushing to a wife, but discovering your husband is a secret homosexual I think is a worse shock. Women have to admit to the complete impossibility of the marriage. Perhaps to admit that it never was a marriage.

The number of these marriages is probably greater than one would expect. In February 1996 the Defense Department budget bill for the military contained a clause (later deleted in April) that required all personnel with the HIV virus be discharged. The Pentagon released the figure that the number of service people, male and female, with the HIV virus was 1,049. Of these 1,049 people, more than half were married. How many of those married men would you guess are gay? (The military is so useful for statistics we wouldn't otherwise have any idea of.)

How do you tell if your husband is gay? I think the list has a certain humor. If it's funny, it is because life is funny—because the list is not speculative or creative. It's from the true experience of one woman. She couldn't believe her husband was gay. She was the last to know.

1) At parties he wants you on the other side of the room from him. (He needs the guys' attention.)
2) At parties he wants you to look hot and dance with all the guys. (He needs the guys' attention.)
3) He avoids going to bed when you go to bed.
4) He sleeps in the living room until after you're asleep.
5) He takes a job where he travels all the time. Foreign countries and long trips are especially good.
6) When he comes home he's glad to see you— until bedtime. Then he picks a fight until you're in tears and he can sleep on the sofa.
7) He works "late"— sometimes works "all night." He waits to come home until you're asleep.
8) He likes you to be social and give parties (so he can meet the husbands of your friends).
9) You have very beautiful women friends but he doesn't notice them or know their names.
10) He dances very stiffly, or "apart" from his woman partner. You're never jealous. (There is another gay-man-type who is an excellent light-on-his-feet dancer. He usually doesn't marry. He can be recognized by his tight jeans or natty dressing style.)
11) You walk into a room and see him finding an excuse to touch a man's face. (He never touches yours.)
12) The plumber (carpenter, painter) sees him in the house and thinks he's your interior decorator.

13) He avoids family vacations. If he ends up having to go, he picks a fight, or somehow finds a way to sleep with one of the kids.
14) If forced to share a bed with you, he lies like a stone— unapproachable.
15) He treats you with anger. You don't know why.
16) He has a funny walk for a guy.
17) He waves his cigarette, or his hands, around a lot. His hands tremble, or he may have other twitches. He has a nervous laugh. (The guy is hiding an awfully lot.)
18) He cares about his clothes and hair. (Not yours.) He spends a lot of time looking in the mirror at himself.
19) He is unresponsive to your touch. (This is the most important clue, and the most painful.)
20) He never touches you. But like the Pollyanna you are, you count your blessings, observing that while he's not interested in you, at least he's not flirting with other women— you don't have to worry about losing him. (Wrong! It just won't be to another woman.)

Advice. Lose him.

III

GLOSSARY

IN JANUARY 1996 Ann gave a party at Elizabeth's and her house for us to work on a glossary. When I arrived most of the guests were already there. Ann who usually wears T-shirts was dressed in a loose, emerald green silk blouse and trousers. I hadn't seen her in a while and she was a little heavier. Her eyes were emerald green, picking up the green of her shirt, and her eyelids their own delicate lavender. Her cheeks were naturally rosy, flushed from the rushing around putting on a lavish spread of food. She looked soft and pretty, and, exuding her usual warmth to all the arriving guests, not at all butch. The guests were laughing and drinking and being introduced. Elizabeth arrived from upstairs, moving with the elegance of a queen, stunning in black velvet with gold and jade jewelry and cradling a large gray cat in her arms. I looked around the living room at the people, one very old woman, one very young man, Stella and Ruth Ann, Sandy, Bill and Jim with their little girl Laurie, a mix of men and women in animated conversations, and I thought if a stranger came into this party, he or she would never think these were all gay people. They would think what a nice looking group of people. I was happy to be there, very happy, and very comfortable.

After dinner all the guests except me broke into groups of four to seven people to work on terms and definitions for a glossary. There was much hooting and laughter and fun as they worked. Then we came together and discussed the terms as a group. This week, in March 1997, I played the tape of that discussion—listening to their laughter and kidding made me miss the fun they have together. I had to phone Ann and tell her I miss them.

AUNTIES Older gay men, often wealthy, who can afford to "keep" a young man. This term is not used much anymore. When Tennessee Williams was young and penniless he was appalled by the idea of ever being kept by an auntie. He socialized with "belles," young and attractive homosexual men.

BEAR A hairy gay man.

BEARD A person who escorts a gay person, for cover. This term is especially used by lesbians, e.g., two lesbians get a third person to escort one of them so they don't appear to be together, but it is used by men as well. The escort does not have to be of the opposite sex, i.e., a third woman can be the beard for a lesbian couple. The term beard is thought to come from the theatrical world, as in a false beard for a disguise.

BELLE An attractive young homosexual man. Not used much anymore. A term used by homosexuals.

BREEDERS What gay people call heterosexuals.

BULLDYKE Very derogatory name for a lesbian with masculine traits. "It's like being called an animal, a gorilla."

BUTCH A lesbian with masculine tendencies and mannerisms. Today the fad and the pressure among young lesbians is for everyone to look butch. Sandy says, "Couples try for the androgynous look, they go around like twins—it's silly." Butch is a very acceptable descriptive term.

CHICKENHAWK An old gay man who likes young gay men. He swoops down on them.

CHURCH "Do you go to my church?" or "We're members of the same church." A way to identify a fellow gay person.

CLOSET A place to hide. Gay people are "in the closet" if they're pretending to be heterosexual.

COMFORTABLE SHOES As in "she wears comfortable shoes." A way to let people know someone is a lesbian, because lesbians used to wear Birkenstock sandals.

COMING OUT Deciding not to hide one's gay sexual orientation any longer. Making a choice to live honestly as who one is.

CROSS-DRESSER A man who likes to dress up in women's clothes occasionally. Not necessarily gay. Cross-dressers can be anyone who dresses as the opposite sex but usually refers to the kinky habit of some men who like to dress up and act like women, usually in the privacy of their homes, often with the consent of their wives.

DOROTHY A way to identify if a person is a fellow gay person. You ask, "Are you a friend of Dorothy?" This refers to Dorothy in *The Wizard of Oz* because gay men love Judy Garland's singing (and Barbra Streisand's).

DICK An old gay guy. Versus Peter for a young gay guy.

DRAG QUEEN A gay man who dresses up in female attire for effect. Very theatrical, for entertainment. Comments in the room for drag queens ran to "they're some of the nicest people I know."

DUCK A gay person. Or "quack quack." What a gay couple say to each other when they spot another gay person, meaning "if he looks like one, and acts like one . . ."

DYKE This can be a general term for lesbians. In the gay world it is used for masculine lesbians. From non-gays, it's a derogatory term. Ruth Ann said, "We can call each other dykes, but we don't like other people to call us that. 'Lesbian' is P.C." (politically correct).

BABY DYKE A young lesbian. Often means a young lesbian trying very hard to look butch. Or, a newly-out lesbian, called "in training," i.e., doesn't know quite how to act the new role. Sandy says, "Oh, it just means young girls. When we go out and see them we say, 'Look at the baby dykes—aren't they cute?'"

DIESEL DYKE Mature dyke. Full-out dyke—eighteen wheels!

DYKES ON BIKES Lesbians who ride motorcycles. They traditionally open Pride Parades with a roar of power.

ELSIE L.C., the lesbian connection. Like Dorothy. "Are you a friend of Elsie?" To identify a gay person.

FAG A gay man. The term can be used among gay men, but is usually an insult when used by heterosexual men.

FAGGOT Always an insult because of its use by straight men as an insult. Faggot meant firewood and refers back to the days when gay men were burned at the stake.

FAG-HAG A heterosexual woman who likes to hang out with good-looking gay men in gay bars. She likes men but fears heterosexual men. She feels safe with gay men. Jake said, "They're usually fat, and troubled, women. We like them and treat them nicely—tell them they have pretty eyes. They like the male attention." I said that many very large women consciously or unconsciously use their fat to make themselves sexually unattractive to men—they're women who were raped or abused as children and fear the sexuality of straight men.

FAIRY Effeminate gay man. Light on his feet—as if having

fairy wings.

FAMILY The gay community. To identify a fellow gay person you can ask, "Are you a member of the family?" From the reality that for many gay people the only family they have is the gay community.

FEM A lesbian who is feminine in dress and manner.

FLAMER An outrageously out gay man. Has an attitude, like a drag queen without the dress. Or a man whose gay mannerisms become exaggerated when he drinks too much alcohol.

GAY Homosexual person. A lighter and happier word used in the homosexual community.

GAY-DAR Sounds like radar. The ability to detect a gay person.

"GIRL" Gay man speaking to gay man. As in "Girl, you won't believe what happened to me." Also "sweeetie". Gay men say that this word now widely used in black-talk originated in the gay community.

HOMOSEXUAL A person of either sex whose sexual orientation is for the same sex. A natural sexual orientation one is born with.

HOMOPHOBIA Fear of homosexuals.

JOHN A john or a trick means a one-night stand. A term borrowed from prostitutes.

L.C. The lesbian connection. See Elsie.

LESBIAN Female homosexuals. Young radical lesbians prefer to be identified with this word to separate them from gay men, i.e., to give them more identity as females. Older lesbians prefer to be called gay.

LESBOS A Greek island. The word lesbian derived from this island's name because the sixth century B.C. poet Sappho lived on the island, had a school for girls, and wrote classical lyric love poetry (of which only fragments remain). There is no proof that she was a lesbian.

LIPSTICK LESBIAN A feminine lesbian (as opposed to butch). Wears makeup. Also called a high-heel lesbian.

MARY A name for a gay man when you don't know his name. This is an insult if done by a straight man, but is used in a friendly manner among gay men. (Jake says he has one friend who always phones and greets him with, "Maaary! How's it going?")

M.C.C. Metropolitan Community Church where many gay people go. "Haven't I seen you at MCC?" is a way to identify a gay person.

NELLIE A generic name for an effeminate gay man. Used as an insult by straight men. The word comes from the old name for a female horse. Isaac Mizrahi in the film *Unzipped* tells how he was standing up cheering at a baseball game and a man behind him yelled, "Hey, Nellie, down in front."

NON-GAY Gay people's word for straight. Straight connotes something good as opposed to not being straight being something wrong. Gay people are trying to orient their language to be positive. They like the phrase "gaily forward" for "straight ahead."

OUT Not hiding one's homosexual identity; specifically, not pretending to be heterosexual.

OUTING When a group of people reveal the gay sexual orientation of a homosexual who's been hiding it (been "in the closet").

OUT-THERE Refers to a flamboyant homosexual. He's really "Out there."

PEDERAST A man who sexually abuses little boys, has anal intercourse with them. A sexual perversion.

PEDOPHILE A person whose sexual preference is children. A sexual perversion not related to homosexuality. Normal homosexuals like normal heterosexuals are not pedophiles. At the glossary meeting the men said, "We are tired of people thinking all gay men are pedophiles. We are not, we are not, we are not." In fact, they said, most pedophiles are white, heterosexual men.

PETER A young gay man. As opposed to Dick, an old gay man.

PITCHER/CATCHER Denotes sex role: top or bottom.

PROFESSIONAL DRAG A lesbian who wears skirts and makeup for professional reasons at work.

QUEEN An older gay man. Usually feminine. Also can mean a campy or an "uppity homo."

QUEER Homosexual. This is what the group said about this word: semi-derogatory, less derogatory than fag or faggot; prehistoric word (1812); from psychiatry, means not normal. The word is getting more popular, becoming a descriptive word. Many gays today are detoxifying it by embracing it.

REVOLVING DOOR A person who is conveniently straight or gay.

SAPPHO Sixth century B.C. poet who lived on the Greek island Lesbos. She had a school for girls and is sometimes identified as a lesbian though there is no proof she was.

STONEBUTCH Archaic term. Means a lesbian that makes sexual love but does not receive it. Comments were: Pity them; There aren't many anymore, but there used to be.

STRAIGHT Heterosexual.

SWISH A gay man who's obviously gay. A touch of flamboyance or too fashionable dress.

SWITCHHITTER Versatile. Someone who can take either position for sex. (See pitcher/catcher.)

TEAROOM Meeting men in the men's restroom. "I met him in a tearoom."

TOOLBELTS Lesbians who are masculine in their interests. Name comes from their liking professions where they wear toolbelts. They like tools, like jobs with uniforms (opposite of lipstick lesbians). This is an okay descriptive term (not insulting like bulldyke).

TRANSSEXUAL A person who wants to be the opposite sex, to the extent of undergoing surgery to achieve this. These people are not homosexuals—they consider themselves people who are born with the wrong body for their inner self. I.e., a man believes he is psychologically a woman mistakenly in a man's body.

TRANSVESTITE A person who dresses like the opposite sex and goes out in public and tries to pass as the opposite sex. This is usually a man seeking to live emotionally and sexually as a woman. Not necessarily a homosexual.

ZELS Professional surfer chicks. Now becoming a general name for lesbians. Sounds like "les" (lesbians) backwards.

One topic that came up frequently was the generational differences in the gay community in both vocabulary and behavior. Younger women don't like the word "gay." They prefer lesbian. Older women don't like the word lesbian, they prefer gay. Older women use the word dyke generically, younger women don't. Younger women like to dress androgynously and butch, older women prefer dressing more naturally to their roles and preferences.

Jake said older gay men don't like mixing with gay women, but younger gay men do. Younger gays share the same bars and social events with lesbians and enjoy the mixed company. Jake's observation on the two groups rang true to my own. He said the men are more campy and flamboyant—have a high camp, creative culture. They're funny, have colorful talk. The women are more reserved, their humor is more toward the droll.

Jake is a successful hair stylist—a good-looking blond man with a tiny gap in his teeth, he looks like a male Lauren Hutton, and is very verbal and intelligent. He also has that excess of exuberance from lots of testosterone. When men arrived at the gathering he jumped to his feet, held their heads between his hands, and pressed a greeting kiss on their lips. The men receiving these kisses obviously didn't want them—they looked startled and uncomfortable. It reminded me of all the unwanted embraces women get from men in just such a manner, unexpected and unavoidable—and after it's done it's too late to make a fuss.

Jake said that when gay men's relationships break up they never want to see each other again, whereas women stay in a social group and regroup with different partners. "Women swap," he said, "They stay in groups. Men leave the state." The group discussed the reasons for this. Men's testosterone—i.e., aggressive nature? The fact that women have a smaller group pool to choose partners from? They weren't sure but agreed the observation of this difference in social behavior was correct. Ann talked about women tending to have calm, ordered lives. "With men," she said, "you're dealing with two sets of testosterone in a relationship, it's a formula for disaster—both want to dominate, both want trophy mates, both will exchange a mate easily for a trophy."

Throughout the evening people talked and laughed and joked and shouted to get their points in. Cracks were made, the witty irresistible remark, but no one took offense. There was no snideness, no distrust, the laugh was paramount. But at other times they got quiet, wanting to hear a point of view. "Does it mean that now?" they would say.

Jake said the gay community is moving away from specialized vocabulary to mainstream slang, sharing vocabulary with many other groups, particularly the black culture. "I miss the old days," he said with a moment of nostalgia, "It was kind of fun, living in a secret subculture. We had our own jokes, laughed at people's clothes—you knew what doors to go through. Now it's more open—between races—vocabularies overlap, and are interchangeable. They're taking our fun words."

IV

Two Men and A Baby

BILL AND JIM were at the glossary party with their nineteen-month-old daughter Laurie. I'd first seen them in the photo album at Ruth Ann and Stella's. In every picture one of them was holding the little girl with such obvious tenderness that I could see how much they love her. I'd hoped to meet them someday because I was interested in the idea of two gay men raising a child.

Jim and Bill are nice looking men. Jim has dark hair and handsome features, Bill is a little round at the waist, with prematurely gray hair cut short and neat, and rosy cheeks. They both have warmth and wit and laughter that comes easily. Their ages could be twenty-six to thirty-two, and they are the best mothers I've ever seen. At every moment the best interest of the child is their paramount concern. The child is deeply loved but not spoiled (Jim said, Well, she does have a lot of jewelry). She played quietly with Ann's two poodles. She was confident and secure around the many strangers milling about the rooms. She never fussed about anything. Looking like a pretty doll, in a frilly dress, with gold bracelet, necklace, and earrings and Shirley Temple blond curls, she posed with people who wanted a picture taken with her—then she scooted off to play or find the dogs. From time to time she went to one of her daddies to be picked up and held briefly.

Jim and Bill are happy to tell me the story of how they

came to be fathers. No mother ever talked more excitedly about the birth of her child than these two kind men to whom raising a family was a dream they never expected to come true. Nineteen months later they still delight in every detail of her arrival.

Jim is a cousin to the birth mother who took drugs and was not considered by the State (Social Services) fit to raise the child. The grandparents asked Jim and Bill if they would adopt and raise the baby. Jim and Bill said, "Give us one day to get ready. We'll get her tomorrow." The social worker said, "You have to get her today, or she'll be moved to a residential home." They said, "We're coming."

They rushed to the hospital, got formula instructions from the nurse, and left with a daughter. "We stopped at Mervyn's (department store) on the way home and bought everything we needed. Meanwhile all the grandparents were getting furniture together." Laurie has three sets of grandparents, two of them care for her on weekdays when her fathers are working. She has "a village."

Jim and Bill are out in the world every day, carrying their daughter around—the mall, the grocery store, the church, the synagogue. People say to them, "Oh, I see it's Mom's day off and you and your brother have the baby for the day." Jim and Bill say, "No, she's ours. We're her fathers." They say people are very supportive.

Her fathers both noticed "she's getting tired." They both said "time for pajamas" which they did together, and shortly after they both, with a glance at each other and a glance at the child, said "time to take her home and put her to bed." The dinner party guests were all invited to walk outside with them and see their new family van.

Both these men have the tenderness, patience, interest, and ability to nurture of the best mothers I've ever seen. And both have all the strength, authority, male energy, and protectiveness of the traditional father. They laughed at the prospect of her teen years. Bill said, "Can you imagine the poor boyfriend when *two* stern fathers meet him at the door?" Jim said, "Boyfriend? She goes to school in Switzerland!"

A few days after the glossary party a newspaper article against the concept of gay marriage brought a flood of anti-gay family letters from readers. One angry man wrote: "the danger is how will children relate to authority when there is no single authority in the home? Where will a daughter find a mother figure?" He said a homosexual partnership "cannot be more than an emotional attachment—a marriage needs procreation to survive the ups and downs." What does he mean by "procreation to survive"? Sex? No, he can't mean that. Giving birth? He hasn't done that, and I've never met a mother who wouldn't prefer just picking up her baby at the hospital. NO adoptive parent would say you need to "procreate" to love or parent your child, and we all know plenty of people who have "procreated" and have bad marriages and are lousy parents.

Parenting has nothing to do with anything but the character of the parents and their ability to love—endlessly, patiently—and their willingness to nurture, protect, guide, and provide. None of these character qualities is in any way attached to any particular gender or genderblend.

The original editorial article, by a leader of the Christian Action Network, said the purpose of State bequeathed benefits for married couples are for children, therefore the State has no interest in the marriage of homosexuals. In truth, according to figures estimated by the Family Law group of the American Bar Association, there are four million gay and lesbian parents raising eight to ten million children. The State should want to protect these children's families too. The old Anglican marriage ceremony stated: marriage is to ensure a protective family for children and keep people from engaging in lust as they would be inclined to do outside the institution of marriage. On these religious grounds marriage would be very good for the families with same-sex parents as well.

The man who wrote the angry letter against gay families said such a family is "unnatural." Maybe the real difference between him and me is that I've seen Jim and Bill and their daughter Laurie. I saw two loving, decent, dedicated parents, and one secure, well-cared-for child.

Perhaps most of the majority heterosexual population will never feel comfortable with the word "marriage" for same-sex couples; maybe "domestic partnership" would be acceptable. Jim and Bill have been partners for almost ten years now. For families like this to be bound legally by State and church would benefit and protect the children and serve the moral and social good of society. Although the courts are moving slowly in this direction, society is moving much faster. More than 450 U.S. corporations recognize domestic partnerships.[4]

Jim and Bill are both legally adoptive parents of Laurie now. (For the adoption she wore "a blue velvet dress with a pink yolk and white shoes.") Thus they don't have the problem of most gay parents without legal partnerships where a surviving parent can lose the child. Jim and Bill have been approached to be a sort of "poster family" for gay families. Jim said, "Although we realize this is an important issue, we have to refuse—it's not in Laurie's best interest for us to give up our family privacy."

---

[4] The scare cry against domestic partnerships, that they will destroy the institution of marriage, is silly; heterosexuals will still marry heterosexuals. The idea is so nonsensical that it doesn't seem worth responding to, yet it is the main rallying cry of those against domestic partnerships.

V

TIME LINE

I READ RANDY SHILTS' book *Conduct Unbecoming: Gays and Lesbians in the U.S. Military* (St. Martin's Press, 1993) and realized how important a history of attitudes towards homosexuality is to understanding where we are now. To write his book Shilts interviewed 1,100 people and got 15,000 pages of previously unreleased documents through 50 requests under the Freedom of Information Act. The book includes the history of social and political movements from the late forties to the time of the Persian Gulf War in 1990. The military proves to be a reflection of America's attitudes towards gays. Shilts found the military was always glad to have gay soldiers in times of war or when manpower needs were greatest. (The numbers in parentheses in this section indicate a page in his book. Sometimes words and phrases are his, particularly in the court rulings, in the interest of accuracy and because it's hard to paraphrase Shilts—his writing is so precise.)

THERE HAVE ALWAYS been gays in the military. Shilts documents high and low ranking ones beginning with the American Revolution. High ranking ones were accepted, like the Prussian General Baron von Steuben who is credited with helping Washington win the war. (11) Low ranking ones were "drummed" out. (Literally followed by drummer boys.)

1916 The first military laws to punish homosexual soldiers. Homosexuality is treated as a crime and soldiers are imprisoned for five to six years. (15)

WORLD WAR II changed homosexuality from a crime to a sickness. Now there are psychiatrists who say homosexuality is not "normal." (16)

IN NAZI GERMANY homosexuals were rounded up and sent to concentration camps. Many homosexuals joined the army to hide. Estimates of those killed range from 50,000 to 300,000. When the Allies liberated the death camps, homosexuals who had survived were sent to prisons by some American and British judges who considered homosexuality a crime. The years they spent in the death camps did not count toward their prison sentence time. (381) (See Richard Plant's *The Pink Triangle*.)

1943 Homosexuals are banned from all branches of the military. (17) Homosexuals were often the bravest and most daring soldiers. They were men intent on proving their manhood.

1948 President Truman racially integrates the military. He needed the black urban vote for reelection and liberals and civil rights groups were demanding an integrated military which Republican opponent Thomas Dewey was promising. (189)

Dewey had put pressure on Roosevelt in the 1944 election forcing him to let the first black units into combat, open training schools to blacks, allow black women into the WAVES and open more positions for black officers.

Up until this time the Pentagon had argued that letting blacks serve with whites would harm order and morale (the same argument used today against gays). When the forces were integrated they found out this was not true. A study showed that 77 percent of enlisted men changed their attitude toward blacks for the better after serving with them. None reported a less favorable attitude. (189)

POST-WORLD WAR II EUROPE WAC Sergeant Johnnie Phelps was serving on General Eisenhower's staff when he told her there were reports of lesbians in the WAC battalion. He wanted their names so he could get rid of them. Phelps estimated that 95 percent of the 900 women serving in the battalion were lesbian. She said, "I'll make your list, but you've got to know that when you get the list back, my name's going to be first." Then Eisenhower's secretary who was in the room said, "If the General pleases, Sergeant Phelps will have to be second on the list. I'm going to type it. My name will be first." Eisenhower looked at them and said, "Forget that order." (108)

1950 Homosexuality is linked to the idea of treason. This came from a Senate committee that included Senator Joseph McCarthy. Their report "Sex Perverts as Security Risks" decided they were, although the only example they found was an Austrian in the Hapsburg dynasty. (105)

FBI Director J. Edgar Hoover began a campaign to rid government of gays. His policy of harassment of gays lasted forty years. He equated homosexuality with disloyalty. (107) The irony of his persecution of gays (he kept extensive files on them) is that he and his companion, Clyde Tolson, FBI Associate Director, were widely known in Washington circles and Southern California gay circles to be a gay couple. (109)

1953 New President Eisenhower issues an executive order saying "sexual perversion" is a basis for terminating and not hiring federal employees. (107) Eisenhower had played the McCarthyism/subversives card for votes. (108)
  In 1991 the Department of Defense did a study which concluded that homosexuals were not security risks and that Hoover had been wrong. Still the policy of gays as security risks was not changed. (112)

1959 Dr. Franklin Kameny, a Harvard educated astronomer working for the Army Map Service, is fired under the Civil Service Commission rules that no homosexual may work for the U.S. government. He begins to work for three goals: to end the rule that gays cannot work for the government, to end discrimination against gays having security clearances, and to end the exclusion of gays from the military. The Supreme Court turned down his own case for review in 1961. (194)

1965 The anti-Vietnam war movement was beginning. By 1966 there was a shortage of manpower. You could not get out of being drafted by saying you were gay. You had to give proof. The catch-22 was if you did give proof (affidavit from sex partner or psychiatrist), you could go to prison. Confessing to a homosexual act was a felony in forty-nine of the fifty states, punishable by as much as twenty years in prison. (65)

MAY 1968 Perry Watkins is inducted into the U.S. Army. He had checked "yes" in the box for "homosexual tendencies." (60) Both a physician and a psychiatrist questioned him—he said he was gay—and cleared him for induction. Months later he met a gay draftee who told him he was being released for being gay so Perry asked to be released under the no gays policy but was refused. Perry was black. Shilts sees significance in the fact that blacks found getting out of the draft more difficult than whites. (64-65)

1968 A year of social upheaval. In April the assassination of Reverend Martin Luther King started race riots. Robert Kennedy was assassinated in June. There were riots in Miami in August at the Republican convention when Richard Nixon and Spiro Agnew were nominated and later at the Democratic convention in Chicago when Hubert Humphrey was nominated. The Beatles released their song, "Revolution." In Atlantic City protesting at the Miss America pageant was a group of women who called themselves "feminists." Young blacks were forming militant groups, and the best selling novel was Gore Vidal's *Myra Breckenridge,* a story about a cheerful transsexual. Homosexuality was first mentioned in a Presidential campaign speech. Governor Ronald Reagan of California said it was a "tragic disease" and should be kept illegal. (74-75)

JUNE 1969 The riots at Stonewall Inn in New York City. Police raided a bar and began dragging gay men out into the streets and into police vans. These raids were common. What was different this night was that the "queers" fought back for the first time. For the next four nights protesters, from college students to political activists, joined the protest against the police. Drag "queens" faced the police with a kick dance line. The colorful protest became a tourist attraction. The words "gay power" were heard for the first time. "Stonewall" marks the beginning of the gay rights movement. From the gentle people who had never fought back came a new movement of young gay radicals. (92)

1970 The feminist movement blossoms. Kate Millett's book *Sexual Politics* gives the movement a vocabulary: *male chauvinism, patriarchy, male supremacy,* and the one that really horrified many men, *Ms.* Their agenda made sense. Abortion was illegal. A woman had to have written permission from her husband to apply for credit or incorporate a business. Legally women were their husbands' chattel. The Equal Rights Amendment, in committee since 1923, made it out to the House floor for a vote. It didn't pass. (142)

The impetus of the movement came apart when Millett who was married was asked if she was a lesbian. She answered yes. A schism came in the movement. Gloria Steinem and Susan Brownmiller stood by Millett, saying the women's movement was for all women. Betty Friedan and other feminist leaders were homophobic, believing that lesbians would harm the movement. (144) As it was many men who feared the movement wanted to believe that every woman who had the temerity to want equal rights and access to jobs was a lesbian. This legacy is still so much with us today that many women avoid the word "feminist." E.g., Yes, I want equal pay for the work I do, but I'm not a feminist.

Many people believe that "feminist" and "lesbian" are synonymous with "hating men"—WRONG, there is no such connection.

JANUARY 22, 1973 *Roe vs. Wade.* The United States Supreme

Court votes 7-2 to overturn all state laws restricting abortion in the first three months of pregnancy.

JANUARY 27, 1973 Official end of the Vietnam war when the peace treaty is signed in Paris by Secretary of State William Rogers and North Vietnamese representative Nguyen Duy Trinh. Hours later the U.S. military draft is ended. (177)
 Now not enough men are volunteering for the military, so opportunities for women increase dramatically. (182)

1973 The American Psychiatric Association removes homosexuality from its list of mental disorders.

NOVEMBER 1974 The Dutch Armed Forces receive official notice not to discriminate against homosexuals. In 1969 the Dutch government had conducted a study determining that homosexuality is an orientation set before birth or in the early years of life, that it has been present throughout history, and may be regarded as normal in the same way left-handedness is normal. Gay people were said to be a minority deserving civil rights protection. (193)

MARCH 1975 The American Civil Liberties Union begins a test case to get the U.S. Supreme Court to hear a gay civil rights case. Frank Kameny has found a perfect man for this test case: Technical Sergeant Leonard Matlovich—three tours of Vietnam, the Bronze Star, a Purple Heart, two Air Force commendation medals, a recent Air Force Meritorious Service Medal, and eleven years of unblemished service. (198) Matlovich took a letter to his commanding officer saying he was a homosexual and requesting to continue his military career. (203) Air Force policy stated homosexuals may be retained in "unusual circumstances." The ACLU attorney David Addlestone would argue Matlovich's retention on this vague wording, on the equal-protection clause of the Fourteenth Amendment, and the privacy interpretation of the Ninth Amendment. (202)

MAY 1975 T/Sergeant Matlovich receives a letter notifying him he is being discharged.

JUNE 29, 1975 At a gay pride march in New York City to commemorate the sixth anniversary of the Stonewall riots, T/Sergeant Matlovich delivers the saying he was already famous for from television and print interviews: "The military gave me a medal for killing two men, and wants to discharge me for loving one." (212) In August he would be on the cover of *Time* magazine, in his Air Force uniform with the caption "I am a homosexual."

JULY 3, 1975 The U.S. Civil Service Commission ends its policy of forbidding the employment of gay people in federal jobs. This followed a federal court decision that there must be a connection between employee conduct and the ability to perform the job to have a ban—no connection could be found between homosexuality and job performance. (214)

This legally lifted the barriers Eisenhower had put in place during the McCarthy era (214), however changing a law does not change what an organization does in all cases. If a person could not be fired for being gay, he could be fired for not showing up for work, for example. One man who worked on a ship as a civilian was not allowed to come on board to do his job. (224)

MID-'70S One of the largest migrations since the Dustbowl was taking place. From all over the country gay people were migrating to cities like San Francisco by the thousands per year, escaping from the small hometowns that were inhospitable to them. They rebuilt and revitalized the older areas of cities they settled in and the new word "gentrification" described the phenomenon of formerly rundown areas that were now chic. (274)

(This past year in San Diego one section of the city made incentives and pleas for gay people to move into their area. They wanted what the gay community had done for the now bustling and attractive Hillcrest area.)

JULY 1975 Congressman Ed Koch petitions the Department of Defense for the elusive 639-page Navy document called the Crittenden Report, a 1957 study on homosexuals in the Navy that the Navy had been denying existed. The Department of Defense responded it knew of no such report. (281) Navy attorneys found this report in Pentagon files in 1976. The report said no correlation was found between homosexuality and ability or attainments in the Navy. The study found no sound basis to think homosexuals were security risks, in fact the report stated "There is some information to indicate that homosexuals are quite good security risks." The report requested the Navy to not make discharges for homosexuality "less than honorable" and advised the Navy to liberalize its policies at a rate even with the mores of the civilian society. (282)

SEPTEMBER 1975 T/Sergeant Leonard Matlovich is given a "general" discharge for "unfitness" by the Air Force Administrative Discharge Board. (239)

OCTOBER 1975 Camp Mercer, South Korea. Specialist Five Perry Watkins' discharge hearing for being gay. Perry's commanding officer had discovered in Perry's records that he was homosexual and felt compelled to process him for a discharge following Army regulations, even though he liked Perry and admired his work. (218) Perry had reenlisted in 1971. His commanding officer had read in his papers about a hearing held in 1968 when Perry was nearly raped because of his homosexuality and had asked to be let out of the Army for his own safety. (118) That hearing board had concluded that Perry could not prove his homosexuality. (83)

The discharge hearing board in Korea this time returned its verdict in thirty minutes. They voted to retain Perry Watkins. They said there was no evidence that his behavior had affected unit performance or morale or his own job performance. Reflecting on Leonard Matlovich's recent discharge Perry decided that the military did not want to remove all homosexuals from its ranks, it just wanted to give the impression it did. (243)

MARCH 1976 *Doe vs. Commonwealth's Attorney.* The case challenging the constitutionality of the Commonwealth of Virginia's statute outlawing "crimes against nature." The plaintiffs argued that the law caused people with otherwise impeccable lives to live in jeopardy and fear and they had a right to privacy. (283) The lower court, a panel of three judges, two who were elderly and brought out of retirement for the case, ruled two-to-one to keep the statute. The old men voted for it, not on the Constitution as a basis but on the Bible, quoting from Leviticus. The U.S. Supreme Court voted 9-3 to not hear the case. They gave no legal rationale, infuriating the three members who voted to hear the case and Constitutional law experts. *Time* magazine said that the Supreme Court supported a criminal law that made 80% of American adults felons. The Virginia law was against sodomy (oral or anal sex) between all people, heterosexual or homosexual. (284)

JULY 16, 1976 Federal Court Judge Gerhard Gesell cited the Commonwealth case in ruling against Leonard Matlovich's reinstatement in the Air Force saying there was no Constitutional right to homosexual activity. He went on to plead with the military to change its policy as the Civil Service had done. The ACLU dropped the case. But Matlovich would continue his fight with another attorney. (285-286)

JANUARY 1977 Dade County Commission, governing the area of greater Miami, voted to enact a gay civil rights act, the first major city south of the Mason-Dixon line to do so. Forty cities had gay civil rights ordinances and by February nineteen states had repealed sodomy laws. (295)

FEBRUARY 1977 A federal district court in San Francisco rules the the Navy's mandatory discharges for gays is unconstitutional. (293) In spite of the setback to gay civil rights from the 1976 Supreme Court rejection, federal courts continued to rule strongly in favor of gay civil rights.

PRESIDENT CARTER'S amnesty program for Vietnam-era draft evaders, deserters, and service members included upgrading less-than-honorable discharges given to gays. (295)

JUNE 1977 In Dade County orange juice queen Anita Bryant leads a campaign to overturn the new gay civil rights law. Her tactics were those of ignorance that preyed upon people's fears. Her slogan, "They can't reproduce, so they must recruit" is a myth still with us. (298) (People are born with their sexual orientation so they cannot be persuaded to "switch." Homosexuals do "reproduce" because most of them live in hiding from the society that's hostile to them by marrying heterosexuals.)

After overturning Dade County's gay civil rights law, Anita promised to carry her "Save Our Children" campaign against gay people across the country. She said gay people are "dangerous to our children, dangerous to our freedom of religion and freedom of choice, dangerous to our survival as one nation under God." (300) She pulled out all the emotional stops on the "fear" organ. She left a legacy of ignorance, hate and fear. Gay rights stopped becoming popular and became controversial. California quickly passed a law banning gay marriage. (302)

NOVEMBER 1977 Harvey Milk is elected to the San Francisco Board of Supervisors. He is the first openly gay public official. (303)

MIAMI TAUGHT the minority Christian fundamentalists they can win elections. They move their crusade "out of the revival tent and into the political mainstream." (303) Jerry Falwell began organizing his Moral Majority and Jesse Helms began preparing to run for the U.S. Senate in 1978.

JUNE 25, 1978 The San Francisco Gay Freedom Day parade has an estimated 375,000 marchers, the largest demonstration for a political cause since the anti-Vietnam war demonstrations. Two new symbols are seen—the rainbow flag symbolizing the diversity of people; and the inverted pink triangle, the symbol Hitler made homosexuals wear in concentration camps. (311-312)

JULY 1978 Federal Judge John Sirica rules the law preventing women from serving on ships is unconstitutional. (315)

NOVEMBER 1978 Supervisor Harvey Milk and Mayor George Moscone are assassinated by anti-gay politician and former supervisor Dan White. No gays were permitted on the jury which found White guilty of not murder but voluntary manslaughter for which he would serve only five years in jail. (313)

MAY 1980 Judge Terence Evans rules that barring gays from serving in the Army violates the First, Fifth, and Ninth amendments of the Constitution. He orders the Army to reinstate schoolteacher Miriam Ben-Shalom into the Army Reserves. There was no evidence of homosexual conduct, but Judge Evans said if there were, the federal government would have to prove it made her unfit for the Army Reserves. (347)

SEPTEMBER 1980 Judge Gerhard Gesell rules Leonard Matlovich be reinstated into the U.S. Air Force, at the rank he would have achieved had he not been discharged in 1975, and with back pay and no impediment to re-enlistment. (362)

The Pentagon offers Matlovich a cash settlement if he doesn't return. (363) Matlovich's attorneys advise him to take the settlement offer. They said the Supreme Court was becoming more conservative and his chances there wouldn't be good.

October 1980 Federal Judge Anthony Kennedy in San Francisco rules that the discrimination against gays by the military is constitutional. Not wise, he said, but constitutional. (366)

The Army refuses to obey Judge Evans' order to reinstate Miriam Ben-Shalom in the Army Reserves.

The Pentagon has a task force working to write new regulations that have no wording that might allow gays.

In the 1980 presidential campaign evangelical preachers use gay rights against President Carter, saying he is a president for gays. They used the slogan "the gays in San Francisco elected a mayor, now they're going to elect a president." Ironically, Carter had shown little interest in gay issues. (368-370)

Reagan was supported by the New Right. The Republican platform endorsed the Family Protection Act which included: no federal funds could be used to buy textbooks in which women are portrayed in nontraditional roles or to support programs for women battered by their husbands. Reagan supported overturning *Roe vs. Wade*. George Bush campaigned as pro-choice but changed his position when he became Reagan's running mate. This backlash to the social changes of the '60s and '70s would influence the next two decades' presidential elections. (368-369)

With Reagan's election Matlovich's attorneys convinced him to accept a settlement from the Air Force and not continue his case. He received $160,000 tax-free. Matlovich hoped to use it to start a business and a new life. (371, 366)

JANUARY 1981 The exiting Deputy Director of Defense Graham Claytor issues a new directive to the military on homosexuals. The new policy allows no gays in the military, no exceptions. (379) The definition of a homosexual now included "desire" or "intent" to engage in homosexuality. Shilts says "The military had, in effect, banned homosexual thoughts." (380) This was one of the last acts under the Carter administration. Four days later, Ronald Reagan was inaugurated.

For the next decade there would be horrible purges and persecutions of gay military people under this directive. Women in the services particularly suffered. (382)

MARCH 1982 Military doctors quietly treat their first AIDS patient at Letterman Army Medical Center in San Francisco, one of the first 300 in the nation. (408)

THE REAGAN administration closes down the Office of Domestic Violence, the agency to protect women from abusive husbands. The pro-family people considered this agency to be anti-family. (408)

JUNE 1982 The Equal Rights Amendment for women fails to pass—three states short of the thirty-eight states required for ratification. Spokesmen against it, including "traditional woman" Phyllis Schlafly used scare tactics such as saying the amendment would advance gay rights, including same-sex marriages. (416) Schlafly's son's revelation that he is gay never softened his mother's anti-gay rhetoric.

IN THE '80S as women entered the workplace in traditionally male roles, men referred to any assertive woman as a "dyke." Lesbianism, previously ignored, now became a symbol of heterosexual men's fear of losing their dominance and identity. Sexual harassment in the workplace proliferated as men sought to have their heterosexuality affirmed. (417)

SEXUAL HARASSMENT and paranoia about lesbians was extreme in the military where the presence and influence of women was growing. (417) There was much forced sex (rape). If the woman resisted, or reported the incident, she was called a lesbian (meaning, does not like sex with men). Such an accusation could bring a discharge. Being a character witness for an accused woman cost women their jobs and eventually their careers. Associating with a suspected lesbian was used as grounds for discharge. Young women were put in prison until they "named names" of "possible" lesbians. Women were suspect if they played softball or were good athletes. One woman was tried because she had a *Vogue* magazine in her locker. (She was a fashionable dresser.) She was asked if she "got off" looking at pictures of women. Her fiancé and a former boyfriend testified that they had had sex with her and she had enjoyed it. Female anatomy diagrams were brought into hearing rooms to show what accused women supposedly did. False statements, made up by investigators, were entered as evidence against women. In the *USS Norton Sound* purge eight of the nine black women on ship were accused of homosexuality for "flaunt(ing) their power and authority over the other females on the ship" their accuser said. (336-37, 344, 350-351, 354, 587, 597, 608, 628, 629, 630, 631, 633, 652-653)

In 1988 in one of the most devastating purges of women from the military, at Parris Island Marine Training Depot in South Carolina, the Marine Corps lost 10% of its female drill instructors and an estimated sixty-five women, many of senior rank. (630-631) In this purge Lance Corporal Barbara Baum was sentenced to one year in prison (the prosecutor asked for the maximum thirty-five years) (611) and a dishonorable discharge with the promise she would be released if she named names (the investigators were after higher ranking women). When she finally broke down and answered questions (she could give only "hearsay" evidence; she'd "heard" someone might be a lesbian) she was not released. She ended up serving six months in prison. Her life was devastated by the harassment, the imprisonment and the suffering she experienced from being finally broken so that she named names and harmed other women. (598-639)

Fear of loss of jobs to women, not fear of lesbians, was the real reason for the purges of women from the military in the '80s. Marines didn't want women doing men's jobs and Navy men didn't want women on their ships. (Actually Navy wives were happy when the women on ships were lesbians.) (5, 322, 339, 495)

OCTOBER 1982 Perry Watkins is refused reenlistment on the grounds he is gay. A federal judge orders his reenlistment and he continues to serve. (425)

1983 Major Robert Redfield, the Army's expert on viral diseases, sees three women with AIDS, married to servicemen with AIDS. He realizes that the disease is not confined to homosexuals and that the problem is going to be staggering in its effects on society. (433)

AIDS was going to make the gay population visible. For more than a decade gay activists had a saying that if every gay person turned purple on one day, prejudice toward gay people would end because people would realize how many people they know and like are gay. Now a sort of visibility was arriving in a horrible way. (434) (Remember the nation's shock at Rock Hudson's AIDS?)

APRIL 1984 Federal Judge D. Brock Hornby rules that the Army, who had disenrolled a girl from ROTC because she said she was a lesbian, must allow for First Amendment rights to free speech. (450) This decision was reversed on appeal after the *Dronenberg* decision. (See below.)

MAY 1984 The Army discharges Perry Watkins in Germany, giving him only a few hours to make a plane to the States. They wanted him out fast so his attorney couldn't get a restraining order. (447)

AUGUST 1984 The *Dronenberg* ruling. Jim Dronenberg was a Korean language specialist at the Defense Language Institute in Monterey. Charged with sexual misconduct (two private, consensual sexual encounters) his lawyers argued he had a right to privacy, as established in the courts in contraception, miscegenation, and abortion, that the government had never shown that anti-gay laws fulfilled any military use, and that anti-sodomy laws applied only to homosexuals and not to heterosexuals deprived them of "equal protection under the law." (451)

Appeals Court Justice Robert Bork, writing for the three-member panel (which included Antonin Scalia, now on the Supreme Court), said "Private consensual homosexual conduct is not constitutionally protected."

He said any judicial attempt to extend civil rights to include gays represented the invention of new civil rights. He criticized the Supreme Court for creating new rights in *Roe vs. Wade*. (451)

Many legal scholars felt Bork and Scalia were advertising themselves for the Supreme Court and Reagan's promise to overturn *Roe vs. Wade*. (452)

The Dronenberg case signaled the courts' sharp turn to the right.

FEDERAL JUDGE Barbara Rothstein rules against Perry Watkin's reenlistment, based on Dronenberg. She said Army regulations, though irrational and lacking wisdom, are constitutional. (453)

IN APRIL 1984 researchers isolated the HTLV-III virus (later named HIV). In March of 1985, when a test for the virus became available, the Pentagon ordered the military to test all blood for the virus. What would be done with the information of who had the virus was a troubling question. (483) Army doctors argued that the infected personnel be kept and treated for the valuable medical research the Army could do under their controlled circumstances on this little understood virus and the course of the disease. (484) Most high officials wanted HTLV-III infected personnel out of the military. Others argued that they shouldn't waste all that training if the person could still perform his job. (502)

MARCH 31, 1986 *Bowers vs. Hardwick*. The first case involving homosexuality to be fully argued in the Supreme Court. Hardwick had been arrested in his own bedroom. A policeman had come to the house during a party and asked for Hardwick. A guest pointed to the bedroom and the policeman entered. Although he came to serve a warrant for intoxication, a matter which Hardwick had already cleared with the court, he saw Hardwick having oral sex and arrested him under Georgia's sodomy law. (522)

At first the Court was divided 4-4. In favor of retaining sodomy laws were Justices Byron White, Sandra Day O'Connor, William Rehnquist and Chief Justice Warren Burger. Their position was that we'd always had these laws, i.e., they are part of our culture. The opposing opinion, that adults have the right to conduct their sexual lives in private without interference from the State, was taken by Justices Harry Blackmun, William Brennan, John Paul Stevens, and Thurgood Marshall. Justice Lewis Powell was undecided. (523) Finally Powell sided with those voting to extend rights of privacy to gay people. Then days later he changed his mind and switched his vote. According to Shilts, court observers believed Powell did not want to be known as the justice who legalized homosexuality. (523)

When the decision was announced, June 30, 1986, Harvard law professor Laurence Tribe, who'd argued the case not on morality, but on privacy, responded that the issue was not what Hardwick was doing in his bedroom, but what the State of Georgia was doing in Hardwick's bedroom. (541)

Chief Justice Warren Burger made clear that although sodomy laws applied to both heterosexuals and homosexuals, the Court ruling was for homosexuals only and did not relate to the broader issue of the State controlling sexual conduct. In his dissent Justice Harry Blackmun ridiculed the Court majority's "obsessive focus on homosexuality" and said other laws on the books for generations, laws against miscegenation, abortion, and for school segregation, had been ruled unconstitutional. (540) He said homosexual orientation was not a matter of choice, but an integral part of an individual's personality, and there may be many "right" ways to define an intimate relationship in the diversity of a nation such as ours. (540)

After *Bowers vs. Hardwick* the decision was used in gay litigation to the harm of gay people. Whether in regard to employment discrimination, or imprisonment by the military, the courts referred to this case and pointed out that gays do not have rights. (541)

LATE 1986 HTLV-III name changed to HIV.

LATE 1987 The number of military personnel known to have HIV is 3,336. This number did not include dependents, family members, or civilian Department of Defense workers. (549)

Doctors were surprised at the number of high ranking officers and Pentagon officials with HIV. At least five colonels at Westpoint tested positive. The Pentagon was long known in Washington, D.C. gay circles to have a disproportionate number of gays. Gay men were dedicated to their careers and did not have traditional family concerns. High ranking persons with AIDS included a four-star general and a rear admiral. Their infection was kept secret. (549)

The possible damaging effect on the functioning of the Pentagon and possible bad publicity caused the military to abort its plan to discharge HIV infected personnel. (550)

BY 1987 sixty-four nations, mostly industrialized Western nations, had legalized homosexuality. The European

Court of Human Rights ruled in 1981 that restricting private gay sex by consenting adults was a violation of privacy under the European Convention of Human Rights. (578) Many Middle-Eastern and Far East cultures traditionally accepted homosexual relationships for men under the idea that men can do whatever they wish sexually (like the ancient Greeks) as long as they marry and produce heirs. (Maybe the U.S. is not so different after all.)

By the late 1980s gays were accepted in most Western armies except the USSR and Great Britain, and these countries related historically to Great Britain: the Union of South Africa, the United States, and New Zealand. Britain had legalized all sexual activity between consenting adults in 1967, but exempted the military. New Zealand did the same in 1986. (580)

OCTOBER 10, 1987 The march on Washington, D.C. for Lesbian and Gay Rights—the largest protest in Washington since the anti-war demonstrations of April 1970. A half million people walked to the Capitol to demand a gay civil rights law and more AIDS research. The AIDS Memorial Quilt was unfolded on the lawn near the Washington Monument. It contained nearly two thousand panels commemorating those who had died in the first six years of the AIDS epidemic. Among the names were Rock Hudson, Liberace, and Michael Bennett. Some panels had Army jackets, Marine shirts, and military medals—Purple Hearts, Bronze Stars and a Silver Star. Each panel was six feet by three feet, the size of a grave. (584)

FEBRUARY 1988 A three-member panel of U.S. Court of Appeals judges rule that Perry Watkins should be reinstated in the Army and that the government had failed to show that their anti-homosexual regulations serve any "compelling government interest." Further the decision said homosexuals represent a "suspect class" which means in legal terminology that they've been historically unfairly discriminated against because of an "immutable characteristic" and their cases should be given extra scrutiny to make sure they are receiving the Equal Protection insured in the Fourteenth Amendment. (641) The Reagan administration appealed the ruling. (642)

JUNE 15, 1988 Marine Lance Corporal Barbara Baum is taken in handcuffs, with her arms locked to a black belt around her waist, from Parris Island Marine Corps Training Depot, South Carolina, through the Savannah public airport and flown to the Marine Corps prison in Quantico, Virginia. She had been found guilty of fifteen felonies. The only thing she had actually done was refuse to name names of possible lesbians. (608, 613)

JUNE 22, 1988 Leonard Matlovich dies of AIDS. He was forty-four years old. His funeral was held on July 4, Independence Day, as he'd wished. His body was carried by Civil War-style caisson drawn by two horses down Pennsylvania Avenue to the Washington Congressional Cemetery. Perry Watkins spoke at the grave site about the dream of equality which Leonard had helped advance by his courage. Minutes before the twenty-one gun salute for a fallen soldier, the Air Force honor guard removed the American flag from his coffin. They refused to participate if he had an American flag, the symbol he'd most loved in his life. (624)

His gravestone is black granite with two pink triangles engraved on it. It has no name, but says: A GAY VIET-

NAM VETERAN. At the top is written NEVER FORGET, and under that NEVER AGAIN. Also etched on the stone is his famous saying: *When I was in the military, they gave me a medal for killing two men, and a discharge for loving one.* (583)

Ironically, and appreciated by Lenny Matlovich, his grave is in the same row and just eight sites away from J. Edgar Hoover and his companion Clyde Tolson, a few sites further on, the two famous gays who'd caused nearly a half century of harassment for gay Americans. (624)

NOVEMBER 1988 The Gay and Lesbian Military Freedom Project is formed to help gay military personnel under investigation. They attempted to draw attention to the Parris Island investigation as two women, Cheryl Jameson and Glenda Jones, remained in jail. (640)

SEPTEMBER 1988 The Army Reserves finally lets Miriam Ben-Shalom reenlist. It had been stalling for eight years obeying the 1980 ruling. In August Federal Judge Myron Gordon had finally threatened a $500-a-day contempt of court fine if the Reserves did not comply. The Army announced it would appeal. In January 1989, Judge Gordon wrote in reviewing the case that the military policies against gays were "basically irrational," violated the Constitution, and served no compelling government interest. (642)

DECEMBER 1988 The PERSEREC report is completed. This study ordered by the Defense Department concluded that gays are not a security risk, are able to observe others' privacy and not make inappropriate sexual advances, and that homosexuality is biologically determined, probably in the embryo stage of life, but at least in the first years of life. The study said the military's fears that gays undermine order, discipline and morale are unfounded and recommended programs to combat discrimination. (647-648)

The study said homosexuality occurs in all mammal species and therefore cannot be considered "unnatural" in the biological sense. It concluded that the fear of homosexuals as security risks is a "social construction" created during the McCarthy era and fanned by the "personal eccentricities" of FBI Director J. Edgar Hoover. (647, 112)

Defense Department officials were upset with the study's conclusions and managed to hide the report by renaming it a "draft." Then when inquiries were made about the "report" they could say that such a "report" did not exist. A saying in Washington at that time was that the Xerox machine was the most important weapon against government deception.

Eventually someone copied the report and leaked it, then more copies were made and got into circulation. (649)

DECEMBER 12, 1988 Barbara Baum is released from prison. Later when she confided in a few people and told them the government had put her in prison for being a lesbian, they could hardly believe it. (638, 646)

MAY 1989 Colonel Margarethe Cammermeyer, chief nurse for the Washington state National Guard, is considered for chief nurse of the National Guard for the whole country and a promotion to general. Because she is required to attend the War College, the Defense Investigative Services does a security check and asks Cammermeyer if she is a homosexual. She answered yes. The Army was informed and took steps to end her distinguished twenty-eight year career which included serving in Vietnam during the TET offensive and winning a Bronze Star, a Meritorious Service Medal, and two Army Achievement medals. With the support of her superior officers and the Governor of Washington, Cammermeyer decided to fight for her career. (683)

EFFORTS TO OUST gays from the military were actually endangering national security. The National Security Agency was losing its Middle-Eastern language specialists in the purges. Civilians at NSA said if the U.S. went to war in the Middle East they would suffer from the losses of these men who were their experts in Arab languages. (684)

FEBRUARY 15, 1990 The U.S. Court of Military Review rules that Barbara Baum had not received a fair trial due to lack of evidence and because her constitutional rights had been violated. Her discharge was changed to honorable. But Barbara had lost her career, her friends, and her "life," as she'd never forgiven herself for breaking under the pressure of prison. (695)

FEBRUARY 26, 1990 The long awaited Supreme Court test of the military's policy against gays came in the case of the discharges of Army Reservist Miriam Ben-Shalom and Navy Ensign James Woodward. Without comment or legal rationale the Court refused to hear the case, thus letting stand lower court rulings. (697)

MARCH–MAY 1990 College campuses and public opinion support young ROTC men who'd received their education and wished to serve and were not only being discharged but ordered to pay back the cost of their educations, even though they did not know they were gay when they enlisted. Several colleges threatened to oust the ROTC program from their campuses. However, need for federal programs and funding made them back down. At least the nationwide publicity of the problem made the military back down from demanding the young men repay the government their college scholarship money. (686, 687, 699, 700, 703, 704, 709)

Defense Secretary Richard Cheney had ordered the Joint Chiefs of Staff to stop trying to get back the tuition money from ROTC men. He'd also heard about the witch-hunt tactics used against gays and said he wanted no more gay purges on his watch. When asked if he would rescind the military policy excluding gays, he responded, "I pilot a big ship. It takes a long time to turn it around." (708)

MAY 1990 The eleven judge U.S. Court of Appeals panel in San Francisco orders the Army to reinstate Perry Watkins.

NOVEMBER 1990 The Bush administration appeals to the Supreme Court to review the Watkins decision. For months the court took no action, causing some observers to believe the court, with one empty seat, was evenly divided on the case. Then when Justice David Souter was appointed a ruling came. In one sentence it refused to review the case. The Court of Appeals ruling to reinstate Perry Watkins into the Army would stand. (729) This ruling touched only on Perry Watkins who had been used by the Army for sixteen years of service while they knew he was gay. It did not touch on the constitutional issues of the Miriam Ben-Shalom case that would have set a precedent for other gays in the military. Nevertheless, the Supreme Court, for the first time, had ordered the military to accept an openly gay soldier. (729)

Nine days later attorneys in the Defense Department advised the Pentagon not to deny security clearances on the fact that a person is gay. They also said Defense investigators should stop quizzing gays about specific sexual practices—they should be treated with the same respect for personal privacy as heterosexuals. (730)

The Pentagon kept these recommendations secret. The Defense Department continued to insist on the necessity of its anti-gay policy, and their investigators continued to pry into the private lives of gays who applied for security clearances. (730)

AUGUST 1991 Dr. Simon LeVay of Salk Institute in San Diego publishes his study in *Science* journal showing differences in the brain structure of gay men from heterosexual men. Originally UCLA had done a brain structure study showing that men had an area in the hypothalmus twice the size of that area in women's brains. The area was the one known to control sexual activity. LeVay looked at the brains of nineteen homosexual male cadavers, sixteen heterosexual male cadavers, and six heterosexual female cadavers. In the heterosexual males the sexual activity area of the hypothalmus was twice the size of that area in the homosexual males' brains. This made an argument that homosexuals are born homosexual. Although some people said the brain structure differences could be a result of "lifestyle," this was the first of several important studies to come in the next few years showing that sexuality is biologically set before birth. This challenged the belief of many experts who still insisted homosexuality in males is the result of a boy's relationship to a dominating mother and weak father. (These experts don't seem to talk about the "environmental pressures" causing lesbians, furthering in my mind Ann Bishop's premise that people aren't interested in lesbians because men don't feel threatened by them.)

AUGUST 1992 Randy Shilts comes down with pneumonia and his HIV becomes full blown AIDS. Shilts was the first crusader for homosexuals to stop unsafe sexual practices when AIDS first became known in 1982. For his campaigns to educate the gay community he was spurned by his own community. He could not walk on the streets of the Castro district of San Francisco without being spit upon. He felt if people stopped the unsafe sexual practices in 1982, they would be safe. He refused to be tested himself until after he finished his book on the AIDS epidemic, *And the Band Played On*. He didn't want his perspective to be colored by personal emotion. On the day he turned in his manuscript he went to his doctor for the test and discovered that he was one of the few people who'd been infected prior to 1982.

PRESIDENTIAL CAMPAIGN 1992 Bill Clinton promises that if elected he will lift the ban on gays in the military. Shilts rushes to complete his book *Conduct Unbecoming: Gays and Lesbians in the U.S. Military*. At Christmas, in the hospital with a collapsed lung, he dictated the final pages.

SPRING 1993 *Conduct Unbecoming* is published in the middle of President Clinton's debate with the Pentagon and Congress over his plan to allow gays in the military.

Not knowing who Shilts was or that I would write this book, I heard him interviewed on National Public Radio (I think it was Terry Gross on *Fresh Air*). I sat in the parking lot of the supermarket listening, fascinated by this marvelous, witty man and the subject.

I remember he was asked about the fact from his book that the military specialty area with the highest proportion of gays is Intelligence. Shilts laughed and said he asked gays in Intelligence why they thought that was, and they laughed and said, "Who can better keep a secret?" It was my first experience of the wit and humor with which gay people view and accept their own difficult lives in a homophobic society.

SUMMER 1993 President Clinton and Senator Sam Nunn work out a compromise in military policy. Gays will be able to serve if they don't say they are gay, and the military is not supposed to ask them. This is called the "don't ask, don't tell" policy.

Ironically, the "don't ask, don't tell" policy is exactly what Shilts showed the military always was. The military has always had more than an average share of the gay people in our society, but the secret was that everyone was supposed to pretend they weren't there — unless you wanted to get rid of someone.

JULY 1993 A new study gives more support to the idea that homosexuals are born homosexual. The National Cancer Institute of Biochemistry discovers that homosexuality follows the X chromosome in males. A study of seventy-six gay men found 7.5% of their maternal uncles and male cousins were gay. The estimated average in the general population is 2%. (These percentages are based on people who acknowledge they are gay and are "out" or open about their being gay. In actuality the percentages would be much higher.) A study of the DNA of forty pairs of homosexual brothers showed thirty-three pairs shared the same sequences of DNA in a particular area of the X chromosome. Homosexuality was the only trait the thirty-three pairs of brothers were found to share. Males have an X and a Y chromosome with the X coming from the mother.

JUNE 1994 Federal District Judge Thomas Zilly orders the U.S. Army to reinstate Colonel Margarethe Cammermeyer, twenty-six year veteran discharged in 1992 for saying she was a lesbian. The judge said the dismissal was out of prejudice and fear of homosexuals and such feelings are "impermissible bases for government policy" under the equal protection clause of the Constitution.

JULY 1994 The Employment Non-discrimination bill is introduced by Senators Edward Kennedy, D-Mass., and John Chafee, R-Rhode Island. The bill is to allow gay people equal treatment on the job. It followed a postal employee's suit against the U.S. Postal Service for the abuse and harassment he suffered on the job as a result of being homosexual. In court he discovered that discrimination against gay men is not against the law. (This bill was allowed to "die" in committee in 1994. It was reintroduced in 1995 but is once again being "held" in committee which will prevent a vote once more. This information is from Sen. Barbara Boxer's office in January, 1996.)

AUGUST 25, 1994 A Domestic Partners bill is passed in California. The bill states that unmarried couples (heterosexual and homosexual) can get hospital visitations rights, be named conservators if one of them is incapacitated, and more easily will property to one another if they register with the state as Domestic Partners. The bill was supported by senior citizens who often live together for companionship without being married.

NOVEMBER 1994 A key passageway in the brain is found to be larger in gay men than in heterosexual men. The finding suggests that sexual orientation may be part of a larger package of brain characteristics that could give gay men different patterns of skills than heterosexual men. The research was presented at the annual meeting of the Society for Neuroscience by Sandra Witelson of McMaster University, Hamilton, Ontario. Other studies have shown that gay men perform less well than heterosexual men at spatial tasks but better at verbal tasks. The new study may illustrate that the differences in the gay brain versus the heterosexual brain are biological rather than possibly the result of experience.

(Please notice that the studies on homosexuality are thus far all on men. Once more, lesbians feel forgotten, or invisible. The same focus on males was historically true about medical studies in general until very recently. Studies all were about men's health. I was surprised when medical studies began to be done on women to discover that heart disease is the leading cause of death for women. Even gay men have more political power than women; more money is spent on AIDS research than on breast cancer research. In 1996 the figures for Federal Government research money are $1.3 billion for AIDS, and $313 million for breast cancer.)

NOVEMBER 1994 The U.S. Court of Appeals in the District of Columbia upholds 7-3 the U.S. Naval Academy's 1987 dismissal of Joseph Steffan for admitting he is a homosexual. Judge Laurence Silberman writing the majority opinion said if Steffan says he is homosexual, then he probably engaged in homosexual activity. Patricia Ward, for the minority, said that his being dismissed for acknowledging his sexual orientation was "not rationally related to a legitimate government goal." She wrote that the ruling "runs deeply against our constitutional grain."

DECEMBER 6, 1994 The American Medical Association reverses its thirteen-year-old policy that recommended efforts to turn gay people into heterosexual people. Its new policy calls for a non-judgmental recognition of the patient's sexual orientation and states that gay people have a right to respect and concern for their lives and values from physicians. The new policy resulted from a meeting between AMA leaders and officials of the Gay and Lesbian Medical Association.

There was an interesting organization about this time of Christian young men to convert gay men to heterosexuals. The organization conceded failure and folded when the two organizing men ran off together.

Also, in Encino, California, the Thomas Aquinas Psychology Clinic, devoted to reversing homosexual orientation, said they have achieved no "cures" yet and therapy would be for a lifetime. (*Newsweek*, Feb. 24, '92) (Thomas Aquinas spoke strongly against homosexuality.)

DECEMBER 1994 Canadian researchers discover a link between the number of ridges in fingerprints and homosexuality. Since fingerprints are completely developed in human fetuses in the sixteenth week after conception, this was one more indication that sexual orientation is established before birth.

AUGUST 4, 1995 President Clinton by executive order repeals the forty-two-year-old federal policy that homosexuality is grounds for the denial of security clearances allowing access to classified information.

OCTOBER 1995 A gay rights case *Romero vs. Evans* goes to the Supreme Court, the first case they will hear since *Bowers vs. Hardwick,* 1986. The issue is the constitutionality of Colorado's Amendment 2, passed by the people of Colorado in 1992, which prevents gay people from having any anti-discrimination rights in the state of Colorado. This law was a response to human rights ordinances in the cities Boulder, Denver, and Aspen that barred discrimination in jobs, housing, and public accommodations based on sexual orientation. Amendment 2 was pushed through to its 53% passage vote by the Colorado for Family Values group which says groups are waiting in eight other states to push for similar bans should Amendment 2 win approval in the Supreme Court.

Presently nine states and the District of Columbia, and 157 cities and counties have laws prohibiting discrimination based on sexual orientation.

The Colorado Supreme Court ruled Amendment 2 is a violation of the fundamental right of any group to participate equally in the political process.

On October 10 Colorado Solicitor General Timothy Tymkovich arguing before the U.S. Supreme Court said the amendment is a valid judgment that homosexuals should not receive legal protection he termed as "special rights" not available to the public in general.

Jean Dubofsky, arguing against the amendment on behalf of the three Colorado cities and six gay Colorado residents, said the amendment prevents the right of every person to be free of arbitrary discrimination and the right of ordinary protection under the law. Angela Romero is a nineteen-year veteran employee of the Denver Police Department whose career and safety became jeopardized after her colleagues found out she was a lesbian. She was downgraded to patrol duty and her colleagues were refusing to help her on police calls.

Since the 5-4 *Bowers vs. Hardwick* decision six of the justices on the Supreme Court have been replaced, and Justice Lewis Powell who voted with majority has said he made a mistake in doing so. In court on October 10 Justice Antonin Scalia and Chief Justice William Rehnquist made clear their sympathy with the Colorado state argument. Justices Sandra Day O'Connor and Anthony Kennedy appeared troubled by the state's argument. Kennedy was concerned that the amendment prevents Colorado courts from hearing discrimination claims brought by gay people. (Linda Greenhouse, New York Times News Service) O'Connor voted with the majority in 1986.

A ruling is expected by July 1996.

OCTOBER 1995 A new study repeats the evidence of the 1993 study that gay men receive a gay gene on the X chromosome from the mother. Researchers looked for the same effect in women but did not find it. The study was led by Dean Hamer of the National Cancer Institute and reported in the November issue of *Nature Genetics*. The

University of Colorado and Whitehead Institute for Biomedical Research, Cambridge, Massachusetts, also participated in the study. Hamer said probably other biological factors like hormones also influence sexual orientation.

Thirty-two pairs of homosexual brothers were studied, and twenty-two pairs shared the same genetic material. Where there was a heterosexual brother, nine out the eleven had different genetic material.

NOVEMBER 1995 Researchers report that men who want to become women (transsexuals) have brain structure in the sexual behavior region of the brain that matches the brain structure of women. Dick Swaab of the Netherlands Institute for Brain Research said the brain differences are probably a result of interaction between sex hormones and the developing brain. Reported in *Nature*.

DECEMBER 1995 Same-sex marriages are in the news with the *Baehr vs. Lewin* case in Hawaii. In 1993 the Hawaii Supreme Court ruled that the complaint of sex discrimination was valid but sent the case back to the lower courts for study and trial to see if the State can find any compelling reason to prohibit same-sex marriages. The case is expected to go to trial in July of 1996. This week a panel appointed by the governor is expected to recommend the legalization of same-sex marriages, or at least a legal "domestic partnership" having the benefits and obligations of marriage for couples. This news rushed through mainland newspapers because in the U.S. marriage in one state must be recognized in every state. Same-sex marriages in Hawaii would have to be recognized in, say, California.

JANUARY 24, 1996 Sacramento, California. The Republican-controlled Assembly Judiciary Committee approved a measure to prevent California from recognizing same-sex marriages. The author of the bill, Pete Knight, said the couples would then be eligible for family insurance benefits which would put an unfair mandate on businesses. Outside the hearing room, Knight said that same-sex marriages would weaken the traditional concept of marriage between men and women and "I don't think we need to degrade that."

FEBRUARY 10, 1996 President Clinton signs a Defense budget bill that includes a clause discharging HIV-positive personnel. He signed the bill because of the military pay raises and positive aspects of the bill. His administration will seek to change the HIV discharge section in the legislature and the courts.

The Pentagon says there are 1,049 active-duty HIV-positive personnel, and more than half of these are married.

MARCH 1996 Researchers and military doctors say the discharge of infected personnel will halt some of the nation's most important studies of the disease. The military has the world's most complete records of the spread of the virus because of their ability to screen their personnel and require regular medical follow-ups.

The Chairman of the Joint Chiefs of Staff, General John Shalikashvili denounced the law as wasting the expensive training and experience of valued personnel.

APRIL 1996 The new federal budget agreement includes the repeal of the law requiring the discharge of service members with the HIV virus.

THE TIME LINE can end when all citizens of the United States have the right promised in the Fourteenth Amendment of Equal Protection of the laws.

MAY 20, 1996 The United States Supreme Court rules that Colorado Amendment 2 preventing civil rights for gays is unconstitutional. The court said the amendment improperly singled out gays and denied them protections from discrimination in employment, housing and public accommodations that are granted to everyone else.

Justice Anthony M. Kennedy wrote for the majority saying a state "cannot so deem a class of persons a stranger to its laws."

For the majority were Kennedy, John Paul Stevens, Sandra Day O'Connor, David H. Souter, Ruth Bader Ginsberg, and Stephen G. Breyer.

Writing the dissent Justice Antonin Scalia said the decision "has no foundation in American constitutional law" and that Colorado Amendment 2 was designed to prevent the "deterioration of the sexual morality favored by a majority of Coloradans." Also for the dissent were Chief Justice William H. Rehnquist and Justice Clarence Thomas.

ADDENDA

JULY 9, 1997 On this day Hawaii begins giving many of the legal benefits of marriage to couples who cannot legally marry: the right to share medical insurance and state pensions, inheritance rights, the right to joint property ownership, and the right to sue for wrongful death.

Couples do not have to live together to apply for benefits. They only have to be eighteen and barred legally from marrying. This would include gay couples, siblings, roommates, widowed mother and son or daughter. The state also passed a proposal to amend the state constitution to ban gay marriages. The benefits package and the amendment proposal are Hawaii's answer to the 1993 Hawaii Supreme Court ruling that under the state constitution it is unlawful to deny marriage licenses to same-sex couples.

ALSO, THIS JULY another Federal District Court judge ruled that the "don't ask, don't tell" compromise about gays in the military that President Clinton was forced to make with the Pentagon in 1993 is unconstitutional because it abridges the First Amendment right of free speech. This will be appealed by the government.

"Don't ask, don't tell" should go. We do relate to people around us sexually, so it's important sometimes to know who people are. It's nice if a guy can say to a woman who's getting a crush on him that he's gay, then she can say, "OK, cool," and they can be friends. Or if a woman knows her friend is a lesbian she won't make her do the "girl talk about guys" thing, or keep fixing her up on dates the woman doesn't want but is afraid to refuse.

Where sexual orientations aren't obvious, people ought to be able to say, "I'm gay." The policy should be socially correct, just good manners: "Don't ask unless you're friends (or have an appropriate reason), and when you tell, please don't SHOUT."

Epilogue

LESBIAN MYTHS
DELUSION AND DISILLUSION

JULY 1997

THIS BOOK was not supposed to have an epilogue—I didn't know there were lesbian myths. The book was being typeset when something happened that made another chapter necessary.

It was a perfect May day, the kind that makes me love California. Chris Briscoe was inking the final drawings for the book. Andrew Gill phoned and said he had the concept for the Amazon cover drawn and would come on Friday to show it to me. I had just come back from Catherine's, the typesetter, late in the afternoon and began washing lettuce for a salad for the lunch I'd missed. The phone rang and I let the answer-machine pick it up. A woman's voice said she was an attorney for Elizabeth Gilad and Ann Bishop and she wanted to talk to me about stopping publication of my book. I picked up the phone, "What?"

She threatened me with a lawsuit if I didn't turn control of the content of my book over to Ann and Elizabeth. She said, "I have your manuscript here on my desk. We demand the removal of the two appendices which are homophobic." She also said a group of people had "read the manuscript and made a list of certain characterizations of lesbians they want changed."

I told her, "If they control the images in the book, then

they'll have a book for lesbians by lesbians and only lesbians will read it. They'll have some sort of cottoncandy fantasy. That was never the intent of the book. If that's what they want, they can write their own book. But heterosexuals won't read it."

She started listing the grounds on which they would sue me if I didn't give them control of the book. "Broken contract . . ." the list was lengthy. She said, "They were told the book would educate people about lesbians."

"It does educate people about lesbians."

She said, "Homophobic people will read the book."

I said, "Then they'll get educated, won't they? Have you read the book?"

She said, "No, I haven't read it."

"It's a very loving book and positive book," I said. "And tell Ann and Elizabeth I'm shocked. I thought they were my friends. Friends pick up a phone and call if they have a problem. They don't have an attorney phone with threats. Make sure they get that message."

She said, "Oh, they'll get it, for sure."

I realized they were probably sitting there listening. It was just about the time Liz gets off work.

I phoned Catherine and told her about the threats. She told her partner Paul. She said, "Paul says you need another chapter, one from a different perspective." At first it didn't sink in what he meant until someone else said, "I guess you don't think they're so wonderful now." As people around me reacted I was surprised at the anger toward lesbians. Jeanne said, "They pretended to be your friends—invited you to their parties, but they were just using you to write this book. Well, they're no friends." Others said, "Lesbian bitches. You can't trust them." "Bitches with testosterone." "Lesbians are backstabbers."

Tom said, "John and I warned you Ann was going to betray you—you didn't believe us. At last it happened."

He looked at me sternly—child to parent.

"Dogs and children always know. From now on let us choose your friends."

I knew all these lesbian myths—lesbians are backstabbers, and you can't trust a lesbian—were the angry reactions of people who felt betrayed. We all do it. Look for the weakest point to hurl an insult when you're angry—looks, race, religion, ethnicity, class ("I always knew you were a snob," or redneck), sex ("that's just like a man," or woman). Men, if they can't find a sore point to insult another male, will attack his mother. Every guy has a mother. The playground "Your mother wears combat boots" is one of the least offensive of a colorful bag of mother insults. Still I wondered about these feelings that lesbians cannot be trusted. Most stereotype insults have that grain of truth in them that gives them their sting.

Later the mood turned lighter and to humor. "Well, you won't have to give complimentary books." "No talk-show visits for them now."

That evening I said to Tom, "I'm confused. It's an enigma. Is there any truth in these lesbian insults?"

Tom who earlier had been very angry said calmly, "There's no enigma. You know it—it's what you always say. It's a matter of character."

I began to wonder if the woman who phoned really was an attorney. Attorneys are not supposed to call you on the phone and threaten you—they get disbarred for that. The next morning I looked for her in the phone book but she wasn't there. I phoned the number she'd left on my machine and said, "You said you have my manuscript on your desk.

That's copyrighted material and I want it back, and all other copies that were made. I gave no artistic control of my book to Liz and Ann and I'm not in their employ or under contract to them. Give me your address and I'll put that in writing." I didn't hear from her. After several days I sent a letter to Ann and Elizabeth asking for my copyrighted manuscript back and saying I would look at the list of changes they wanted. Frankly I was curious, as were my friends. We couldn't guess where in the text they didn't like how lesbians were characterized. I said to Jeanne, "Maybe they didn't like my saying Patsy made me think of John Wayne."

She said, "But they dress that way. Why wouldn't they like it?"

On Friday twenty-year-old Andrew Gill came over with his cover drawing. (I'd known he could draw since I drove him home from church youth group when he was in ninth grade and he left his school notebook in my car. It had a few school notes and pages of drawings.) I'd had a concept for the cover, an Amazon without a face—indicating we don't know much about lesbians, that they're faceless to us—often we don't know they are lesbians. I thought she could be surrounded by, or bursting through, puzzle pieces, showing the book breaks through the puzzle of who she is. Andrew had found a different way to show the puzzle of the lesbian—he put the mystery in her face. This Amazon's expression was Enigma.

"Andrew, she is so beautiful," I said.

He sat at the kitchen table drawing—armor on her, a quiver of arrows. We talked about the threats on the phone. Andrew said matter-of-factly, "They can't tell you what to put in your book. That's your First Amendment right. If they don't like your book, they can write their own." We talked about when the movie *Basic Instinct* came out and lesbians objected that the killer was a lesbian. Lesbians picketed the theatres with placards saying, THE KILLER IS A LESBIAN. People ran to the theaters to see the film. Andrew and I laughed that heterosexual women didn't picket when the killer in *Fatal Attraction* was a heterosexual woman. It seemed so silly—they protest too much.

How did they get my manuscript? I did the friend thing—against the advice of Tom and John. At the beginning of April I called Ann to ask how her mother was and told her the book was finished. She said Elizabeth wanted to see her chapter. I laughed and said, "Tell her I kept my promise. There's no sex in it. And nothing she didn't say." Still Ann insisted until finally I said okay, I'd drive out with it.

Tom and John said, "Don't give it to her, she'll betray you. She can't be trusted. We've always known it and you can't see it."

I said, "She's our friend. We have to trust her." Actually her insistence on the phone made me uncomfortable too, but I felt I should give her the benefit of the doubt. "Besides," I reasoned to Tom and John (and myself), "Elizabeth will see her chapter is just what she actually said and then she won't worry. I can do that for her."

When I got to the house, Ann's behavior was very nervous. She paced. She chainsmoked. Conversation was small small-talk. I had all those uncomfortable little galvanic skin responses that tell you something is wrong. She kept going over to her mother and kissing her. I was surprised and said, "Has your relationship with your mother changed?"

"No," she said, "but I find this is very effective—it gets me responses that are useful." Actually, her mother looked very confused at the kisses, albeit she does have memory problems.

Ann looked at the manuscript and said, "I'll make copies of this and give it to people so they can make changes."

I said, in some alarm, "No. You don't understand. This is art not soup. (Borrowing Lily Tomlin's line.) We can't have everyone's finger in it. Communal art is an oxymoron—it doesn't exist. The book is done. If you start asking people to make changes it will never be done. Listen, it's okay for Liz to see her chapter, because you insisted. But no one else. You have to promise not to show it to anyone or tell anyone it's here, or I can't leave the book with you."

She said, rather oddly, and without looking at me, as she put the manuscript on top of the refrigerator, "My policy is 'don't ask, don't tell,' but I won't lie if someone asks me if I have it." (My god, such scruples, huh? Tom said, "I can hear her now, 'Ask me if I have anything you might like to read.'")

"Well, just don't show it to anyone but Liz."

By the time I got home I knew Tom and John were right—Ann couldn't be trusted. I'd wanted so much to believe in her. I had no idea what she would do, but I knew I should get the book back. The next day I phoned and said I was coming out to get the manuscript. When I got there Ann said Liz was upset that she might be identified by her family's nationality and the mention of specific jewelry she wore. Also, she said Liz said the penance of going on your knees begging for bread wasn't done in *her* monastery. I made a joke about making her Irish, as that would put her in a larger pool of nuns, but I said, tell Liz I will change those things, and that no one is going to know her except the small group of friends who are in the book. "Tell her her message is important. It will help people—many people will come to the turn." Ann said, "She doesn't care about that."

Ann said Liz also said that it was customers, not the tellers, in the bank who remarked about her "costume." I didn't think that needed to be changed and Ann agreed. Ann said Liz said I'd named her religious order—I hadn't. Ann always spoke for Elizabeth. Liz seemed to want that protection from the outside world and Ann drew importance from providing it. Ann herself seemed dreamily happy about the chapter—she asked me why I chose the name Elizabeth. "I like that name," she said. "That was the name of my lover before Liz."

When I got home I realized Ann had photocopied the manuscript—she had mistakenly given me the copy. Tom and John said, well, they'd warned me. But we didn't know what she'd do with it—maybe just keep it and read it. I did rewrite Liz's chapter, losing interesting details, making her family vaguely "European," but trying to keep the full story of her character and her message as she'd portrayed it.

More than a week passed after the phone call from the woman lawyer. Then I got a letter from her, full of threats. Tom read it. He couldn't believe the venom. "How do these people sleep at night?" he said. "Two pages, single-spaced. That's a lot of work."

The letter said the two appendices "completely misrepresent the lesbian and gay community by characterizing lesbians and gay men as totally lacking in moral character and integrity, suggesting they routinely prey on the unsuspecting 'straight' with the intention of misleading them and taking advantage of their innocent vulnerability.

"These appendices serve to reinforce erroneous negative stereotypes and totally ignore the fact that the gay scenarios presented are not the norm for the lesbian and gay community in the 1990s. You state that . . . you feel they must be included to attract the interest of homophobes so they will presumably purchase the book and read it, becoming educated in the process. My clients find this patently absurd and note that you never mentioned your intention to proselytize in this fashion."

Of course I never said that to her. Proselytize, what? I told Tom, "I see this woman lawyer fanning the flames of billable hours. My impulse is to phone Liz and Ann and warn them—never trust anyone who says 'patently absurd.'"

"You can't, Mom. You can't help them. Ann's not your student anymore."

And I knew he was right. I know how people are when they make you into an enemy. They never see anything you do as it is again. They forever see all your actions through the dark and distorting glasses of their paranoia.

The letter's next point was "(you) mis-characterize (sic) their lives and perspectives in a truly objectionable fashion." I didn't see how this could be when I transcribed their words verbatim from the tapes.

She went on to tell me to review my manuscript and contact her telling my proposed changes. Then she gave a list of the threatened legal actions Ann and Liz would take against me if I published the book without giving them control of the content. I know you're curious, so here it is: "breach of contract, intentional and negligent misrepresentation, false promise, invasion of privacy, false light, intentional and negligent infliction of emotional distress and fraud." She said I could "avoid this only by making significant changes in the manuscript or by choosing not to publish it at all."

Ann said that last day at her mother's house that Liz was concerned her family might recognize her in the book. In the lawyer's letter she must be the one who now wants more "privacy." Yet if they bring a lawsuit she surely will become the most famous lesbian ex-Mother Superior in the country. I can't quite see her wanting to walk into a courtroom and announce to a jury, "My name is _____. I'm a lesbian ex-Mother Superior and I'm suing for more privacy." "Yes, Ma'am. And will you tell us just where you were Mother Superior." It makes no sense. In the last phone conversation I had with Ann she was not at all concerned with privacy. I asked her if she wanted her pseudonym or her real name on the acknowledgment page. She said, obviously pleased, "Whatever."

A week later I received another letter from the lawyer saying Liz and Ann "do not want any direct contact with you" and to communicate with them through her (and her amazing "telephone game" that makes what one says no longer recognizable—fodder for her lawyerly "cleverness"). She went on to say "you mention that (Liz) did, in fact, have review rights." No. She went further on to say I had said other things which I had not. Billable hours. I slipped the letter into the file with the first letter and the tape of the threatening phone call. I put her twisted ideas, words, and threats out of my mind.

Her letter said she's waiting for me to send her the list of changes I propose to make. I never got their list of wanted changes. She's still waiting.

The problem is, when someone betrays you, for a while you become wary of that whole class of people. Because I had a bad and cruel husband, for a long time I feared and distrusted men, and I love men. I just wasn't sure I could tell the good ones from the bad ones. Sometimes Tom or John had to remind me, "Hey, we're men." Well, they always knew I loved them—they just wanted me to not be afraid of all men.

Now I had a very bad taste in my mouth about lesbians, for Ann and Liz, and particularly for their lesbian lawyer and her wildly imaginative concoctions. At first my distaste for lesbians extended to all my favorite lesbian celebrities, actresses and comediennes, who look like lesbians. This upset me—I knew my feelings were wrong and out-of-proportion and would go away but I didn't like having them, however temporarily. But it's a human condition, an emotional response as scientifically predictable as a chemical reaction in the lab.

Interestingly, I had none of these feelings of distaste for gay men. As came out at the glossary party, gay men are much more open than the reclusive and quiet lesbian women. Oddly, or not oddly, gay men have that chatty, emotional openness of women friends, and lesbians have that "something's wrong, I'll withdraw and sulk about you" attitude of men. (Generalizing here.) So let's look at disillusion and delusion.

I had the illusion that Liz and Ann were my friends and they were not. (I trusted them but they didn't trust me.) So now I'm dis-illusioned. That was my only disillusion—and maybe my surprise at their not understanding, and not wanting to understand, the book. Being dis-illusioned, or betrayed, is always painful and one has no choice but to go through that pain. Like being nine months pregnant, there's only one way out. (I once had a friend who in the uncomfortable ninth month of pregnancy screamed at her doctor that she didn't want to have this baby—she'd changed her mind—it was going to be too hard.) I knew the pain would pass and it's better to know the truth than to live in illusion. In retrospect I never even feel angry about betrayal. It always feels somehow foreordained. And it is, by character.

That gives me compassion for the betrayer.

From the pain of my dis-illusioning came something of value. (Tom said, "Betrayal is always illuminating.") It's good to lose friends who aren't friends, but, more importantly here, I became aware of the lesbian myths, and exploring them would make the book more complete in its truth of the lesbian experience. And what's happened doesn't change the truth of their stories. Their stories are true as they told them. (When Ann said Liz wasn't truthful in saying she had no sexual relationship with her first partner, I said I wouldn't question or change that. Liz told me "her truth," and I wrote it down as she told it. As with Ruth Ann and Stella's first sexual encounter, sometimes two people have two truths.)

Why do people believe lesbians are "backstabbers" and "can't be trusted?" I think it has to do with their reclusiveness that is mentioned other places in the book. And with their "ex-clusive community"—a tendency to socialize only with each other and exclude themselves from the larger society. Remember Jill said she and Jonnie were different in this respect, staying away from the insular lesbian community and choosing their friends on interest and character only.

I remember the lesbian couples I've known in the neighborhoods I've lived in from college on. One member of the couple always seemed to be in the house, peering out from behind the curtains, while the other would chat with me in the front yard. I thought of that person behind the curtains as a shadow person. It was a little eerie to me, a little creepy—why did she act afraid of the outside world? Why did she scurry, head down, from car to house, while the other woman, the butch one, was always the "man in the yard," who leaned on her rake and said hello when I passed? I asked Ann about this once when we were together. She said, "It's not always the fem partner who hides in the house. With Liz and me, I'm the one hiding in the house, she's the one out in the yard." (But she doesn't make phone calls or speak for herself.)

It was an answer, but not to the question I was trying to ask. I was asking, "Why is *anyone* hiding?"

I know the answer now. They have a delusion. They have homophobia-phobia. They fear homophobia where it does not exist. When I was nearly finished with the book and began to talk to local publishers, they always asked, "What is the book about?"

Gulp. Cough. How would they react? I'd heard Christian Fundamentalists and Far-Rightists on cable TV spouting some pretty hateful verbiage. I would bravely swallow and think I would now share in the hatred that lesbians face everyday—I would do that as a sign of my solidarity with their suffering. What happened? I never ran into that attitude at all—even at a religious press. What I got was: "great topic." And then a lot of questions. "Are you a lesbian?" "Is anyone in your family a lesbian?" "Can homosexuality be inherited?" "My bother's son is gay, can I get a book for my brother—I keep telling him to accept his son—maybe if he understood." "My ex-husband is gay. Fifteen years and I didn't know. He was military—so tough. Now he's running around in bizarre clothes—why is that?"

Everyone was interested. Everyone was open. At least to wanting to know the truth—just like my friend Sherry in the "Anniversary Waltz" chapter. Remember Ann's saying she had stayed away from children because a lesbian had told her people don't want lesbians near their children because they "fear them." Ann's own experience later showed her that's not true. It's a lesbian myth. Lesbians believe they are feared and they are not.

I have compassion for Ann and her fears and for the strangely reclusive and inbred lesbian community that feeds and grows those fears. I had compassion for Ann when she told me in her story that she "appears" different for different circumstances—plays roles. She could "shrink down" to appear a non-threatening woman around men. But in lesbian clubs, she said, "I puff myself up—to look fierce. I dance in a circle around my women friends so people will know they have a protector." (Why do they need a protector in a lesbian club? It seems more that it's a role she enjoys playing in the safety of the club—the male protector.)

So I feel I know part of what happened. Liz got cold feet about being in the book—became concerned her family would recognize her, that she would lose her avowed non-lesbian status (although her family knows), and so Ann puffed up her chest, told Liz she would protect her, and hired a lawyer. And on the way, she thought, she could exert control over what she at some time had begun to think of as "her book."

All my friends and the people who knew about the book were supportive and curious. They shared stories about the gay people who'd been in their lives. No one showed any homophobia. Even my most conservative friends, Jeanne and Nick, aren't homophobic. Just uncomfortable with certain ideas. Jeanne says they talked it over and agree they "think homosexuality is wrong." They don't actually "think" it's wrong, it "feels" wrong—the thought of it feels wrong to them. As it does to me. The other sexual orientation always feels wrong to people. Remember Ted's saying to Fred about Fred's having sex with his wife? "Eyuuuw. How could you DO it? I could NEVER do it." And Fred replied, "I shut my eyes and thought about men."

Knowledge that there are other sexual orientations will never make us comfortable with their sexual practices. Nature sees to that. So no one has to be scared that understanding sexual orientation (education) will turn us into a morally amorphous society. Nick says he hires lesbians at his company. "I don't mind hiring them or working with them—until they start wearing their Act Up T-shirts and putting little rainbow flags on the desk and bringing their sexual politics into the workplace. Then everyone gets uncomfortable. Okay, they're homosexual. But do we have to talk about it?"

Seems fair enough to me. Heterosexuals don't announce their sexuality and want to discuss it (I know some of you are making jokes here, but you know what I mean—politicize it). One day, weeks before the "May surprise," Jeanne and I were sitting on the upstairs steps in her house talking about our kids and life as we always do. Something made us laugh hard and we were holding hands and rocking with laughter. When we stopped laughing we let go of each other's hands and she, ever aware of my book, said, "If you were a lesbian, I would still be your friend . . . but you couldn't hold my hand anymore."

So, lesbians lighten up a little and join the rest of us. Remember the first thing Ann said to me, about the military—only men are homophobic about gay men, you never hear about women fearing lesbians in the military, saying they won't bunk with them or shower with them. HETEROSEXUAL WOMEN DON'T FEAR LESBIANS. It's a lesbian myth that they do.

Why do lesbians have this myth? Why do they think the dreaded appendix "Fox in the Hen House" portrays lesbians as "predators on vulnerable heterosexual women"? No heterosexual woman who read the book saw that appendix that way. It just reminded them of their own similar stories of in-the-closet lesbian friends. They chuckled or shook their head, wondering why the lesbian woman thought the heterosexual woman would ever think they would be interested.

This is the point. Many lesbian women evidently, and particularly those in the closet, know so little about sexuality and their own sexual orientation that they do get crushes on heterosexual women thinking wrongly that someday that sexual interest might be returned. Evidently Ann and Liz and their lesbian lawyer think that. It's a myth. A heterosexual woman will never be attracted sexually to a lesbian. All heterosexual women know this. They don't know that lesbian women don't know it. On an Oprah show in May a lesbian activist leader, enthusiastically waving her arms, asked Oprah, "Why don't women open up their female friendships to the added dimension of sexual experience?"

Oprah responded with shock, "Because I'm not the teeniest bit interested in having sex with my girlfriends." She held up her thumb and forefinger pressed tightly together to illustrate, "not the eeensiest, teensiest bit."

"Fox in the Henhouse" is about the sad delusion of lesbian women-in-the-closet who do not understand sexual orientation. It's about education in that respect. I didn't know that lesbians "out" in the gay community also hold that delusion. The appendix is about "gays in the 1990s" in spite of what Ann and her lawyer say. It's the true story of my three friends and my friend Maryann's friend in the '90s. Did we feel "preyed upon and vulnerable"? No. I felt sad that the women didn't want to be friends when they found out I wasn't interested in a sexual relationship. Did Maryann feel victimized? Well, when I said, "Maryann, you'd better tell her you know she's a lesbian and make it clear to her you'll never return her sexual interest in you."

Maryann twisted her bracelets and looked uncomfortable. "But I don't want her to go away—I mean, really, she does so much for me. She picks my kids up at school. She repairs my car when it's broken."

So, who's the victim here.

Is the appendix "The Last to Know," about the pain of a marriage between a closet-homosexual man and a heterosexual woman, something that doesn't happen in the '90s? No, it still happens and will continue to happen until people understand sexual orientation and accept others' sexual orientations. Until that time parents' disapproval of homosexuality will force their gay sons to hide their sexual identity and marry. Society, as in the form of corporations who require executives be "family men" to be promoted, will force gay men to marry.

And yes, the woman is innocent, and she is a victim. He knows she wouldn't marry him if she knew the truth, and he needs the marriage for his public face. But the man is a victim too. Of our societal ignorance. And that's what this appendix is for. To bring home the pain of these marriages for all concerned. Divorce attorneys say their experience is that these are chaotic and bizarre marriages. One told me, "The kids are wild, the woman cries all the time—no one knows why."

Except the husband. It's all very, very sad. And that's the truth, the whole truth. One woman abandoned in her forties said, "He stole my life."

The young generation today is much more knowledgeable than mine was. I had gay boyfriends in high school and college. I didn't know they were gay. They were great friends, good dressers, good dancers, witty and fun. But I never understood why the relationships didn't progress to kissing. Jeanne said she was shopping with her thirteen-year-old last week and they saw a really cute guy. Her daughter asked her, "Mom, is he too good to be true?"

Jeanne said she looked. Clothes perfect. Styled hair, jewelry. "Yep," she said, "I think so." I said every mother should make sure her teen daughters see the movie *Clueless*. Alicia Silverstone's character, a fashion-conscious teen, falls for the coolest looking, dressing guy in school, and later finds out he's gay.

Straight guys have rough edges somewhere. Comedian Chris Rock says guys never can get girls until some girl chooses them and cleans them up—then girls want them. John was home last weekend and couldn't find any clean socks. Finally he found in a basket of clothes he'd brought from school some rose colored socks—not his. He put them on laughing, "Oh, migosh. What will people think?"

I said, "Well, you might want to change that (bright) blue shirt."

He cocked his head at me, "Right, matching shirt and socks. Then everyone will think I'm gay."

The next generations will have more knowledge about sexuality and the situations of the two appendices will become more a thing of the past. I wish I had known my dance partners were gay, or they could have told me. We could have gone on dancing. We could have stayed best friends, but they felt they had to go away at a certain point and I didn't know why.

Even men fearing homosexuals is changing. In both his first and second year of college Tom had a homosexual roommate in the suite. The first year it was a tall African-American boy. The second year an Asian boy. All the suitemates knew the boys were gay, and they weren't uncomfortable. The odd thing was the gay boys thought no one knew they were gay, and they were uncomfortable, trying to hide they were gay. I see that a lot. People know people are gay, and it's okay. But the gay people don't know it's okay. Tom was angry with Ann that first night after the threatening phone call.

He said, "When I see Ann I'm going to say let's go a round. Man-to-man."

"You can't do that," I said, "she's a woman."

"She tries to act like a man," he said. "She's a bulldyke."

"But she's still a woman," I said.

But this week Tom's talking about wanting to go on the road to sell the book. "I really enjoy talking to gay people." And he does. All my friends do too. *Ellen* was Jeanne's favorite TV show even after I risked telling her two years ago that Ellen DeGeneres is gay. Only now does she say she won't watch the show in the future. Now that the Ellen character has come out on the show Jeanne is afraid she'll see something that will make her uncomfortable. I don't think she will. The show had the gay male couple and everyone loved their characters. Tom said, "Heterosexual people will never go to lesbian movies." I said, "You saw *Bound.*"

He said, "That's not a lesbian movie. That's a movie by guys for guys. Guys are kind of kinky. Voyeuristic. They like chick fights, lesbian love scenes. It's more a power thing, an entertainment. It was only ten minutes at the beginning of the movie—then it's an action movie."

So I got the film and watched it. I minded it—the whole movie made me uncomfortable. John said he saw it and was uncomfortable. Sexuality is complicated. I want the book to tell the whole truth, as much as I could find, because truth buys freedom. Freedom is not in illusion. It's in truth.

Maya Angelou (in *The Heart of a Woman*) tells an old story

about the slave who wanted to buy his freedom from his master. He worked weekends for another farmer for pay and finally saved one thousand dollars. He went to his master and asked how much a slave costs. The master said, Oh, a young strong slave is worth about 800 to 1200 dollars. "But you're old, and you served me well. I'll sell you your freedom for $600." The old slave thought it over and decided not to buy his freedom. He told himself, "The cost of freedom is a little too high for me today."

Tom says, "I don't understand that story. He had enough money. Why didn't he buy his freedom?" I tried to explain to him that for some people the cost of their freedom is too high. He doesn't understand that concept—because he's young and free—and I'm glad he doesn't understand.

For Ann the cost of freedom—the whole truth—is too high. So she wants an expurgated, sanitized, image-controlled book. And, in the vernacular of the young, she thought she could pimp herself a book.

The first week in June, after I received the first letter, I went to church and heard a sermon that fit this story exactly. The priest told us that that week a hummingbird had gotten into his garage, and although he opened the big double front door, the little hummingbird wouldn't fly out. It went to the side door of the garage and kept banging its head on the small panes of glass. The priest said he could imagine the hummingbird thinking, "They've tricked me with a false opening." The priest's wife and son were yelling at him, "Do something. Do something," for they all thought the hummingbird was killing itself by flying against the window. Because nothing else was working, the priest, a big, kind man, decided to risk really frightening the small bird and he grabbed its tailfeathers and hurled it through the open door.

He imagined the little bird telling its family, "Then the big one grabbed me, but I managed to get away." He had been saved by a kindly hand but did not know it. Now the priest had a point to his story, but like all good stories, it fits many places. Ann wants a book without the whole truth. That's not going to help give gay people their freedom—that's the door with the "false" exit. The big, wide open way to freedom is the truth and the whole truth.

Chris Briscoe's reaction when I told her about Ann's threats and complaints was, "They're so defensive. I don't see it at all."

Catherine said, "They're so defensive. It shows the social culture of the '90s that lesbians are so afraid."

I look at the beautiful photograph of the Wounded Amazon sculpture that will be the frontispiece of the book. I think of lesbian women retreating from the world. Still wounded women.

Myths grow out of fears. They're stories we make up to explain what we fear. Lesbians believe we fear them. That makes them fear us. They retreat to their closed circle of initiates, building the myth to heterosexuals that lesbians are different, alien. Sexually they're hybrids. Behaviorally they're genderblends. That acknowledged, they don't have to be any different. Gay people are sometimes picked on by bullies, but bullies pick on anyone they think will be a victim. Gay people can stop being victims. Most everyone will stand up for you.

I have compassion for gay people. I love you guys. But, hey, I'm throwing you out the big door.

I gratefully thank the following talented people for their generosity and support of this book: artist Chris Briscoe; artist Andrew Gill; Nikki Thelen, proofreader; Paul Bayfield and Phyllis Carter of ColorType, production; Marv Walsh, printer's rep; Roger Newman, publisher; and John J. Murphey, copyright, trademark, and patent attorney.

And Tom and John, for sharing my learning experience with grace, intelligence, and strength.

This is the Last Great Revolution in America—for civil rights and human rights. In the '70s in the women's movement we had a saying: When your granddaughter asks, "What did you do in the revolution?" what will you answer?
Martha Mattson, October, 1997

Martha Mattson grew up in western Michigan and received an M.A. degree in literature from the University of Michigan in 1968. She lives in Southern California.

To order copies of this book send check or money order with your name, address, and phone number to Amazon Press, P.O. Box 26383, San Diego, CA 92196-0383. Cost per book is $16.95 plus $3.00 shipping for the first book, $2.00 shipping for each additional book. (California residents add 7.75% sales tax, making total per book $18.26.) Special rates available for quantity orders.